# US Infantry Weapons In Combat

*Personal Experiences from World War II and Korea*

By Mark G. Goodwin

Foreword by Scott A. Duff

# US Infantry Weapons In Combat

All rights reserved. No part of this book may be reproduced or transmitted in any form or by any means, electronic or mechanical, including photocopying, recording or by any information storage and retrieval system without the written permission from the author, except in the case of brief quotations embodied in critical essays and reviews.

Copyright © 2005 by Mark G. Goodwin

Second Printing - April 2006

ISBN 1-888722-15-0

Published by:

Scott A. Duff Publications
P. O. Box 414
Export, PA 15632

724-327-8246

www.scott-duff.com

Printed by:
South Greensburg Printing Co., Inc.
Greensburg, PA 15601

# Contents

- v **Illustrations**
- vii **Foreword**
- ix **Preface**
- xiii **Acknowledgements**
- 1 **Darrell "Shifty" Powers** • World War II - ETO • Army, 101st Airborne Division
- 12 **Bill Trexler** • Army • World War II – ETO • Army, 9th Infantry Division
- 17 **Neal Burdette** • Army • World War II - ETO • Army, 26th Infantry Division
- 21 **Harrell Roberts** • Korean War • Marine Corps, 1st Marine Regiment
- 27 **Charlie Feeback** • World War II – PTO • Army, 24th Infantry Division
- 30 **Sam Shaw** • World War II – ETO • Army, 63rd Infantry Division
- 33 **Walter Klink** • Korean War • Army, 25th Division
- 38 **Robert Mort** • World War II – PTO • Marine Corps, 4th Marine Division • Korean War • 1st Marine Division
- 42 **Frank Fulford** • Korean War • Army, 2nd Division
- 45 **O.B. Hill** • World War II – ETO • Army, 82nd Airborne Division
- 47 **John Hooper** • World War II • Army – ETO • 29th Division
- 51 **Wayne Stephens** • Korean War • Army, 2nd Division
- 54 **Clinton Riddle** • World War II – ETO • Army, 82nd Airborne Division
- 58 **Don Dencker** • World War II – PTO • Army, 96th Division
- 61 **James Ray Deaton** • World War II – ETO • Army, 3rd Division & 9th Division
- 64 **Clifford Savage** • World War II – ETO • Army, 99th Division
- 66 **Inman Richard** • Korean War • Army, 2nd Division
- 69 **Thor Ronningen** • World War II – ETO • Army, 99th Division
- 73 **John Boitano** • World War II – ETO • Army, 101st Airborne Division
- 77 **Everett "Bud" Hampton** • World War II – PTO • Marine Corps, 4th Marine Division • Korean War • 7th Marines
- 80 **Hank Hanahoe** • World War II – ETO • Army, 9th Division
- 82 **Jack Walentine** • Korean War • Army, 25th Division
- 92 **Gaylen Kittlesen** • World War II – PTO • Army, 503rd Regimental Combat Team & Alamo Scouts
- 94 **Morris Williams** • World War II – ETO • Army, 26th Infantry Division
- 97 **Robert Seiler** • World War II – PTO • Army, 96th Infantry Division
- 100 **Lawrence Moore** • Korean War • Marine Corps, 1st Marine Regiment
- 104 **Harry Hagstad** • World War II – ETO • Army, 99th Division
- 105 **Thomas Shoen, Jr.** • World War II – PTO • Army, 11th Airborne Division
- 110 **Jim Haahr** • World War II – ETO • Army, 26th Infantry Division
- 114 **Terry Tennant** • Korean War • Army, 3rd Division
- 117 **Henry Turner** • World War II – ETO • Army, 29th Division
- 120 **T.C. Mataxis** • World War II – ETO • Army, 70th Infantry Division • Korean War • Army, 7th Infantry Division

125 **Gerald Cosgrove** • World War II - PTO • Marine Corps, 4th Marine Division
129 **John Nothnagle** • World War II – ETO • Army, 70th Division
131 **Marion Throne** • World War II – ETO • Army, 3rd Division • Korean War • Army, 2nd Division
134 **Ray Aebischer** • World War II – ETO • Army, 101st Airborne Division • Korean War • Army, 7th Division
138 **Robert Young** • Korean War • Army, 2nd Infantry Division
141 **Radford Carroll** • World War II – ETO • Army, 99th Division
145 **Paul Cain** • World War II – PTO • Army, 24th Division
149 **Richard Finkbone** • World War II – ETO • Army, 94th Infantry Division
152 **Win Scott** • Korean War • Marine Corps, 1st Marine Division
155 **David Clymer** • World War II – ETO  Army, 26th Division
157 **Donald Van Roosen** • World War II – ETO • Army, 29th Division
161 **John "Red" Lawrence** • World War II – PTO • Marine Corp. –22nd Marines/ 6th Marine Division
165 **Robert Cashion** • Korean War • Army, 7th Division
167 **Earle Slyder** • World War II – ETO • Army, 99th Infantry Division
171 **John Shirley** • World War II – ETO • Army, 3rd Infantry Division
175 **Gerald Gwaltney** • World War II – PTO • Marine Corps, 4th Marine Division
179 **Bob Nesbitt** • Korean War • Army, 187th Regimental Combat Team (Airborne)
181 **Rudy Haynes** • World War II – ETO • Army, 83rd Division
185 **Howard Gaertner** • World War II – ETO • Army, 9th Division
187 **Oliver Green** • Korean War • Army, 3rd Infantry Division
191 **Bill True** • World War II – ETO • Army, 101st Airborne Division
193 **Len Lazarick** • World War II – PTO • Army, 96th Division
198 **Jim Kendall** • World War II – ETO • Army, 103rd Infantry Division
201 **John Taylor** • Korean War • Army, 40th Infantry Division
203 **Don Owens** • World War II – ETO • Army, 94th Infantry Division
206 **Tom Bartelson** • World War II and Korean War • Marine Corp., 1st Marine Division
210 **Bud Warnecke** • World War II – ETO • Army, 82nd Airborne Division • Korean War • Army, 5th Combat Regiment Team
213 **Earl E. Green** • Korean War • Army, 25th Infantry Division
216 **Ralph Carmichael** • World War II – ETO • Army, 1st Infantry Division
219 **J.J. Witmeyer** • World War II – ETO • Army, 79th Division
222 **Jim Foster** • World War II – PTO • Army, 96th Division & 86th Division.
223 **Lawrence D. Schubert** • World War II – ETO • Army, 1st Infantry Division
225 **Tom Twomey** • Korean War • 3rd Infantry Division
231 **Glossary**
232 **About the Author**
233 **List of Publications**

## Firearms Illustrations

3.   M1 Rifle (Garand)
12.  Quad .50 Cal. Anti-Aircraft Gun
13.  M7 Grenade Launcher
14.  M1 Carbine
18.  M1918A2 Browning Automatic Rifle (BAR)
27.  M1A1 Thompson Submachine Gun
31.  M1919A6 .30 Cal. Browning Machine Gun
38.  Model 50 Reising Submachine Gun
40.  USMC Ka-Bar Knife
48.  M3 Trench Knife
59.  81 mm Mortar
65.  M1917A1 .30 Cal. Browning Water-Cooled Machine Gun
70.  M1903A4 Sniper Rifle
78.  M1903 Rifle
84.  M1C Sniper Rifle
89.  Winchester M97 Trench Gun
96.  M1A1 Bazooka
106. M1A1 Carbine
109. Griswold Bag
115. M3A1 Submachine Gun (Grease Gun)
123. M2 .50 Cal. Browning Machine Gun
135. M1A1 Carbine
150. Hand Grenades
162. Bayonets
178. Rifle Grenades
195. M2-2 Flame Thrower
199. M1917 Rifle
202. M2 Carbine
205. M9A1 2.36-inch Bazooka
218. M1911A1 .45 Cal. Pistol

# Foreword

The first thing that the reader must know about this book is that it is a gun book. It is not simply war stories, but is a series of interviews with soldiers and Marines specifically relating their experiences with the US infantry weapons in combat during World War II and in the Korean War. We decided to include both wars as basically both saw the same weapons used. As I first read the manuscript I was fascinated by the dramatically differing opinions. One man loved the M1 rifle and hated the M1 carbine while the next loved the M1 carbine and hated the M1 rifle. One thought that the Garand was too heavy and that the carbine was light and handy. The next thought that the carbine didn't have enough stopping power and he would only carry a Garand. Based upon his personal experiences each man had his own opinion of the weapons that he had used during these wars and relates those observations to the reader.

The author first gave me a copy of the draft manuscript while we were at a gun show in eastern Pennsylvania. After a five-hour drive home from the show on Sunday and after unloading the truck, I had the opportunity to sit down in my easy chair to read a few sections of the manuscript. When I finished the last interview I realized that it was 1:00 AM and that I had been reading for hours! Once I began, I could not put this book down. You have been warned.

What the men interviewed had to say about US infantry weapons fascinated me. So much of what we collectors think we know about the use of US infantry weapons in combat has been derived from two sources: movies and books. Some movies, like "Band of Brothers" are very accurate, others are not. Even though "Saving Private Ryan" was a wonderful movie, who can forget the fictitious quick-change scopes on the M1903 sniper rifle? The general history books of these wars rarely contain the in-depth details of infantry weapons that would be of interest to collectors. The stories about US infantry weapons contained in this book are the real hands-on experiences of the men who actually used them for their intended purposes.

Like the author and many other collectors in our age group, my interest in US infantry weapons of World War II and Korea began with watching movies like "Sands of Iwo Jima". In the late 1950s and early 1960s I spent hour upon hour leafing through my father's Korean War era Guidebook for Marines. Then in October of 1962 the television show "Combat" debuted. My Dad and I never missed an episode. I was hooked on Garands, carbines, Thompson submachine guns, BARs, and .45 pistols! I knew that when I grew up I would own some of those weapons.

I bought my first GI .45 in 1981 and my first M1 Garand in 1985. Thus began my collecting of US infantry weapons of World War II and Korea. As my enthusiasm for collecting these arms grew, so did my study of the history of these wars. The natural progression then moved to the individual men who carried these weapons.

Because my Father had been a Marine during the Korean War, I started collecting Marines Corps uniforms and 782 gear. When in 1992 I learned that my future father-in-law, Thomas Shoen, Jr., had been a paratrooper in World War II. I had to have an M1A1 carbine, jump boots, and a M1942 jump suit. In conversations with collectors I have found that many of us collect the firearms that we do because our dad, grandfathers, or uncles carried them in World War II and Korea. With that motivation it quickly becomes a personal quest to collect these artifacts.

Often times, upon acquiring a new model of martial arm, the collector develops a greater curiosity of that weapon that goes far beyond simply owning an example. He wants to learn how to disassemble, inspect and reassemble it. He wants to know what those numbers stamped on the parts mean. He may also choose to develop proficiency in firing it. But what does he know about that weapons use in combat? Like many of you I know the mechanics and collectible aspects of these arms. But even though I had written several books on collecting and maintaining these weapons, I knew little about their actual performance in combat. Through the interviews published in Mark's book, collectors and shooters of World War II and Korea US infantry weapons now have an insight into the combat usage of these arms in the words of the men who used them.

The opinions of the individual interviewees may differ, and sometimes greatly, but it is their personal experiences that they lived, recalled and related to the author. Mark Goodwin has provided a great service by sharing those interviews in print. I hope that when you sit down to begin reading this book that you are as enthralled as I was and cannot put it down.

Scott A. Duff
Export, Pennsylvania
2005

# Preface

My interest in US infantry weapons began early in life. I think it started with the TV show "Combat" that was on in the 1960s. I remember it came on every Tuesday night and I never missed it. From that show, it seemed obvious to me the weapons the American soldiers had were far superior to the ones used by the Germans. It was from watching that show that I quickly came to know the types of infantry weapons used by our soldiers in World War Two. The Thompson submachine gun that Sergeant Saunders carried and used with such effect seemed like the ultimate weapon. It was like he never missed with it. It had a very distinctive sound and it seemed to shoot forever. I noticed that the M1 rifles the American soldiers used fired faster than the German's bolt-action rifles. They looked better and even sounded better to me. Then there was the BAR, it was big and looked heavy, but it seemed so powerful. Those weapons in the hands of the American soldiers just seemed to be the best weapons in the world. After all, how could America send its soldiers into combat with anything less than the "best in the world"? Later, as I got older and learned more about these weapons, I understood that it wasn't always the case. Of course, these days there always seems to be a debate on the strengths and weaknesses of those weapons.

One of the big events in the small town that I grew up in was the annual Memorial Day parade. I remember the soldiers, who were probably National Guard troops, who marched in the parade. I immediately recognized their M1 rifles. I marched with one platoon of soldiers the whole parade route. When they had completed the march, they were waiting to board trucks to go back to their base. There was a crowd of us kids hanging around them and they were joking with all of us. One of them handed me his rifle and said "Here kid, here's a souvenir for you." I grabbed the rifle, surprised at its weight and pivoted to take off with it. But, they were ready for that and quickly caught me by my collar. They all got a big laugh from that, as did I. But I was thrilled that I had briefly held an M1 rifle.

I wouldn't touch another one for nearly 20 years. While checking out a gun shop in Alabama in 1982, I was surprised to see an M1 rifle for sale in the rifle rack. I'd never seen an M1 for sale before. The shop owner saw me gazing at the rifle. He removed it from the rack and handed it to me. He must have sensed he was close to a sale. "Come on, I have a range out back, why don't you try it out." He grabbed a few clips of ammunition and we went out to the back of his store to a small range. He fired off a clip, reloaded the rifle and handed it to me. My experience with military rifles at that time was with the M16A1; the recoil of a full sized 30.06 cartridge rifle surprised me. But then again, I liked everything about it. The recoil, the sound and the way the clip "clanged" out after the final round in the clip was fired. That was when "the bug" bit me. I thought the shop owner was very clever for allowing me to shoot the rifle. I was sold; I bought the M1 for a pretty hefty sum. At the time, I didn't care, I wanted that rifle. It was the first US military rifle I owned and it was my most prized possession for many years. A few years later, I purchased a second M1 rifle through the Department of Civilian Marksmanship (DCM). Then over the years I acquired other M1s, carbines and M1903s. That first rifle has always been my personal favorite.

It seems over the last few years, collecting and shooting of World War Two era weapons has gained tremendous popularity. This popularity has spawned a great interest in the use and history of these weapons. I've listened in on many conversations from people who were far too young to ever have carried any of those legendary weapons in combat. I'd hear different things about how certain weapons were used, how some were far more popular or effective than others. It made me wonder what the real story was. Over time, I think a lot of us have developed some preconceived ideas on how things were done. But the armed forces in World War Two and during the Korean War were so large, there was bound to be some different stories. How much weapons training did the average soldier or Marine receive before they went into combat? Did they have confidence in the weapons they were issued as they entered combat? Did they clean their weapons every day? How much ammunition did they carry? It made me wonder what the men who carried these weapons in combat had to say. So I simply decided to ask some of them.

In this "information age" I was able to locate many veterans organizations, which greatly aided me in contacting veterans of World War Two and Korea. I tried as much as possible to contact veterans from different units and who served in different theaters. I wanted to get a good cross section of individual experiences with the different issue weapons.

I've read many "oral history" type books, as there are many in print. I've always enjoyed reading about the regular GI or Marine in the foxhole. These men had no idea of the grand strategy or the plan of battle at the time. Often, they knew nothing at all. They just did their jobs, when the time came they left the safety of their foxholes and moved forward. Some were superbly trained when they went into battle and others were not. It was these "average" Soldiers and Marines that I wanted to talk to.

One of the challenges of this project has been keeping perspective on training and experiences these veterans had with their weapons. I spoke to many former soldiers and Marines that had some fascinating stories, but they didn't focus around weapons use. My problem is, I enjoy hearing about everything. As I transcribed these interviews, I tried to weave as much of their experiences into the final product without straying too far off subject.

Just about all these interviews were conducted over the phone. Although, I did receive some letters from veterans about their experiences and decided to include them. Some of the best interviews in this book began with the statement " I don't know if I have anything to say that would be of interest to you." It even got to the point where if they said that I knew I was going to hear some great stuff. For some, the memories from events that occurred almost 60 years ago have faded. As you read through these interviews, you can sense that with some of these men. They often weren't able to remember some of the small details. For others, a few simple questions opened doors to a wealth of great information and they seemingly remembered everything.

It's important to remember these men are in their 70s and 80s and time does take a toll on one's recollections. I did not double-check the accuracy of dates or places in reference to historical facts. This is not meant to be a history book; it's a collection of experiences with the infantry weapons of that era. Also, keep in mind that the generation that these men came from isn't overly concerned with "political correctness." In some of these interviews, you'll hear Germans referred to as "Krauts," Japanese as "Japs" and Chinese as "Gooks." For most of these men, those terms were the names given to enemies and are not necessarily meant as derogatory terms. Although for some the 50 plus years that have passed have not erased the sadness and bitterness of having friends and comrades killed. I haven't had to experience that and can't condemn them for their feelings. Time does not heal all wounds.

I think as you read these interviews you'll hear some interesting things. I certainly learned a lot just from listening. Some of the men were amazed that I had so much interest in what they thought were trivial things. If nothing else, I think it's safe to assume that there was not one simple method for doing any one thing. Often you will hear historians or weapons "experts" state that German weapons were superior to American weapons. I can tell you that many of the men I spoke to didn't feel like they had been armed with inferior weapons. However, they did learn, sometimes the hard way, about the quality of some of the weapons they faced.

It was a real treat to talk to these men. So many of them didn't think what they did in World War Two or Korea was anything special. They were just "doing their job." I guess in simple terms, they were, but I don't know what the world would have been like today if they hadn't done their job. I do sense the pride they all seem to feel about what they accomplished while they served. It is a well-deserved pride. I hope you enjoy reading these interviews as much as I enjoyed conducting them.

Mark G. Goodwin
Fayetteville, North Carolina
2005

# Acknowledgments

I want to start by thanking all the veterans who took the time to talk to me.

I spent 20 years in the US Army and the veterans of World War Two, Korea and Vietnam were my mentors. I've always had tremendous respect for them. I never take for granted what they did for this country. You'll notice as you read these interviews that many of these men bled for our country. As it's been said, "Freedom isn't free." Our veterans have paid the price of our freedom over the years.

I want to thank my family and friends for all their encouragement as I worked on this project. As it was, I underestimated the time and work it takes to complete a project like this and that support and encouragement was very helpful.

I want to give special thanks to Donna Ridgeway, Frances Goodwin and Carolyn Kendall for all their help in editing the text from the interviews.

I appreciate the photographs provided by Bruce N. Canfield, Scott A. Duff, Frank Iannamico, Robert G. Segel, and LeRoy Wade.

I also want to extend thanks to Scott Duff for all his help. I got the idea for this project a few years ago and mentioned it to him to get his opinion on whether it would be a worthy endeavor. He basically told me if I wrote it, he'd publish it. His initial and continuous enthusiasm for this project really helped me decide to do it and motivated me to complete it.

Darrell "Shifty" Powers, Company E, 506th Parachute Infantry Regiment, 101st Airborne Division of the "Band of Brothers".

Personal Experiences

> **Darrell "Shifty" Powers** *enlisted in the U.S. Army in early 1942 in Portsmouth, VA. He volunteered for the Paratroops and was sent to Camp Toccoa, GA. where he was assigned to E Company, 506th Parachute Infantry Regiment. The story of Easy Company has been described in Stephen Ambrose's excellent book, "Band of Brothers" and in the HBO miniseries of the same title. The Regiment became one of the three infantry regiments assigned to the 101st Airborne Division during World War Two. After intensive training in the US, the 506th moved to England and continued to train for the invasion of Europe. Mr. Powers made combat jumps with Easy Company into France on June 6th 1944 and into Holland on September 17th 1944. He also fought in the "Battle of the Bulge" around Bastogne and into Germany before the war ended. Injured in a vehicle accident while in Germany, he spent time in various hospitals until being released from a military hospital in Nashville, TN in the summer of 1945. He was at home on leave when the atomic bombs were dropped on Japan. Not long after the war ended he was discharged from the Army from his home state of Virginia.*

The 506th was actually formed down at Toccoa. As we came in they would fill up the companies. When I came in I was assigned to Easy Company, which is what they were filling up at the time. They would fill up the first platoon, and then they'd start with the second platoon down through the third platoon. When I got there they were filling third platoon and that's the platoon I was in. I stayed in third platoon throughout the war.

One of the first details I was on, me and two or three other guys; was cleaning the cosmoline off of some machine guns. Of course, before that I'd never seen a machine gun. They were air–cooled .30 caliber machine guns. We had a Sergeant there watching us, but he didn't stay around long. As we took them apart we would clean the parts and lay them out so we could put them back together. We used gasoline to clean the parts. We were issued rifles within the first week or two we were there. They were brand new M1 rifles and we had to clean the cosmoline off of those too.

We did dry firing at Toccoa and we also did our qualifying there. But, we didn't do it on the Toccoa base, we went over to, I believe Clemson College. I guess it was 10 to 15 miles from Toccoa; we walked over there. They had a good firing range there, a known distance type range. I'm not sure, but I believe the targets were set up at 100 and 300 yards. We spent about a week there doing rifle training.

*Darrell "Shifty" Powers of the "Band of Brothers" with M1 rifle.*

We took turns practicing aiming and dry firing. It usually took three people for one person to dry fire. We had a little stool like box and one person would sit on that, I guess maybe twenty yards away, not very far. He had a little round disk on a stick and that disk had a hole in the center of it. He would sit a straddle of the box. As for the other two guys, the one that was doing the dry firing would be lying on the ground and he'd have the rifle laying across a sand bag. He wouldn't touch the rifle; he just had it pointing at the box. From then on he would sight the rifle without touching it and the guy on the box would move that little disk around. When you thought you had the disk dead on; you would tell him to mark it. And he would take a pencil and mark in the center of that disk in the hole, on a piece of paper that was tacked to the box he was sitting on. The third guy, would be beside the guy doing the sighting, was kind of his helper. His job was to tell the other guy which way to move the disk. The one doing the sighting would say "left" and the other guy would holler for the guy on the box to move the disk left. He would move it real slow and when he got it where you wanted, you'd say, "stop" and he'd stop. Then you say "up" or "down" and he'd move it up or down until he got it right and you'd say "mark." You'd do that three times and then he would check the paper. The ideal thing was to get a triangular pattern from your marks on the paper.

For the sight picture on the M1, you put your sight post on the bottom of the target, a six o'clock hold. All my life, when shooting a rifle, I'd been used to putting the sight post on the center of a target. It took a while to get used to using the six o'clock hold.

*M1 rifle, often referred to as the "Garand," after the name of the inventor, John Garand. Photo courtesy of Scott A. Duff.*

One thing they taught us, was instead of putting your right hand around the stock over the trigger, they wanted you to stick your right thumb out to the right and let it lay along the stock. I couldn't do that. I always gripped it with my hand so I had more control of the trigger pull. I shot the way I wanted to on the range.

They taught us to shoot from the prone position, the kneeling position and the standing position. And they taught us how to shoot with the sling wrapped around our arm. The sling does make it steadier while target shooting. I don't remember if we were required to use the sling when firing or not. I believe it was up to each individual. I don't even remember if I used it or not. I kept a sling on my rifle during the war, but I never used the sling to shoot in combat.

Best I remember; they didn't give us much practice shooting. They might have given us a clip to zero the rifle in, but there was very little firing before we qualified. Once I got my rifle zeroed in, I never messed with the sights the whole time I had it. I used Kentucky windage all the way.

In our company of 140 guys, I was one of two of us who qualified expert. I think I had an advantage because people in the south fired rifles more than they did up north. I'd been around weapons since I was 12 years old, I guess. My father was an excellent shot, he taught me a lot of things. We had quite a few people from New York, Pennsylvania, Maryland and a lot of places up there. I know a lot of times you could watch some of those people shooting and you could see the bullet hitting the ground half way to the target.

McClung (Earl McClung) and I had a conversation about shooting one time. He wasn't with us when we fired for record at Toccoa, but he was an expert rifleman. You talk about shooting rifles; he could really make one talk. When shooting off hand, in a standing position, I would aim above the target and let it ease down. Let the weight of the rifle bring it down and fire. He would aim below the target and ease it up and fire. I asked him why and he said "If you do it like I do it, you can see the target all the time." Which is true, but I couldn't fire that way. I always thought that the tension of bringing that rifle up would cause you to jerk or something.

Later, it was probably at Camp MacKall, we fired the machine gun, the Thompson and the mortar. We weren't really trained on the mortar and machine gun as we were with the rifle. The machine gunners and the mortar men were trained according to their job, but we did work with them some. I shot the carbine, but I never did have too much confidence in it. I guess the carbine was like a lot of other rifles; you could get a good one or a bad one. The carbine that I fired, you couldn't adjust the rear sights like you could on an M1. So if you got one that was off, it was off. I liked to be able to move that rear sight left or right to get it zeroed. Up and down you could figure out using Kentucky windage, if you fired a lot.

We were in England a pretty good while before the invasion. We didn't do a whole lot of firing on target ranges. We did some firing at pop up targets. They would set those up at different ranges, some would be close and some would be further out. Some of them might pop up 20 to 30 yards right in front of you, then another would pop up to the right at 40 yards and then further on, another would pop up on the left. Shooting at the pop up targets was enjoyable. At that time I had extra good eyesight and I could spot the targets easily. There was a competition thing for first, second and third platoons. They would set these targets up with papers on them. They'd run one platoon through, collect the papers and set up for another bunch. The thing was, a rabbit would jump up and everyone would start shooting at the rabbit. So they didn't really score anyone on account of that.

I'll tell you, you had to know how to shoot known distances because during combat you would have targets like that. And then in combat you were liable to have pop up targets. I think out of the two, I believe the known distance firing was the best training. But, both types of shooting should be required during any rifle training.

For the D-Day jump, I carried all the required stuff and anything edible that I could get. We had quite a bit of stuff on us. I jumped with my rifle loaded and the safety on. I carried it down under the harness, the parachute harness that goes across your chest. When you jumped you wrapped your arms around it. I had jumped the rifle so many times holding it like that; I couldn't see any advantage of trying something new when I knew the old way worked. I didn't go in for that leg bag business. I don't know if anyone was forced to wear a leg bag, they had a choice. I was never asked if I wanted a leg bag and I wouldn't have taken one if asked. I was kind of amazed that some of the other people took those leg bags, because they had never jumped them before.

I just carried the ten ammunition clips in my belt, which was 80 rounds. And I believe that I had one more clip in the pocket on my shoulder. I think I had two hand grenades, about four or five pounds of plastic explosive and some detonators. On one of my jumps, I jumped all of that, plus 250 rounds of machine gun ammunition. I volunteered to jump it. You took your shirt off and wrapped it around your stomach and chest with cloth belts; then you put your shirt back on. That's the way you jumped it.

When we went into Normandy, we were told we'd be there three days. I figured that I could make eighty rounds last for three days. There was always an opportunity to get re-supplied with ammunition from the people coming in on the beach. I figured eighty rounds would be enough.

We'd done all that training in England and we were all hopped up. We had trained so long, we were anxious to go. On D-Day, when we got in the plane, we didn't know what to expect. We got over Normandy and the ack ack started coming up. The shrapnel started coming through the plane and the machine gun bullets started going through the plane. We couldn't hardly wait to get out of there. I was tickled to death to jump out of that plane and most of the time I'm not too tickled to jump.

As I went out the door, the motor was on fire. I was either the last man or the next to the last man to jump; I was real fortunate to get out. The plane was going a whole lot faster than it should have been. Of course, I couldn't blame the pilots too much, if I'd of been them I'd be wanting to get out of there too. The Germans shot at us on the way down, but we weren't too awful high.

After the jump, I joined up with two guys from my plane and we wandered around. We were quite fortunate, we didn't run into any Germans and they didn't run into us. We spent the rest of the night pulling a roadblock with another group of paratroopers. We were kind of a mixed group, I think some were from A Company and some of them were from the 82$^{nd}$. Of course we were in an area we weren't really supposed to be in. On the road intersection where we had that roadblock, the Navy had on their fire list. They shelled us for the rest of the morning as it got time for the troops to come in. It had to be the Navy because the Germans didn't know where we were; we didn't know where we were.

That morning, on D-Day, we walked all that day and got close to the beach. We decided it was getting late and we didn't want to go in there after dark and get shot by friendly fire. We held up in a little bombed out building and stayed the night. The next morning we went down to the beach and the Beach Master had a list of where the companies were and he knew where Easy Company was. We walked a couple of miles and joined them.

We stayed with the company for a couple of days, waiting on guys to come in and join up with us. The guys would trickle in two or three at a time. When we got what they thought was enough people, then we moved on to Carentan on D-Day plus two or three.

After we took that little town Carentan, we drove the Germans out of there and we followed them up a road to an intersection. They had some reinforcements up there. Of course, that was all hedgerow country. The Germans were across a field behind a hedgerow on their side of the field and we'd be behind the hedgerow on our side of the field. The Germans would be shooting at us and we'd shoot at them, but you couldn't see them and they couldn't see us on account of the cover. So you would fire at places where they were firing from, you fired a lot of rounds then. You could see the bushes shaking from where they were shooting and you'd look for the obvious places where a soldier would be firing from. The more rounds that were going in to a position, the more demoralizing it would be. We couldn't drive them any further and they couldn't drive us back. We fought there back and forth for quite a while, then we finally got some reinforcements up from the beach and we got relieved from there.

Holland was a beautiful jump. The day was real nice, the sun was shining and it was warm. There wasn't much firing going on, not much ack ack, very little small arms fire, if any. The big advantage was the day jump, at nighttime you can't meet up with everybody. With the day jump, the Captain threw an orange smoke grenade out and that's where we were supposed to gather up. So, we had a good jump there, it just went off so smoothly.

In Holland, most of the fighting was done after dark; we did a lot of patrols. We didn't move around much in the daytime. It was very flat and the Germans would see you and shell you. Well, I was a Sergeant then and the Lieutenant told me to take two men into a field to set up a listening post after dark. We got out in the middle of that field and set up. I told the two guys with me to look at the shrub bushes in the field and remember where they are. And I told them not to stare at them because if they stared at them it would look like they were moving. Well, I pulled my watch and I laid down to rest. About the time I laid down, the other guy started firing his M1. I jumped up with my rifle and I said "Where they at!" And he said, "Right there, see them!" I said "That's those bushes I told you about, grab your gear!" We grabbed our gear and ran across the field and jumped into a ditch. About that same time, "crump, crump," mortars hit right where we had been. The Germans had seen the muzzle flash of his rifle and zeroed right in on our listening post.

We had come back from Holland to this little camp in France. There was no training there, we stood formations and they checked rifles, stuff like that. We were getting ready to have a football game. One of the battalion's was playing another battalion in football and we were looking forward to that. We hadn't had much to eat and they had promised us a big turkey dinner for Christmas. I remember I was sitting with Buck Taylor and he was teaching me to play chess. I was just starting to learn when they came in and told us "Grab your stuff, we're going." We didn't have time to get too upset over it. I don't know where any of the guys were issued ammunition in France. I'm pretty sure I wasn't, I just had what I had in my belt when I came back from Holland. I believe I had five or six clips.

So, when we first got to Bastogne, we were short on ammunition; so we had to be careful with it. The Germans would fire, harass us and shell us. They tried to run over us, but they couldn't. They were in a hurry, so they decided to split and moved around us. They would send patrols in and you would have some firing going on then. We kind of conserved our ammunition and didn't have to fire a whole lot right around Bastogne. During the war, I never did run plumb out of ammo, but I came pretty close up in Bastogne.

The fighting around Bastogne was defensive at first; we were fighting from our foxholes. We mostly stayed in our positions, very few patrols went out. Later we were on the offense, we did do quite a bit of firing down around Foy, which was in the Bastogne area. Then after Patton came up with his tanks, we got in front of those tanks and took a couple more towns.

After Bastogne, we knew the war was practically over. We were sent to Haguenau to replace another outfit that had been there. The city had a river running right down the middle of it. The Germans was on one side and we were on the other. We did send out a patrol or two, but as far as I know, they didn't send any patrols in our area. They would fire their artillery at us and ours would fire back at them. They were like us; they knew the war was almost over. After we left out of there we went down to Berchtesgaden, with the war almost over, most of us didn't have to fire our rifles anymore.

As a rifleman, they expected you to carry an M1, but they weren't very strict about it. If you could pick up a Thompson submachine gun you could carry it or a carbine, whatever. Most everybody stayed with the weapon they were familiar with. I swapped one time; we were getting ready to make a jump before Holland. We were out at the airfield, but Patton overran the drop zone. While we were at the airfield, they came out and told us the area we were going to drop in; the Germans had a lot of guard dogs. Well, I'm kind of a little bit scared of dogs, so I talked to another guy about swapping, I gave him my M1 and he gave me his Thompson. I figured I could spray the dogs. They called that jump off, so I went back and swapped back with him. The Thompson was a good weapon, the only fault I heard about the Thompson was that you had to keep them clean or they would jam.

The most amazing thing about that M1 is you could throw that thing down in a mud hole, drag it through it, pick it up and it would fire. It wouldn't jam; it would fire. What we did mostly was keep the outside of it as clean as we could with a rag or something. And we'd clean the bore out as often as we could. Any time we were off the line we'd clean the rifles well. Most of the M1s came with a cleaning rod in the stock and we had some patches. I believe we had a little gun oil too. In combat, when you were right on the line you don't take time out to clean the rifle. You just kept the mud and dirt wiped off the outside of it the best you can. They were outstanding weapons, that rifle worked all the time.

My rifle had a mind of its own. It seemed like I could just point that thing and tell it what I wanted it to hit and it would hit it. It was one of the most remarkable rifles I ever fired. One thing I did was I filed the sear in the trigger assembly on my rifle. I wanted a hair trigger and I had it filed down so fine that it would shoot three times when I pulled the trigger. It didn't do it every time, but with an eight-round clip, a lot of times it would shoot the first three rounds.

If you're an expert rifleman in the company and any new thing comes up dealing with the M1, they would send you to learn about it. For example, when they first came out with the grenade launcher for the M1, they had to have someone go down and have an instructor give you one and show you how to use it. Then you'd come back and tell the company how to use it. They would always pick out somebody who was pretty fair with a rifle, which makes sense. We got down to this place when we were in England and they had this guy to tell us about the grenade launcher. He wasn't real familiar with it, he just knew the basic things. He showed us to use a blank shell in the rifle and showed us how to put the launcher on the end of the rifle, which was no big deal. Then you put the grenade on that. He didn't know and we didn't know. With the rifle grenade, you had to use Kentucky windage and kind of lob it in. The grenade didn't fire in a straight line like a bullet. We got them things put on the rifle and he said now you put that up to your shoulder and lob it in to the target. So I put that up to my shoulder and I pulled that trigger and it liked to knock me ten foot back. We didn't know any better. Later on, after firing it a few times like that, we found out you were supposed to put the butt of the rifle on the ground. We had different types of grenades; we had smoke grenades, a fragmentation grenade and one that was a flare.

I was issued a rifle grenade launcher; we had one or two in each squad. I carried one just about the whole time I was over there. I usually carried fragmentation grenades and flares, it depended what I could get a hold of. Most of the time I carried them in my musette bag. The flare was very effective; we would use those at night to check things out. If you heard people moving around, you put that flare up in the air and you could see pretty well by it and it stayed up for a while. We used the fragmentation grenades mostly for machine gun nests; two or three people grouped up or in a spot we'd think was hot or just a place we thought there might be some Germans. Or lob one into a building. You never could get them exactly where you wanted them because you didn't fire them that often. Maybe you would go without shooting one for a week or two. Shooting anything, I'm talking from basketballs right on to rifles, bazookas or whatever; the more you do of it, the better you can do.

I carried a bayonet during the war; we had to have them. We had our bayonet and we had our trench knife, which we carried in our boot. Then you had a switchblade knife that you carried in your coat; there was a zipped pocket near the collar. The purpose for that was in case you got hung up in a tree you could cut yourself out. With all that gear we had on the jump, you couldn't reach down to get the other knifes. But you could get to that one and use it one handed, that's the reason it was a switchblade. I wouldn't fire my rifle with a bayonet on it if I could help it. It didn't have the same feel and it's not really accurate.

As a rule, most of our engagements were anywhere from 100 to 150/200 yards. Occasionally it would be long range. I shot at this German one time when I was at Bastogne. I was out next to the edge of the woods and every morning this guy would come walking around the foot of a little hill, just sauntering along. I guess he was about a good mile away, back then I had excellent eyesight. He must have been going to get water or something. I didn't have a lot of ammunition, but I wanted to see if I could scare him. I kicked the safety off my rifle and using Kentucky windage, I raised up about six feet above his head and I fired. It took so long for the bullet to get there that I could move my head to the side of the gun to see what was happening. Nothing happened. Well, I thought about that all day and the next morning I thought I'm going to try him one more time. This time I held the rifle twice as high as I had the morning before. I fired and looked around and all at once that guy stopped and then he took off just a flying. If I hit him it didn't hurt him bad at that distance, but I never did see him anymore.

When we were going on patrols, you wouldn't have your musette bag on your back, or your sleeping bag or your raincoat. You would have your rifle and ammunition belt. Your shovel went with you all the time. Your bayonet went with you all the time. Your trench knife went with you all the time and your canteen. Everybody knew what they were supposed to take.

I had always taken good care of my rifle. It might have had a little scratch here and there, but it wasn't beat up. If I had that rifle here today, I could clean that stock and get it in top-notch shape in an hour. It was in excellent shape, except for a pit in the bore that gave me problems.

It started down in Toccoa. After we were issued our rifles and we got them all cleaned up. On the first inspection we had, an officer looked us over. They'd make sure you didn't need a haircut and that you'd shaved. Of course we were so young then we didn't have to shave too often. They would check your uniform to make sure it looked right. As soon as he come up, you brought your rifle up at port arms and kicked the breech open. You'd stand there and look him in the eye and try to figure out when he was going to grab that rifle. As soon as you saw his eye flicker, why you'd turn loose the rifle. If you didn't, he'd jerk it out of your hands. From the first time an officer looked down that barrel, they'd say; "Powers, you got a pit in the bore of that rifle, get it out of there." I'd say "Yes, Sir" and it was that way every inspection, same thing, over and over. There ain't no way you can get a pit out of the bore of a rifle, but I always told them I would. The rifle came from the factory that way. It was just a little bitty pit in the bore; it didn't affect the accuracy of the rifle.

When we were in Haguenau, we had replaced another outfit that had been on the line there. After we had been there for a couple of days, I looked over in the corner of one of the buildings and there was a rifle there. So I went over and got it and looked it over. It still had some cosmoline on it, it was a new rifle. I figured whoever had it had been a replacement who never did get the opportunity to clean it. I cleaned the bore out real good and it was bright and shiny. So I laid my rifle down and picked that one up. I never did get to zero it in. After we left Haguenau, most of us didn't have to fire our rifles anymore. I wouldn't have swapped rifles if I hadn't known the war was practically over.

When the war was over they came out with a points system. Anyone with 85 points could be rotated back to the states. Well, I only had 80 points because I didn't have a purple heart. I was one of the two people in the company that fought every day on the line that the company fought on the line. And one of the two people who didn't have a purple heart. The Purple Heart counted for five points. So, I didn't have enough. I was one of the original people there; we had lots of replacements. I was the only original person there that didn't have 85 points.

So, they put names in a hat to draw a name for someone to rotate back to the states and they drew my name. I found out two years later that my name was the only name in that hat. So, I got all my gear ready, I had me a bunch of pistols and stuff. They drove us down to battalion to get our paperwork done, there were four of us, one from each company. We were in the back of a truck and we started around this curve and another GI truck coming up from the opposite way came over to our side of the road and hit us. It threw me out of the truck over the top of the hood and I ended up in the street. I broke a few bones, it messed me up a little. That's the reason I didn't get home early, I think most all the other guys beat me home. I spent about six weeks, maybe a little more, in several hospitals. After I got pretty well straightened out, I got a 30-day leave to go home. While I was home they dropped the atomic bomb on Japan. When my leave was up, they sent me down to Camp Pickett or Camp Lee and I got a discharge.

# US Infantry Weapons In Combat

*Bill Trexler with Quad .50 caliber anti-aircraft gun, 1945.*

> **Bill Trexler** *entered the Army in December 1942 and joined the 99th Division at Camp Van Dorn, MS. He trained with the 99th until being transferred to the ETO as an individual replacement prior to the D-Day invasion. Following the invasion, he was assigned to the 9th Infantry Division as they were fighting around Cherbourg. He served with G Company, 39th Infantry until he was wounded. Once recovered from his wound, he was reclassified and transferred to an anti-aircraft unit. He served with that unit until the end of the war, eventually becoming the company first sergeant. He returned to the US in December 1945 and was discharged.*

I was drafted in December 1942 and went to basic at Camp Van Dorn. I was in the 99th Division as they were training up. Most of the weapons training I did was with the M1 rifle, although we got a little taste of everything. We trained with the pistol, carbine, BAR and a little with the mortar and machine gun. I was a corporal then and corporals were in charge of the BAR team, so I had to qualify with the BAR. I loved the M1 and qualified as an expert with it. It was a great rifle. I don't know why they ever replaced it.

I trained with the 99th Division until April 1944. We were at Camp Maxey, Texas, after doing maneuvers in Louisiana. That's when we were broken up and a lot of us went out as replacements. When I got over to England, I worked on the beach for a couple of weeks unloading ships. They were calling people up every day for replacements. I believe that originally we were earmarked to go to the 1st Division because they expected to have a lot more casualties than they had. They finally started farming us out to whoever needed replacements. I joined G Company, 39th Infantry in France at the end of June.

We saw quite a lot of fighting in the hedgerows before we broke out of that country. I think what kept me alive was my love for the rifle grenade. I always had them handy. You know you always hear those stories about somebody attacking a machine gun with hand grenades? I just took them out using my grenade launcher and a rifle grenade. The rifle grenade looked like a little rocket, it was a great weapon. One time in Averanches, I took out a tank commander and about five of his tank crew from about 600 yards away with a rifle grenade. We were down the bottom of a long hill, hiding behind tombstones in a cemetery. The tanks were stopped on top of the hill. I wondered if I could reach them with a rifle grenade and took a shot at them. They were all standing around up there reading their map and the grenade came down right smack through the map. It was luck! I guess they never heard you weren't supposed to bunch up.

*M7 grenade launcher mounted on M1 rifle. Photo courtesy of Scott A. Duff*

Normally you were only a couple hundred yards away from the target and with a lot of practice the rifle grenades were very accurate. I didn't use a rifle grenade sight; those didn't come out until later. I'd just rest the butt of the rifle on the ground and try to imagine the arc the grenade would fly. I fired them from the shoulder twice and both times I was sorry I did. It really hurt to shoot the grenades from the shoulder, but they were more accurate when you fired them that way. One time, the Germans trapped one of our sergeants and we couldn't get to him. I could see the Germans coming down through the brush for him. I took a chance and fired a rifle grenade at them from the shoulder. I thought I'd dislocated my shoulder, but the grenade landed right in the middle of the Germans and our sergeant was able to get away. Those rifle grenades had a pretty good wallop.

Not very many guys liked to use rifle grenades, but we carried as many as we could. I usually had an ammo bag that would carry about five grenades. I also had the guys in the squad carry some. I kept the launcher on the rifle all the time; you could still fire regular ammunition with it mounted. I normally carried two bandoleers of ammo and four or five clips in my cartridge belt. That much ammo along with a few hand grenades would usually keep us going all day, although a few times we got in spots where we would only have one clip left. The sergeants would tell us "When you fire that last clip, somebody better drop." With the M1, you could engage targets out to 500 yards. Since I had qualified as expert with the M1, I could hit targets that far out.

I remember one day in Normandy, our sergeant crept up on a hedgerow and stuck his head up. He saw three Germans walking down a trail with a machine gun; they were going to set it up on a corner of the hedgerow. He went to fire at them with his rifle and it went "click" and there he was standing there staring at the three Germans. He had to use his foot on the op rod to cock his M1 again. He finally got it cocked and bang, bang, bang, the three Germans went down. It was the only time I ever saw an M1 hang up.

During combat, I chose which weapon to carry depending on the conditions. I liked the M1 while we were fighting in the hedgerows. When we got in the forest, I liked the carbine. In the towns I had a Thompson submachine gun for a while, which was good, but was heavy to lug around.

When we got into the Hurtgen Forest, I switched to a carbine. I just picked one up along the way and left my M1. We had people who followed us and picked up or destroyed whatever weapons were lying around. In some cases if we were surrounded or something, we destroyed a lot of weapons. The carbine wasn't very accurate; you had to be right on top of them. It was only good out to a couple hundred yards, but in the forest it was close in fighting. When you were close in to them, the carbine would do the job. We got the ammo from the company already loaded in magazines; you could take as many as you wanted. The magazines fit in the cartridge belt and I'd usually carry about a dozen of them.

*M1 carbine. Photo courtesy of Scott A. Duff*

Personal Experiences

I thought both the carbine and the M1 were reliable weapons. We'd clean them whenever we had the chance. We kept a cleaning kit in the butt of the rifle. A lot of times when a replacement got hit, we'd just pick up his clean weapon. We didn't have an attachment to any single weapon. It was just a tool to us.

I thought the BAR was a great weapon, but it took someone that knew how to handle one. It had a tendency to rise up to the right when it was fired; you had to hold it down. Most people hated carrying them, but they were very good in combat. In the unit, when people came in we'd ask them if they had ever shot a BAR and they'd always say they had never seen one before. One time we had a young Chinese boy come in as a replacement and we asked him, "What are you"? He said "I'm a BAR man" and we almost dropped over. He really was a good BAR man too.

I carried a Thompson submachine gun for a while. It was good for close in fighting, but it wasn't very accurate and it was too bulky. It wasn't effective beyond 50 yards as far as I was concerned. At least I couldn't hit anything past that. You had to carry a lot of ammo for it and .45 caliber ammo was heavy. I carried three loaded magazines and had a bag of loose ammunition. Sometimes it was hard to get ammunition for it; I usually had to grub it off of tankers. At one point after we had crossed the Meuse River, we were overrun one night. I lost my extra bag of ammunition and I was running around with only half a clip of ammo. After that, I got rid of the Thompson and picked up an M1.

One day up around Monchau, we were setting up an outpost in a house. I was still carrying the Thompson at the time. I went up the steps to check the second floor. There was a German hiding in one of the rooms and he jumped out and took a swipe at me with a knife. I kicked him and he fell back down the steps. At that moment I was so panicked that I pulled the trigger on my Thompson and emptied the whole magazine at him. I think every round hit him while he was on the way down the steps. Somebody commented that I didn't have to make mincemeat out of him. There were three Germans in that house, the other two tried to get away and they were shot.

I got hit on New Years Eve near Elsenborn Hill, I got a piece of shrapnel in my knee. I was sent first to a hospital in France and then back to England. After I recovered enough I was reassigned to limited service, returned to Europe and assigned to an anti-aircraft unit. The unit had quad-mounted .50 caliber machine guns on tracks. We were right behind the front lines and stupidly one night we decided to try them out. Our infantry was being attacked and we went up and raked the fields in front of them and then pulled back. We got away with it the first time, but the second time we tried it we got caught. One of the officers caught us and all hell broke out. They didn't want us taking the guns forward, they were afraid of losing them. It was a very effective weapon; the infantry loved our support. Most of our men were wounded infantrymen who had been transferred back into service. I doubted whether we could hit a barn on purpose. Only once did we see a German plane and take a shot at it. We didn't hit the plane and later we were told he had his landing gear down, which meant he wanted to surrender. We got in trouble again.

After the war ended, our unit had all those former infantrymen with a whole lot of points. We were stuck in the outfit because the colonel wouldn't let us go. One of our sergeants went to Paris and complained about it. A few days later, General Eisenhower showed up and the fur flew. Everybody with 70 points was supposed to be out of the ETO and most of us were sitting around there with 100 to 110 points. He gave the unit 24 hours to have us out of the ETO and boy we flew! We went right to the boat and they pulled people off to make room for us. Five days later, we were being discharged in Boston. It was November 1945 and I had spent about three years in the Army.

Personal Experiences

*Neal Burdette with BAR.*

> In July 1943 after finishing high school at the age of 17, **Neal Burdette** enlisted into the Army. He went to basic training at Fort Benning, GA and was accepted into the Army Specialized Training Program (ASTP). He attended school in Indiana until the program shut down in February 1944. He was assigned to the 26th Infantry Division and trained with them until going overseas in September. He was wounded by a sniper's bullet in November and evacuated to England. Upon recovery he was reclassified for noncombat duty and served with the Air Corps until he was returned to the US in December 1945. He was discharged in January 1946, but later served with the National Guard for about nine years.

After I enlisted, I was sent to the Infantry School at Fort Benning for basic training. With the Infantry School there we got quite a bit of weapons training. We first trained with Enfield rifles; they didn't have enough M1 rifles for everyone. So we did drill and bayonet training with the Enfields, but we never fired them. Then we had about two weeks of marksmanship training at the range with the M1 and we qualified with it. We also did familiarization training with the carbine, the BAR, machine guns and mortars. We shot the water-cooled M1917 heavy machine gun with .22 adapters. They had .22 ammo in belts and we fired the guns on a 50-foot range. I did some weapons training while I was at the University of Indiana. We didn't do any shooting, but we practiced taking them apart and putting them together.

After the Army closed the ASTP down, I went right from Indiana to the mud of Tennessee. I joined the 26th Division while they were right in the middle of the Tennessee Maneuvers. I was assigned as a BAR man in the 2nd Platoon of C Company, 101st Infantry Regiment. I liked the BAR; it gave you a lot of firepower. My BAR was a M1918A2 with the bipod on the barrel. Although in combat, I got rid of the bipod. I think everybody did. It would catch on things. I kept mine in my pack. I fired the BAR quite a bit during training and qualified with it. We had three-man BAR teams back then. I had an assistant gunner and an ammo bearer, but I always carried the gun. Our squad was made up of a squad leader, a first and second scout, the BAR man and then the ammo bearer and assistant. The rest were rifleman; we only had one BAR in each squad.

*M1918A2 BAR with bipod folded. Garand Stand collection. Photo courtesy of Bruce N. Canfield.*

We got over to France in September 1944. In combat, I wore a six-pocket BAR belt that held two magazines in each pocket. But in one pocket, I carried a small box like leather case that had all kinds of spare parts for the gun. So I only had ten magazines in the belt and one in the gun. The assistant gunner and ammo bearer carried extra magazines for the BAR, as well as ammo for their own weapons. They both carried M1s. My ammo bearer also wore a full BAR belt with magazines. At one time the army had these square shaped canvas bags with a shoulder strap to carry BAR magazines, but I can't remember if either of the guys had one. Both my assistant gunner and ammo bearer were captured in early November. We had taken over a position from another company and they had gone back to get rations and ammo for us. They followed the commo wire down to the ammo point, but on the way back they must have followed a Kraut wire or something because they went the wrong way. They got in front of our lines and were captured.

After they were captured, I was short on ammo. Another guy in the squad filled in for them after that. I had a metal loader that fit over the top of the magazines and he would get stripper clip ammo, the five-round clips for the Springfield, and he'd run those stripper clips down into the magazines. He was pretty good, he always came up with ammo and grenades and kept us well supplied. If we didn't get issued the five-round stripper clips, we'd have to get our ammo from eight-round M1 clips. We got a mix of ball and armor piercing ammunition, but no tracers. I didn't want any tracers. One time we took over a position from part of the 4th Armored Division and I found one of those cloth machine gun belts. It was all wet and the rounds were stuck in the belt. I cut the loops to get the rounds out, threw away all the tracers, then loaded up my empty magazines.

The BAR was very accurate, if you had open terrain you could shoot out to 600 yards. I felt like I could stitch someone at that range. With trigger control, I could shoot one round at a time or two rounds or as many as I wanted. I never had any problems at all with mine; it was a dependable weapon. You had to keep it pretty clean, but I didn't think it was hard to maintain. I kept a can of bore cleaner and a little can of oil in the belt pocket with the leather case. I would have to borrow a cleaning rod to clean the bore.

The one big attack we made while I was there, we ran the Krauts off of Hill 310 in France. We all lined up around the back of an old church with all our automatic weapons. We started firing to keep the Krauts pinned down. There was also artillery and mortar fire hitting the hill too. While we fired, another platoon walked down this little valley and then went up the hill. We kept firing until they got on the top of the hill and we were afraid we were going to hit them. Then we quit firing and took off right after them. I fired about six or eight magazines during the attack. My assistant was lying right there beside me and when I'd drop an empty magazine from the gun, he would reload it. He was reloading them as fast as I was firing them. He was a cool and calm guy under fire. The Krauts were still popping up out of the holes when we overran them. It was like a Fort Benning field problem and it worked just the way it was supposed to work. We just kept up a steady fire and the other platoon did marching fire going up the hill and the Krauts were pinned down in their holes. I remember when I ran up there, I ran past a Kraut machine gun with a big frame mount and a scoped sight. The crew had been captured, we'd kept them so pinned down they couldn't do anything. I came to another hole and these guys popped up and then dropped back down. I wasn't going to run past them and have them behind me, so I stuck the BAR down the hole and fired about five rounds. I'm not sure if I hit them or not, but I went on. We didn't have a single casualty during the attack.

After we took the hill, we received one hell of a counterattack all night long. We had dug in to a Kraut hole that was on the reverse slope of their position. It was a shallow hole. We tried to dig it deeper, but we hit water. During the night we took some heavy artillery fire and then they made their big counterattack. We were pulling the pins on grenades, counting off for three seconds, then throwing them up and ducking down into the hole. They were going off in the air. The Germans were that close. I bet we threw 20 to 25 grenades that night. My assistant was a little skinny guy, where he carried all that stuff, I don't know. At one time during the night, we pulled about 50 to 60 feet back from our hole and fought from the bare ground. We did a lot of shooting that night. We would shoot in the general direction of where we thought they were. We could hear them hollering and screaming. By the time the attacks let up just about everyone was completely out of ammo. The next morning we had a couple of them stacked up about six feet in front of our hole.

I was wounded the day after that big fight, on November 11th, Armistice Day. A German sniper got me. I got shot right through the helmet. I shot left handed with the BAR, so I always wore my helmet cocked to the right side to kind of keep it out of the way. We were on flank security and I saw some Germans who were setting up a machine gun. I turned around to shout at our Sergeant to tell him they were moving a machine gun up. When I turned my head back towards the Germans I got hit. The round went through the helmet and cut a groove in my skull. It gave me a severe concussion. I crawled back a ways and a few guys came up and helped me back to the aid station. They sent me back to a hospital in France for a week or so and then flew me over to England.

I spent a whole lot of time in the hospital in England. I got out in March 1945 and they sent me to the Air Corps on limited duty. I went to the base at Molesworth and I loaded bombs on B-17s. After the war ended, they sent me to Casablanca and I worked several different jobs. I finally got home in December 1945 and was discharged in January 1946.

## Personal Experiences

> **Harrell Roberts** *enlisted in the Marine Corps Reserves in 1949. His unit was called to active duty in the summer of 1950 after the Korean War broke out. After receiving additional training at Camp Pendleton, Mr. Roberts was sent to Korea with the second draft of replacements. He arrived in Korea in November 1950 and was assigned to G Company, 3rd Battalion, 1st Marine Regiment. He was wounded in the fighting around the Chosin Reservoir in December and evacuated to Japan. From there he was sent back to the US for additional medical treatment for his wound. He was medically discharged from the Corps in September 1951.*

I enlisted in the Marine Corps Reserves in March 1949 while I was in high school. It was right after the war; I had been in ROTC during high school. It seemed everyone had relatives in the service and it just seemed like it was the thing to do. Who in the world would have thought there would be another war?

I had no boot camp; I took my training with the company. We had weekly meetings, we met every Monday and then we had summer camp every summer. That summer I went to camp at Camp Lejeune. I was in a reserve infantry company; it was called D Company, 10th Infantry Battalion. It was kind of a unique outfit, about half the people in it were World War Two veterans. There was a lot of experience in the unit, so we got some pretty good information from those people.

For weapons training, we dry fired all the time at the armory and in our maneuver area. It was one of those things I had learned in high school with the old 03s and Enfield rifles we had in ROTC. I could assemble and disassemble M1s, BARs, Carbines and .45s, we had all those weapons in our armory. During summer camp at Camp Lejeune, we had the opportunity to fire for qualification and record with our M1s. I had no problems qualifying with the M1; I qualified the first time. Having grown up shooting .22s, I was a little surprised at the noise it made. It didn't kick too bad, although I remember a few of the boys got a fat lip. They snuggled up to it a little too close.

In the summer of 1950 the Korean War started and there was a headline in the paper "80,000 Marine Reserves Called to Active Duty!" My unit was activated on the 21st of August and we shipped out on the 28th to Camp Pendleton.

At Camp Pendleton I became part of the second replacement draft. At first we were divided up in a training battalion. The World War Two combat veterans and the people who were 19 years of age and had two summer camps were considered combat ready. Can you imagine a 19-year-old kid who has been to two summer camps being combat ready? I had only one summer camp so I went into the second category and went to advanced infantry training. The third category were those who were under 19 and had been to no summer camp. They went to boot camp. While I was at Camp Pendleton, I was issued a rifle and allowed to fire 50 rounds of familiarization with it. It was serial number 2447720 and it was the same weapon that I kept with me the whole time. I had a buddy who was shipped out to radio school right before we left for Korea. The rifle that he had was just like brand new! The stock was beautiful and all the parts were like new. So I stripped down the two rifles, kept my barreled receiver with the serial number on it and put everything new from his rifle on my rifle. He turned in his rifle when he left for school. My rifle worked like a champ for me.

The advanced infantry course was 24 days; they assigned a bunch of us to a weapons company for the training. They had us all lined up and asked "Anyone who knows anything about machine guns fall in over there". "Anyone who knows about mortars, fall in over there." There I stood, I didn't know anything about machine guns or mortars, I'd been in a rifle platoon. So a bunch of us wound up in an assault platoon and our training was with flame throwers, bazookas and demolitions. Then it was off to Korea.

The second replacement draft landed at Wonsan on the 11th of November, Armistice Day. We were divided up into the different units and I went to George Company, 3rd Battalion, 1st Marines. We had to wait in Wonsan for our company, which was over in Majon-ni. They had been trapped down there for 15 days or so. The company had originally landed at Inchon and when they made it back to Wonsan they still had their summer gear on. We had drawn winter stuff while we were in Japan. I remember seeing them in the back of the trucks huddled together with blankets over their shoulders and all of them had beards. They were a horrible looking crew. For a 19-year-old Marine it was a real eye opener.

We were on flat cars going north between Wonsan and Hamhung. It was a narrow gauged train with a wood fire locomotive. We pulled into a marshalling yard someplace and there were a platoon of Army engineers working on the rail lines. We stopped next to a boxcar on another track and leaning against this boxcar was that engineer platoon's weapons. M1s and carbines, the works, everything was right there. Our platoon sergeant looked at us and said, "Listen up people, any of you people who want to survey your weapons now is the time." "Take those leather slings off your rifles right now, get your eye on one of those rifles down there and when I give you the word, make the swap." The army had web slings and we had the leather slings. Then he said, "Do it," and in three minutes time our platoon had surveyed all their weapons. They slapped those web slings on their old rifles and leaned them against the boxcar. I held on to my rifle these guys had been through Inchon and Seoul and their weapons were worn out. They got rid of all their worn out weapons.

George Company pulled into Koto-ri on the 28th of November. The Chinese had cut off the main supply route between Koto-ri and Hagaru. Chesty Puller ordered several separate units under the command of Lieutenant Colonel Drysdale of the Royal Marines to open the main supply route. So the Royal Marines, George Company, Baker Company, 31st Army Regiment, a tank company and a bunch of division headquarters people became "Task Force Drysdale." All of us, about 900 strong shoved off the next morning. The plan was the Army and the division headquarters people would stay on the road with the rolling stock and the Royal Marines and us would work the hills. The Royal Marines took the first hill and we moved through them to the next hill. That was a long day.

My first combat was on that second hill, it was called Telegraph Hill and things got sticky in a hurry. There were a lot of Chinamen there. I knew we were in for a fight and I had my cartridge belt with 80 rounds and two bandoleers plus a pocket full of grenades. I don't think I could have carried much more. There was an abundance of targets on that hill, that's for sure. It was close in fighting; they were probably only 50 to 100 yards from us. The majority of the fighting was at right around 50 yards; we could see those suckers very easily. The Chinese were dug in and we were trying to get to the top of the hill and push them off. We had to clear the hill so the convoy could get by. It wasn't hard to hit people at that range. It was pretty much aimed fire. We got the correct sight picture, took up the slack from the trigger and squeezed it. It was Marine training and it was very effective in that open territory. We really put our training to use that day.

We pushed them back off the hill, but they called everyone back down to the road because they had called an air strike on the hill. The Corsairs came in and laid it on them with 20 mm, rockets and napalm. Back down on the road it was a real mess, in the 11 miles to Hagaru there were nine roadblocks. The road was narrow and the Chinese had all the high ground and they just poured it on us. It was terribly confusing, the column stopped and started, stopped and started. When we stopped we'd be off the vehicles and firing back at the Chinese and then the column would start moving and we'd have to hurry to jump back on a vehicle. We lost considerably in wounded, killed and captured. Just about all the division people and the Army people were captured. We finally got in to Hagaru after dark.

We had a night in Hagaru and it was bitter cold. The next morning we went up East Hill. East Hill was right where the road that runs east of the reservoir and the road that goes up to Yudam-ni forked. It controlled that intersection and the Chinese were determined to have that hill. We lost a lot of men during that day, the Chinese were just pouring fire on us and you couldn't tell where the hell it was coming from. They were on the top of the hill. We never did get to the top of that hill. I was on our left flank and the Chinese had a damned .50 over there and that thing traversed on us all day long. It got a bunch of our guys.

We held all day long and took a good number of casualties. We weren't dug in at all, you couldn't dig in. On top of that hill at 40 below zero, an entrenching tool would not do anything. I broke the handle right off my entrenching tool trying to dig in. About 10:00 that night, you could hear a bunch of stomping of feet and then a bunch of jabbering, then the whistles blew and then the bugles blew. When those bugles blew, church was out! Those suckers came down the hill and then back up at us. We had some tanks down near Hagaru and they shot those star shells up to illuminate things. Then you could see them and pick up some targets, although basically you were aiming down the barrel. You could get off a round every now and then at a good distance when the star shells were up. They came right up to us, but we drove them back. The guys were just popping them down; some of them were only 20 feet away.

About 1:00 AM, they came again. They really came though us that time and breached through our platoon. That .50 was working us over all the time. I was lying prone, leaning over a ledge firing down at the Chinese and all of a sudden, splat! A round caught me in the left wrist. One of the guys tied a tourniquet on my arm to stop the bleeding. I thought I'd better get down to the aid station, so I started down the hill. I only got about ten feet down when I remembered I'd left my rifle up the hill. I went back to get it and when I got back up there, you could hear Chinese jabbering everywhere. When I got back to my position a damned bullet went right through my breeches leg! It didn't hit me, but it put two holes in my trousers. I thought "The hell with that rifle; I'm getting out of here!" The hill was so steep and slippery that I just sat down, reached between my legs and pulled the tail of my parka up and slid down the hill. I got to a road about the same time as a jeep pulled up with ammunition. After they off loaded the ammo, they loaded up the wounded guys and away we went to the aid station in Hagaru.

They worked on me at the aid station, put a splint on my arm and gave me a shot of morphine. There was a stove in the aid station; it was warm in there. I found a place to lie down and went right out. The next morning I came around and they put me on a litter and took me out to the airstrip. I must have flown out on one of the first planes out of Hagaru; it was on a C-46.

They flew me down to the Division hospital at Hamhung. My arm was put in a cast and the doctor told me "Boy, you've got a million dollar wound, you're going home." A couple of days later, I flew to an Army hospital in Osaka, Japan. We went in there right from the field and we were all cruddy and stinking. They got us all in a big receiving room and told us to drop all our ordnance in the middle of the room. I'm not kidding; there must have been a pile of hand grenades that was three feet high! After that they got us washed down and in pajamas. From there, they flew me to the naval hospital in Yakuska and then they flew me to California. I wound up at the naval hospital at the Jacksonville, Florida air station, where I spent six months.

I was sent to the Marine barracks at the naval base at Charleston, South Carolina. I went before a physical evaluation board and they retired me out at 60 percent of corporal's pay. That was in September of 1951 and that was my career in the Marine Corps.

I thought the M1 was the finest weapon that anyone could ever want. You know you normally want to keep a light coat of oil on everything. But in that cold weather, you had to keep that thing as dry as possible. The Chinese used fish oil, although it was probably whale oil on their weapons. It didn't freeze the way our lubricating oil did. But, as long as you kept your weapon dry and worked the bolt now and then, you were all right. The BARs worked pretty good, the carbines weren't worth a flip. They weren't worth a flip anyhow. We didn't use carbines much; even our company commander carried an M1. Anyone who had a carbine got rid of it right quick; they just didn't have the stopping power.

My rifle froze up on me on Telegraph Hill outside Koto-Ri. We were moving forward towards the crest of the hill and when the Chinese came swarming over we had to ease back. We were right down in the snow; there wasn't any cover. The snow was about a foot deep. I looked up and saw a scraggly assed tree up near the crest of the hill. I saw a Chinaman pop up on the left side of the tree and he cranked off a round. He ducked back down and then he popped up on the other side of the tree and cranked off a round. I thought " I got you, you rascal" and I was waiting for him when he came up on the other side. I took up the slack up on the trigger and nothing happened! I looked at my rifle and saw that the bolt was open. What had happened was I'd been firing my rifle while I was lying in the snow and some snow melted in the track for the operating rod and then froze. About that time, our squad sergeant had our fire team move back about 25 yards around to our right flank. We got right up in some rocks there and I field stripped that rifle in a heartbeat! The cold was so brutal I kept my wool glove inserts on. I was able to clean the ice out and get that bolt operating. Then I looked up the hill and saw another Chinaman who couldn't be more than 40 feet away from us. He had a pair of binoculars and he was peering through them. I punched the BAR man and said "Smitty, take a look at that." We dispatched that sucker and my rifle worked fine.

I thought the Chinese were good soldiers; they were very disciplined. They had to be disciplined to behave like they did. They had those long Russian Mosin rifles and the short carbine model with the folding bayonet. They also had those Russian burp guns. They were really something; it had that drum that held 71 rounds and it would really spit them out. Those people also had an abundance of Thompson submachine guns that came from the Chinese Nationalists. There were so many of them that I heard tales that when they made those charges a lot of them didn't have weapons. They just followed the group in front and picked up a weapon when another guy got knocked off.

I think we had superior firepower over the Chinese. The way we were set up with one BAR to every fire team gave us three BARs to the squad. The platoon had nine BARs and a machine gun section with two machine guns. We could put out some fire; the BARs did super work for us.

I remember when I got back from overseas people would ask, "How many guys did you shoot?" In combat you don't know who you shot, it wasn't like in the movies. If the guy drops, you take your eyes off of him and move on to the next guy. There were plenty of targets. I'll tell you one thing; I tried to shoot as many as I could.

Personal Experiences

> **Charlie Feeback** *was drafted in July 1943 and went to Camp Croft, SC for basic training. After his basic training, he was sent to the Pacific Theater and assigned to the 24th Infantry Division in New Guinea. He saw combat in Dutch New Guinea, Palau Island and in the Philippine Islands. During the war, he made six beachhead landings and was wounded three times. He was in the Philippines when the war ended, returned to the US in December 1945 and was discharged.*

I got drafted in 1943 and they sent me to Camp Croft for basic training. Camp Croft was an infantry replacement training camp down near Greenville, South Carolina. We did six weeks of basic and then had advanced training. We didn't do a lot of weapons training. The first weapons we shot during training were .22 caliber rifles, but I can't remember what they were like. Of course we shot M1s on the firing range and we also shot 03s. They used those for shooting rifle grenades. I remember some of the rifles we trained with were pretty worn out. We shot BARs and we trained a little with the 60 mm mortar. I don't remember shooting a machine gun there. Overall, I thought we had some pretty extensive training there.

After basic, I was sent to Fort Meade, Maryland. We were replacements and we didn't do much there. A buddy and I were on the alternate list to go to Europe. They always had alternates in case someone took off or something. We were all standing on the parade field in the snow one day and everyone except my buddy and me got on trucks and took off. So we hitched a ride back to the barracks and were the only ones there for a few days. Then another group came in and they gave us all mosquito nets and we knew where we were going.

M1A1 Thompson submachine gun. Photo courtesy of Frank Iannamico.

# US Infantry Weapons In Combat

I departed the US from New Orleans and landed in New Guinea, where I joined the 24th Division. I joined C Company, 21st Infantry Regiment as a rifleman. I didn't carry the M1 for very long. Right after we landed on Hollandia, one of the scouts in my squad made sergeant and they made me first scout. I was first scout from then on. In our outfit, the first scout carried a Tommy gun. I think in the whole division the only one's who had Tommy guns were the first and second scouts in the rifle squads. You know you see all those movies where the sergeants and all those guys carry Tommy guns? I never saw any of that. They all carried carbines. The officers carried carbines because they couldn't hit anything with a .45 pistol. I had never fired a Tommy gun, so they let me go out and shoot it. I ended up being the company scout most of the time, which means I got shot at a lot. Sometimes the Japs would let me pass though before they opened up and I'd be trapped out there for a while.

I liked the Thompson; it was a good combat weapon. I kept a clip in the gun and two 30-round clips in a pouch. Then I had an extra canteen cover with one of those little waterproof bags that I carried extra .45 ammunition in. All we carried in combat was our weapons, ammunition, a poncho, a canteen, a first-aid kit, a couple of grenades, a spoon and a canteen cup. We didn't need a lot of stuff. You know you see all these movies with those guys with big packs on? I can't understand that, we didn't do anything like that. We were on the move most of the time.

A lot of the fighting that we did was at close range and the Tommy gun was the ideal weapon for that. Sometimes you were right on them and they'd pop out of a hole at you. I remember one time on Mindanao, we were dug in across the road from a few small shacks and this Jap kept shooting at us. When we got across the road I could see where he was. He was down in a hole and he had the hole covered up with a piece of tin from a roof. I stood back and shot him in his hole, then he pulled a grenade out and blew himself up. The battalion commander had come up, he was right behind me when another Jap popped out of a hole and I shot him. He wasn't any more than 25 to 30 yards from me. The Tommy gun was great for close range; you didn't have to be a good shot. If you needed to shoot way off, we had a couple of guys with sniper rifles and the M1s were pretty good for that too. You had to make due with the ammo you carried; you couldn't just shoot wild. A couple of times I used it single shot, which was kind of weird. Sighting with it was out of the question; you kind of held it waist high and fired. That was the secret of hitting something with the Tommy gun. When you shot it you really had to hold it, because it would creep up on you. It would want to go up and to the right, but you got used to it. That gun got wet and muddy many times, but it never failed me. I tried to clean it as much as I could under the circumstances.

Sometimes we experienced some hand to hand fighting. One night we had a Jap jump into a hole with one of the guys. While they were fighting, the Jap bit one of his fingers. The guy killed the Jap, but he had to go to the hospital because of his finger. He went into the hospital the same time I went in after I got wounded, but

I got out before he did. It was like his finger wasn't ever going to heal. It was a hell of a way to get a Purple Heart.

The Japs would normally string their troops out just to aggravate us. There were a lot of them hiding in trees. They were hard to deal with because we couldn't see them. Someone would start shooting at us and we wouldn't know where it was coming from. Once we spotted them, it wasn't hard to get them. If they weren't too far away, the Tommy gun was effective. If they were farther, we'd use M1s or BARs on them.

After I was wounded in May 1945, I had to go back to a hospital on Leyte. When I came back to join my outfit, they gave me one of those grease guns. I wasn't too happy about that. It didn't look like much of a weapon to me. I fired it a few times and I didn't think it compared to the Tommy gun.

When the war ended, you had to have 70 points to go home and I had 80 points. They wouldn't give me my sergeant's rating because of my points. The division was going to Japan for occupation duty. So they sent me home from the Philippines instead of letting me go to Japan. I wanted to go to Japan just to see it. Our ship pulled into San Francisco in December 1945. They put us on a troop train to Fort Knox, Kentucky and I made it home for Christmas.

## US Infantry Weapons In Combat

> **Sam Shaw** *joined the Army in November 1943. He did 18 weeks of infantry basic training at Camp McClellan, AL. He was then sent to Camp Van Dorn, MS to join the 63$^{rd}$ Infantry Division in June 1944. He was assigned to the Heavy Weapons Platoon in L Company, 253$^{rd}$ Infantry Regiment, where he became a machine gunner. After several months of training the division moved to Europe, arriving in November 1944. Mr. Shaw fought with the division through France and Germany and was wounded in January 1945. He returned to duty after six weeks off the line to the same unit and served with them until the end of the war.*

In basic, we were issued the M1903 Springfield rifle. The M1s were being sent elsewhere at that time. I never did shoot the 03. We did our rifle training towards the end of our basic training. When we went to the rifle range to qualify, they had enough M1s where they could take us in small groups to qualify with it. Then they would swap the rifles from one group to another. A sergeant would take us off to the side and show us how to operate it, load it and how to get the clip out. He also showed us how to mash our thumbs real good with the bolt if we didn't get it out of there fast enough. Once I qualified with the M1, they gave me my Springfield back. I also remember training with the bazooka and the .45 caliber automatic pistol.

When I got up to Camp Van Dorn, I was assigned to the heavy weapons platoon in L Company, 253$^{rd}$ Infantry and was put in one of the machine gun sections. The platoon had two squads of light machine guns and two squads of 60 mm mortars. The machine gun was an air-cooled, .30 caliber machine gun. It had a bipod on the end of the barrel and a shoulder stock. There were four men in the squad: a gunner, an assistant gunner and two ammo bearers. I was the gunner. We trained for eight to ten weeks with the gun while we were at Camp Van Dorn before we shipped out. I was comfortable with the machine gun; I got to know it real well during our training.

I had a lot of experience with the machine gun in combat, practically every day we got in some kind of firefight with it. It was a real good gun, but adjusting the headspace was really critical. It was important to set the head space right or when the gun got hot it would rupture a cartridge and jam. We had a ruptured cartridge case get stuck one time and it was during a battle. One of the ammo bearers had changed the barrel and set the spacing too tight. We scrambled around and got the ruptured case extractor in there and got the case out. Nobody got hurt or shot because of the jam. If you got the headspace right it was a reliable weapon. Other than that one time, we never had any failures with the machine guns in the platoon. Since we were right up with the rifleman, we usually engaged targets at the same ranges as they did. I'd say the normal engagement range was about 100 yards.

Personal Experiences

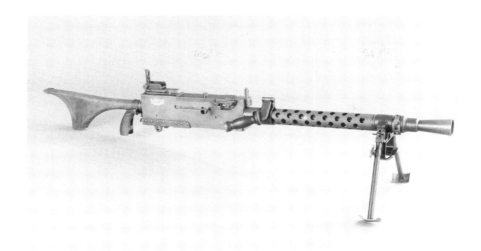

*M1919A6 .30 caliber Browning machine gun. Courtesy of Robert G. Segel.*

Sometimes it was even closer than that. We would sometimes fire the guns so much that they would get hot enough to cause a round to cook off. We would clean the guns as often as we possibly could. When things got quiet, we would run a rod down the bore and clean and oil the gun. Normally, between the four of us, we carried about 1,000 rounds of ammunition for the gun. The ammo bearers carried at least two boxes of ammo each, I think there were about 100 rounds in each box. We kept a full ammo belt in the machine gun, that would be draped over our shoulder when we were carrying the gun. We did that in case we ran into something where we had to get in action quick. You wouldn't have to worry about loading the gun because it was ready. It was a good machine gun, in my opinion. For what we had to use it for it was perfect.

Generally, in the company the two machine guns were split up. We never worked as a pair. Usually one gun would be on one end of the line and the other gun on the other end. Sometimes there was a lot of separation depending on the ground the company was defending.

I also carried a .45 pistol and a carbine. The assistant gunner and myself were issued .45s and the two ammo bearers had M1s. I had told my company commander that I didn't like the .45, but he told me I had to carry it. I mean what good was a .45 at 150 yards? I guess the .45 was all right, but it wasn't meant for front line combat. I wanted a carbine. I found a carbine that had been dropped along a trail. I called the commander and told him that we had acquired the carbine and wanted to keep it and he told me we could. Normally we were expected to turn the weapons we picked up into the company. That carbine sure helped us out. I would switch off with the assistant gunner with it. If one of us was carrying the machine gun then the other would use the carbine when we went into action. I thought the carbine was a good short-range rifle. I'd just as soon have it over an M1. I could thread a needle at 50 yards with it and I felt I could shoot very accurately with it out to 150 yards. You had to use Kentucky windage if you shot any further than that with it.

I recall one time, the 44th Division was getting the hell kicked out of them. We set up in a position by a bridge that was over a small river. The engineers had put charges on the bridge and were supposed to blow it at midnight. The 44th was retreating through our lines and we were to hold off the Krauts once they were through. But something happened with the engineers, they never did come to blow the bridge. During the night, all the 44th boys passed through our lines. When the last bunch passed, one of their lieutenants came by our position and told us that this was the last bunch from the 44th and anything coming now would be the Krauts. We had a lull for about an hour or so and then the Germans came. They came with infantry and three tanks to back them up. I could hear the sounds of their hobnailed boots coming across the bridge and I knew they were Germans. One of our BAR teams challenged them and we had a little gun battle with them. We ran about four or five belts of ammo through the gun. We got eight of them and they retreated back across the bridge. I think what saved us was the bridge was too small for the tanks to get across. We called artillery fire on their tanks and a couple of our tank destroyers came up and fired a few shots at them. We held the position and the Germans who got away went back to their lines. It had been a combat patrol; they had been feeling out to see where we were.

When I returned to the unit after recovering from being wounded, I was made the squad leader. The assistant gunner became the gunner and we got some replacements in for the ammo bearers. I continued to carry a carbine during that time. I stayed with that squad until the end of the war.

Personal Experiences

*Walter Klink (left), taken at Ft. Hood during his refresher training.*

> **Walter Klink** *first enlisted in the Army in late 1945. After receiving basic training and serving as training cadre, he attended Army photographic school. He served in the Signal Corps for a little over three years before he was discharged in 1949. As a member of the inactive reserve, he was recalled to duty during the Korean War. He arrived in Korea in January 1951 and was assigned to the 27th Infantry Regiment in the 25th Division. After four months of combat duty he was wounded during the Chinese Spring Offensive in April 1951. He was evacuated to a hospital in Japan for treatment of his wound and then returned to the US.*

I first joined the Army in November 1945. I'd just turned 18 and I enlisted in order to get the GI Bill and to get into the photographic section of the Signal Corps. That took me almost a year to accomplish. I took basic training at Camp Crowder, Missouri. While there we trained with the grease gun, the carbine and the M1. I was a pretty good shot, I made expert with the M1 on the range at 200 yards. Specifically, I recall shooting 176 out of whatever the top score was, I think 190. If you shot expert they made you cadre. That's how hard up they were to find people to train the new troops who were being drafted. After I became cadre, just for fun I went through the rapid-fire sequence: nine rounds in three positions at 200 yards at a head and shoulders target. I shot 27 out of 27. That drew a crowd toward the end.

My 15 minutes of fame. The bottom line is simple: The M1 was a damn fine weapon and if you did what you were taught, it could put out deadly accurate fire. I taught marksmanship for several months before finally getting transferred to the Signal Corps Photo Center in New York City.

I went over to Korea in April 1948 and served with the 123rd Photographic Detachment. After about a year I returned to Fort Lawton, Washington and was discharged in June 1949. I was in the inactive Army Reserve and I was recalled to duty during the Korean War. The Army worked that very cleverly. They didn't want to call up too many reserve units because that would impact towns and small cities. So mostly they called up the inactive guys like me who were sitting in college. There were no exceptions, so off we went.

I was recalled in early November 1950. They sent me briefly to Fort Dix, New Jersey and then on to Fort Hood, Texas for refresher training. The refresher training was a joke. The people they had giving us our training were the dregs! They had never been in combat and they were too dumb to send to Europe. All we did was bivouac for a few nights and did some work on the rifle range. It was ridiculous. It all took no more than three weeks. They just needed bodies for infantry replacements. We took a train to Travis Air Force base and they flew us to Japan. We spent a few weeks in Japan, but we didn't do any training there either. Then we took a boat to Korea.

I got to Pusan in early January and they put us on a train to take us up north. I was assigned to G Company, 27th Regiment of the 25th Division. I was not a trained infantryman; my MOSs were 152 and 945, photographic stuff. But when I got to Pusan, I was quickly ushered into the Infantry. The pressing need was for "bodies" because the casualty rate in November and December of 1950 was really bad. This left me in the peculiar position of being a staff sergeant who had to serve as a rifleman rather than squad leader, which would have been more appropriate for my grade. Given the usual attrition, by the time I was hit after four months I'd actually become a squad leader. This period almost completely coincides with the offensive the UN Forces began in January and ended with the Spring Offensive the Chinese mounted in late April of 1951.

Shortly after joining "George" Company, we began the offensive that ended in late April. We alternated with the Turkish Brigade on the line. We attacked in daylight and they held on at night. Their doctrine was different. They looked like rabble when you saw them on the move, but they loved to kill. They lit fires at night so the enemy would know where they were so they'd attack and give the Turks a chance to kill them. It was weird, but we knew they could hold on while we went to sleep to get ready for the next day. I was sorry when our collaboration ended. Then we went back to the usual sleep pattern of two on, two off and God help the guy who went to sleep. That could mean two dead GIs killed in their sleeping bags. We usually had orders that the man on guard had to be out of his sleeping bag. You wanted him cold enough to stay awake.

Mostly, I carried the M1 Garand. I should add that the M1 was hardly ever called the Garand. Most people just referred to it as the M1 and most would not have known that Garand was the designer-inventor. Since we had to climb every hill and mountain in our sector, the extra weight of the Garand was a negative. Sometimes, I'd carry the M2 carbine, the one you could put on full-auto or fire single shot. Those were the only weapons I ever learned to field strip, the M1 and the carbine. For some people the difference in weight between the M1 and the carbine doesn't count for much. But, climbing those hills, every pound made a difference. I briefly carried a captured Thompson submachine gun straight out of a thirties movie. But the damn thing outweighed the Garand by at least three pounds and carrying an adequate supply of .45 caliber ammo made for a heavy load. I never fired it; I gave it to one of the cooks after about two days. Nobody cared if you swapped weapons, although if a squad had all started carrying carbines there would have been an opinion about that.

I wore a standard cartridge belt, but I didn't carry M1 clips in all the pockets. I was more comfortable with a bandoleer slung around my neck. It was easier to get at. With the carbine, I had a banana clip and a few of the smaller clips. I carried about 100 rounds for it. We always carried as many grenades as we could. With us occupying the high ground, they were excellent for rolling down hills during enemy night attacks. They were extremely effective. We had a grenade pouch that carried three grenades and that's what we carried. It was possible to carry two more if you put the handle into your harness. Like General Ridgeway's trademark grenade on his harness. They were less excellent when you had to do a lot of running and they fell out of their pouches. I'd guess the landscape over there is still littered with our grenades.

The basic word back then was the carbine didn't have the knockdown power of the M1. That's hardly surprising given the size of the two slugs. I remember one guy who was a squad leader and could have carried a carbine, but refused to carry it. He wanted the knockdown power of the M1. I never really noticed the difference; I didn't have any bad experiences with the carbine. There was one night when we were attacked in a very narrow, confined area and I was very glad I had an M1 that night. They got a whole lot closer to us than I wanted them to be. I remember shooting at this one guy and he slowly staggered on down a ravine. I apparently hit his grenades and they started to flare while he was stumbling around.

I never had any problems with malfunctions on the M1 or the carbine. I do recall one occasion when another guy's M1 was fouled up. We'd just taken a hill or got most of the way up, when a guy who'd been recovering from pneumonia returned

## US Infantry Weapons In Combat

to the squad. Aside from still being wiped out physically, he'd been handed an M1 by supply and sent up the hill. When he got to me, I checked his rifle and it was totally jammed in a way I couldn't deal with. You couldn't even make it work manually. Somewhere, somehow it had turned into garbage and/or someone had a grudge and handed it to him on purpose. I covered for him until we could get another rifle sent up. That was an uncomfortable hour or so. I could shoot well, but never field stripped an M1 beyond the basic mode we were taught.

The Chinese hit us hard during their big spring offensive in April 1951. Around 0200 they threw an artillery barrage at us, but their spotter screwed up. The barrage went over the front foxholes and landed one hundred yards behind us and did no damage to anybody. Immediately accompanying the barrage were the colored flares and the bugles. The whole ball of wax you hear about. When they hit us that night it was though the ground erupted with Chinese. They managed to get close to us undetected and came at us out of nowhere. I had a rookie in the foxhole with me that night. I had him by the scruff of the neck, pulling him up and down. It was now you shoot and now you get down. I probably fired six or seven clips that night. There was no point throwing it away. You wanted them close enough to have some effect. When a group of them got close enough for us to see, them we'd fire at them. After we'd get them, there'd be another group of them and then another. There was an air-cooled .30 caliber machine gun about ten feet below my hole and there was a tank off to my right. I think they might have broken through if it hadn't been for that tank. There was another machine gun above me, up the ridge about 50 feet. They burned out a barrel that night. I found out later that until they got that barrel changed, there was nothing up there except a .45 caliber Colt pistol! We didn't lose anybody that night, nobody got a scratch! The next morning the place was littered with enemy dead. There was a mountain of brass surrounding that machine gun near my hole. If I learned one thing from all this, it was that marksmanship counted for little in combat. The prime factor was firepower.

I was wounded about a week later. The Chinese attacked us early in the evening and we were spread too thin. Our foxholes were 50 feet apart. They couldn't get any armor up to back us up. The company was overrun and things got real bad. There were no orders and then I heard a voice say "First platoon, let's go." The first platoon was on our left flank and I knew if they were going, we had to do something. I got out of my hole, told my guys to stay calm and keep watch and ran back to where the platoon CP was. About halfway there, I got hit in the shoulder and knocked down. There wasn't any mortar fire, so it had to have been a gunshot. My shoulder was numb, but I couldn't taste any blood, so I knew I wasn't hit in the lungs. I got up and made my way to where the platoon CP was supposed to be, but they had bugged out! I immediately went back and got my guys out of their holes and we took off as a unit. Later, we got in a firefight with Easy Company because nobody knew where anybody was. I got lucky because we ran across a 35th Regiment litter jeep and was evacuated by them.

I first went to an aid station. I laid there and listened to machine gun fire all night. I truly regretted giving my carbine to my assistant squad leader when I left the squad. It wasn't a good feeling being there without a weapon. It took about a day for them to get me to a MASH unit. They cleaned up my wound and put me on a hospital train down to Pusan. They had a triage at Pusan and they sent me to a Swedish hospital ship in Pusan harbor. After a week or so on the ship, I was sent to an Army hospital in Kobe, Japan for more surgery.

After a couple more surgeries, I was healed enough where they sent me to the port to be shipped back to G Company. We were on a bus getting ready to go to Sasebo, when an officer came on and asked if there were any reservists on the bus. I raised my hand along with a half dozen others and he told us to get off the bus, we were going home. They kept us around for three weeks pulling guard duty for no other purpose than to keep us busy. Then they put us on a ship for home. I was released from active duty in July 1951.

# US Infantry Weapons In Combat

> **Robert Mort** enlisted in the Marine Corps in December 1943 when he was 17 years old. He took basic training at Parris Island, SC and was sent to the Pacific where he joined the 4<sup>th</sup> Marine Division. He was in the first wave in the invasion of Iwo Jima on the 19<sup>th</sup> of February 1945. He fought on the island until he was wounded on the 7<sup>th</sup> of March. He was initially evacuated to Guam and then to a Naval hospital in San Diego. He was training for the invasion of Japan when the war ended. He stayed in the Marine Corps after the war and served two years in China and then as a drill instructor at Parris Island. When the Korean War broke out, he was transferred to the First Marine Division and fought with them in Korea before being wounded in November 1950. Mr. Mort served 20 years with the Marine Corps, retiring in 1963.

I enlisted when I was seventeen, all *gung ho* looking to fight Japs. During basic training at Parris Island we fired all the different weapons they were using at that time. We went through there in seven or eight weeks; they needed us out in the Pacific. They had just brought the M1 into the Marine Corps a short time before. Just a few platoons ahead of us had switched to the M1, although we still trained with the 03. I qualified with both the 03 and the M1. I think the 03 was a little bit more accurate, especially at long distances. We shot out to 500 yards on the rifle range. I qualified as an expert with both the 03 and M1. I had been brought up in Ohio and we hunted all through the ages. I had owned a weapon from when I was

*Model 50 Reising submachine gun. Photo courtesy of Frank Iannamico.*

eleven years old. I had shooting experience; I just had to learn to shoot the Marine Corps way. Between the two rifles I preferred the M1, it was one of the better weapons we had. It proved itself time and time again; it took a lot to stop it from working. The 03 was good, but it only had five rounds and you had to work the bolt to load each round. With the M1 you had eight rounds and it fired faster. When the last round fired the clip flew out and you just shoved another one in and it was ready to go. We also trained with the .45, the Reising and Thompson submachine guns. They bought the Reising to replace the Thompson. What a waste of money. We used to drop the sling down and stand on it so it wouldn't rise clear over your head when you fired it. I also fired the BAR and the light .30 machine gun.

After basic, I was sent to the Pacific and joined the 4th Marine Division. I was assigned to C Company, 1st Battalion, 25th Marine Regiment. I was the BAR man. I was the smallest guy in the outfit, so they gave me the BAR. The new guy would get the BAR and after a campaign he could pass it off to someone else. Whatever your assigned weapon was when you had guard duty was the weapon you carried. I had to walk my post for four hours at a time carrying the BAR. It got very heavy! In the company I was with, the gunnery sergeant taught us how to detail strip that weapon down. He'd take all the pieces, put them down on a poncho and shake them up. We had to know what each part was by the feel of it. Then we would reassemble it in the dark.

My BAR was a M1918A2, which was the World War Two model. It only fired fully automatic, where the older one could fire one round at a time or fully automatic. My BAR had a bipod that could be removed. You could screw the flash hider off the muzzle and slide the bipod off, then put the flash hider back on and lock it down tight. If you were going to defend a position you'd use the bipod, otherwise you'd put it up on the back of your pack and strap it down.

They pulled me out of my platoon at the last minute before they went to invade Saipan and Tinian because I was only seventeen! Mrs. Roosevelt didn't like us seventeen-year-olds getting killed. It was pretty frustrating; we had enlisted to fight. They landed on the 15th of June in 44 and I turned 18 on the 29th of June. They put me in the rear echelon to wait until they came back and then we went to Iwo.

When I landed on Iwo, I was carrying my BAR and wore a BAR belt. The belt had six pockets, with two magazines in each pocket. That gave me 12 magazines in the belt and one in the weapon. It was a lot of weight! I wasn't issued a bayonet, but I carried a Ka-Bar. The assistant BAR man, who happened to be the biggest man in the platoon, carried six more magazines for the BAR. He carried a carbine for himself and he had a belt with three pouches for BAR magazines that could be slung over his shoulder.

The BAR was a good weapon; I used mine quite a bit. It was very accurate; you didn't leave anything in front of you with it. If we couldn't see them, we would shoot where we knew the fire was coming from. Other times we had individual targets. When you were in combat, you never saw a BAR lying around. If somebody with a BAR got hit, someone picked it up. Guys didn't want to carry it, but in action you didn't have a problem getting someone to use it. It was a very reliable weapon, although every time you got a chance you took the brush to it and cleaned out the sand. On Iwo we weren't able to break it down to clean it. I had a shaving brush and a toothbrush and I'd keep it clean around the bolt and magazine areas. If we got a chance, we'd take a cleaning rod and run it down the bore.

At night, we'd clear a spot on the parapet of our foxhole and lay the ammo belt and open all the pockets. That way we could get to the magazines quicker. Once we emptied a magazine, we'd put them back in the pocket and we'd reload them later. For a long time, the ammo we got was 03 ammunition in five-round clips. We'd take the clips and press them right into our magazines. Otherwise, we had to take the ammo from the eight-round M1 clips and load them singly. We used a tracer every fifth round and the rest of the ammo was either ball or armor piercing. We used whatever they gave us. I belonged to an assault squad; we had a bazooka, a flame thrower and a demolition man. We were the covering fire for them when they went up. We had three BARs in a 13-man squad and we could put out some heavy fire.

I was wounded on the night of the 7$^{th}$ of March; I almost got through it. We were on an OP about 100 yards in front of our lines. A Jap came in from behind us and dropped three grenades in our hole. They were looking for water mostly; they had run out of water and all they had was the sulfur water from the island. It was really potent; it was like drinking ocean water. All three of us on the OP were wounded. I came out the luckiest, the other guys were wounded much worse than I was. When they came out and took us from the hole back to our lines, I was the last one out and the Jap came in to get my canteens. All he had was a bayonet and all I had was my Ka-Bar. I made it and he didn't.

I was evacuated out on one of the first plane loads of wounded after they had secured one of the airstrips. I was flown to a hospital in Guam and then they put us

USMC Ka-Bar knife with leather scabbard. Photo courtesy of Scott A. Duff.

on one of those small aircraft carriers and took us to San Diego. I recovered in the big naval hospital there. When I got out of the hospital I went up to Camp Pendleton; they were forming an armored division for the landing on Japan. We were still forming when the war ended.

I stayed in the Corps after the war. I went to China and served with the 4th Marines for almost two years. Then I came back and they sent me to Parris Island to be a drill sergeant. After that, I was stationed at the Boston Navy Yard when the Korean War began. I was transferred to Camp Lejeune and we formed D Company, 7th Marines. Then we joined the 1st Marine Division at Camp Pendleton, California as it was formed. The Division was sent overseas to Korea.

Our first action in Korea was the battle for Seoul. I was a squad leader then and I carried one of the new M2 carbines. They would fire full automatic. It was a good weapon for house-to-house fighting, but it didn't have shock power for any distance. It was only accurate out to 100 yards. For a lot of the fighting we did, 100 yards would be a long way out. I carried it for one reason, the firepower for close in fighting. I had some banana clips that would hold 30 rounds apiece. I would tape two of them together and have 60 rounds. It didn't take long firing fully automatic to empty a 30-round clip. I kept mine on single shot unless we got into a good skirmish and then I flipped it on automatic. During that close in type fighting, it was a good thing to have other than an old shotgun with double ought buck. The carbine gave me a lot of firepower. I had four banana clips taped together in pairs and I carried a clip pouch with two 15-round clips. I also carried three to four 50-round boxes of ammo in my pack.

We landed in Wonsan, North Korea in October 1950. I remember when they brought back the first Chinese prisoners, I said "Those guys are Chinese" and everyone laughed at me. But I had spent too much time in China not to know. We got in a big fight with them one night; it was the first time we heard the bugles and the whistles. They were using a lot of our weapons. They had our .30 caliber heavies and they also had our lights and some M1s. Different weapons have very distinctive sounds and when you'd hear that old machine gun going off and you'd think "That's ours." We found out real quick that they were using them too. When I was in China we'd re-outfit some of the Nationalist Chinese troops. About two or three weeks later they'd come back from the front lines and they had dropped their weapons and run. That's the way the communists got a lot of our weapons.

I got hit in November; we were north of Hamhung at the time. We got in a fight and I was hit by a burp gun. My parka was full of holes, but there was only one hole in me. A round had hit one of my ribs and went into my lung. They flew me back to an army hospital in Japan. After two purple hearts, they let you go home. I had been wounded earlier down around Seoul; it was a minor wound, but enough for a Purple Heart. They sent me home and I was eventually assigned to Parris Island again.

*Frank Fulford in Korea with captured Russian rifle.*

**Frank Fulford** *joined the Army in September 1949. He had trained to be a transportation specialist and was passing through Fort Lewis, WA on his way to Japan when the Korean War broke out. He was quickly reclassified as an infantryman and assigned to the 2$^{nd}$ Division. He became a BAR man in C Company, 1$^{st}$ Battalion, 38$^{th}$ Infantry Regiment. The division was shipped over to Korea and took its place in the line around the Pusan Perimeter. He spent about 13 months in combat with the 2$^{nd}$ Division enduring the withering Chinese attacks and the costly retreat through the "gauntlet" near Kunu-ri during the harsh winter of 1951. Mr. Fulford later joined the National Guard and served in an artillery unit. He retired as a major after 32 years of military service.*

During basic training, the only weapon I trained with was the M1. I didn't train with any other weapons until I joined the 2$^{nd}$ Division. I was a small guy in my unit and they used to pick on us, so they gave me the BAR. I was glad they did. I trained with it a few months while we were at Fort Lewis before we shipped out for Korea. I also fired a grease gun, but I didn't think too much of it. I qualified with the pistol too. Since I was a BAR man, I was issued a pistol.

When we arrived in Korea, we went right up on the line in the Pusan Perimeter. On our first night on the line we had a couple of heavy attacks and I probably fired about a thousand rounds through my BAR. We were lucky that we had brought plenty of ammunition up to our hole. I fired all night and my assistant kept loading magazines for me. The ammo we got for the BAR came in cardboard boxes with 20 rounds in each box. We didn't have those loaders they have now with the M16 rifle, where you could strip the rounds right into the magazine. We had to load them into the magazines one round at a time. The next morning the barrel of my BAR was all discolored, so I went down to an ordnance unit and had them change the barrel for me. It was pretty simple and it didn't take long.

I really loved that BAR; I felt it had saved my life a few times. It was quite accurate too. Most of the engagements were at 100 to 200 yards and from those ranges it was deadly. You just couldn't miss. It had two cyclic rates of fire, 650 or 450 rounds per minute. Usually 450 was sufficient, it would help hold down shooting the rounds too fast. I was good enough with it where I could fire single shots by controlling the trigger pull.

The North Koreans would zero in on our automatic weapons. They'd make probing attacks to locate them. We learned not to fire the automatic weapons during those probing attacks. You could tell when the main attack came and then we'd cut loose. On the attack, the BAR was a great weapon. You could really keep some heads down with it. When we attacked, the BAR would be in the center of our line. It was a good reliable weapon; I fired thousands of rounds through mine and only had to take immediate action with it to clear a jam one time. It was heavy and the ammunition was heavy, but it gave you a lot of firepower.

During the breakout from the Pusan Perimeter, the 1st Cavalry Division was in the lead and we were clearing up behind them. I was on our flank one time and I saw a few North Koreans running through some trees and fired at them. I dropped a few of them and then 14 of those rascals came out of the bushes and surrendered. It surprised the heck out of me. They had heard that BAR talking and they came out and threw their weapons down. I had my assistant take the prisoners back to the road and went in to check to see if there were any more of them hiding. One other North Korean came out and tried to run. I called for him to stop but he wouldn't and he met his maker.

After a few months, I was promoted to assistant squad leader and they gave me a scoped M1 sniper rifle. It was a nice brand new rifle, covered with cosmoline. It came with scope and a cheek pad. Just like that, I was a sniper. No training, just here's your rifle, go zero it. That rifle was a honey; I could reach out and touch someone with it. I had quite a few takedowns with that rifle. One time I saw a gook that was about 500 yards away across a valley. I took him down with one shot. I held a little bit over his head, fired and watched him fall. I used that rifle for several months, but then I had a problem with it. During the fighting at Kunu-ri, it would only fire one round at a time and I had to slam the bolt back after every shot.

I just didn't have time to clean it. I think we had fired so much that there was a problem with carbon build up in the gas system. It just wasn't blowing back enough gas to cycle the bolt. I threw that rifle away and picked up another one. That one did the same thing, so I found another rifle that worked right. Normally, every time we'd stop for a while we would clean our rifles, but we couldn't do that during Kunu-ri. There was just too much going on. We fired thousands of rounds through those rifles during that fight. It was the only time I ever had a problem with an M1. It was a tough rifle under tough conditions and I don't fault it for the problem I had with it. The M1 paid its way.

Before I completed my tour, I was made a platoon sergeant and acting platoon leader. I started carrying a carbine because I could move around with it better. The carbine couldn't hold a candle to the M1 as far as effectiveness goes. I never had to use it too much, but I didn't like it. You just couldn't reach out with it. Most of the time I was directing the platoon's fire and I wasn't shooting.

> **O.B. Hill** *was a paratrooper with the 1st Battalion, 508th Parachute Infantry Regiment. He joined the Army in 1942, took his basic and infantry training at Camp Walters, TX and then jump school at Fort Benning, GA. He joined the 508th after it had formed in Florida. The Regiment deployed to the UK and trained for several months before joining the 82nd Airborne Division. Mr. Hill made the D-Day jump and was wounded after fighting in France for seven days. He was evacuated to England to recover from his wounds and rejoined his unit in time for the Battle of the Bulge. He was wounded a second time on 26 January 1945. He was discharged from the Army in the summer of 1945.*

When I was in infantry training, we were issued M1903 Springfield rifles. We did our marksmanship training with the 03. During our training, we had classes on the "new" M1 rifle. There weren't enough of them to go around, so we shared rifles. They taught us how to disassemble and assemble the M1 and we got to fire it. I remember that during the class they taught the general principles about the rifle. They told us the speed of the bullet when it left the barrel and the gas pressure in the barrel. I don't think any of that stuff stayed with me once I left the room. I liked the M1 very much, better than the 03. It was semiautomatic and since you didn't have to work the bolt it was easier to fire. It had less recoil and an eight-round clip. After jump school, I reported to the 508th at Camp Blanding, Florida. I was issued an M1 and that was the rifle I carried all the way through the Normandy campaign.

The 508th went over to England and became part of the 82nd Airborne Division. We did quite a bit of training before the invasion. When we made the D-Day jump, our commander encouraged us to carry as much ammunition as we could. So I carried as many extra bandoleers as I possibly could and I'm glad I did. In fact, I didn't wear a reserve chute because I didn't have room for it. I didn't put my M1 in a case; I just pushed it between the harness and my body and jumped with it. We were pretty scattered on the jump. I think I landed about five miles from where I was supposed to be. We formed a group; I had more men from the 508th than any other unit. But there were a few men from the 101st and one from the 505th and one from the 507th in my little group. I think I ended up with 28 men in the group once we all got together.

That night we got in two firefights with the Germans and I lost about half the men I had. After daylight we ran into another group and we joined them. We had no officers, no medics, no communication equipment and no heavy weapons. The heaviest thing we had was our M1s and some grenades. We used a gammon grenade to blow up a French Renault tank the Germans were using. We were in the second floor of a house and it stopped immediately under us. The turret opened and the guy stood up in it. I took the cap off the gammon grenade and handed it to my buddy and he dropped it down the turret in front of the guy. That wiped that tank out. Our group fought for five days behind the enemy lines and then another two days before I was wounded.

As I mentioned, I'm glad that I carried the extra ammo. By the time my group was relieved by a patrol from the 90th Division on the fifth day, I was down to seven rounds of ammunition. Some of the guys were out of ammo and the most anybody had was two clips. It was a bad feeling to be that low on ammo. My buddy and I asked every man if they wanted to give up or if they wanted to stay. Every damned man said that if we've stayed here this long we can stay here forever. I was glad they said that because we had already decided we would stay. That is what I called the "Airborne Spirit." I was wounded on the 13th of June and evacuated to England. I don't know what happened to my rifle after I was wounded, I guess it stayed there.

I missed the operation in Holland while I was recovering in England. I returned to my unit while it was in France, just before the Battle of the Bulge. Since I was an NCO, I was given a choice of what type of weapon I could carry. I could choose between an M1 rifle, a Tommy gun, a regular carbine or a folding stock carbine. I chose to continue to carry the M1 rifle because it was an efficient weapon that had got me through some tough situations. I didn't think having a Tommy gun was much of an advantage.

During the Bulge, I didn't carry as much ammo as I had during the D-Day jump. Since we went into combat as a unit, it wasn't necessary to carry as much. We were given an ample supply to last us for two or three days in case we got isolated, although I never thought we'd get isolated because we were fighting as a unit. At that time I didn't keep the clips in my belt or use bandoleers. I would keep the clips in my pockets and in my musette bag. Any place I had room, I kept clips there. I just thought it was more comfortable to carry the ammo that way and I was able to carry all I needed. I still wore the ammo belt to carry my canteen, entrenching tool and the necessary things.

I fought in the Battle of the Bulge from the 17th of December through the 26th of January, when I was wounded the second time. I was sent to Paris to recuperate this time. I could have gone back to England, but I requested to rejoin the outfit. I got back to the 508th just about as the war ended. I stayed in Germany until August and was rotated home.

The M1 was a reliable weapon. I kept mine clean as much as possible. On the jump into Normandy I landed in water and my rifle got wet. Although it was wet, it worked just fine. However, during a lull the next day I made sure to clean it so I'd be sure it would keep working. Even during the Bulge during the miserable conditions, I cleaned my rifle every time I had the chance and tired to keep the snow and dirt out of it as much as possible. I never had any problems with it.

Personal Experiences

*John Hooper, England, prior to D-Day.*

> Not long after turning 18, **John Hooper** was inducted into the Army in June 1943 and was sent to Camp Fannin, TX for basic training. After completing his training, he was sent to England in February 1944 and assigned to the 29th Division. He was further assigned to the A&P Platoon in the first Battalion of the 115th Infantry Regiment. He landed in Normandy on the 6th of June and fought with the Division across Europe.

Camp Fannin was an infantry replacement training center in east Texas near Tyler. We went through training for all the weapons that were used by the infantry at that time. Firing on the rifle range with the splendid M1 rifle, issued to me the first day in Camp Fannin, was an event I had long looked forward to. Caring for it with almost daily cleaning finally had a purpose. Having been on the high school ROTC rifle team provided just the skill required for me to make expert. I deeply regretted

## US Infantry Weapons In Combat

that range firing was limited to only a few days. I would have enjoyed spending the entire 18 weeks training on the rifle range. Besides the M1 rifle, we also trained with the M1 carbine, the BAR, hand grenades, rifle grenades, the 60 mm mortar, the bazooka and the air and water-cooled machine guns. Our training lasted 18 weeks; we thought it would never end.

I got over to England in February 1944. I went to a replacement pool and from there I was assigned to the 29th Division. Initially, I was assigned to the 60 mm mortar section in the weapons platoon of A Company, 1st Battalion of the 115th Infantry Regiment. I was issued a sleek looking new carbine and a fascinating knife commonly called the M3 trench knife. I had never seen one before then and it seemed to be quite an appealing item. I never thought of it as a weapon, they were just issued to everyone with a carbine.

*M3 trench knife with M8 scabbard. Photo courtesy of Scott A. Duff.*

I settled into extensive mortar training, although live firing of explosive shells was extremely limited. They were obviously saving the stuff for more important use. I heard that those precious rounds cost $15 apiece. Three rounds would have been a months pay for me.

A few months later, I asked to be assigned to the Battalion A&P platoon in Headquarters Company. The Headquarters Company was composed of four separate platoons. One was the anti-tank platoon, one was the reconnaissance platoon, one the communications platoon and then the ammunition and pioneer platoon. My big break came and I was transferred to the A&P platoon. The A&P platoon was required to supply all the ammunition to the rifle companies, search for and neutralize mines, lay mines and barbed wire. They put up all the things that an engineering group would put up. We had people who had previous experience in construction work or with explosives in the platoon. Because we had work to do, the platoon was issued carbines. You can't work very well with a rifle hanging on your shoulder. I thought the carbine was an excellent little weapon. It really squirted the bullets.

On D-Day, we landed at about 8:20 AM at a sector of Omaha Beach we know as Easy Red. Our regiment was to back up the 116th who were the assault troops, so we were carrying extra ammunition. Other than the usual equipment, every one of us carried two bandoleers of M1 rifle ammunition. I also carried twenty pounds of TNT in a waterproofed burlap package we called a satchel charge. We made those by the hundreds and distributed them to other people who were authorized to have them. My carbine in its green plastic waterproof envelope was not immediately functional until I reached the shore, which worried me some. For my carbine, I carried one magazine in the weapon and two in the pouch on my belt. It wasn't until about a month after we had landed that putting the ammunition pouch on the stock of the weapon caught on. A few guys started doing it and then everyone was doing it. It was a convenient way of carrying the pouch, an example of Yankee ingenuity.

The day after we landed, we were moving towards our objective, Saint Laurent-Sur-Mer, a small French town and we ran into an awful lot of fire. The Germans were resisting our advance something fierce. The rifle companies were running out of ammunition. We passed the extra bandoleers we had carried along the line. They were handed from one man to another; it was a conveyer belt of hands passing the ammunition up to the rifle companies. Finally we had to send a squad back to the rear to get more ammunition and my squad was chosen. As we started back to the beach, we passed through a little farmyard. There was an old white horse and a wagon in the yard. We hitched the horse to the wagon and took it down to the beach. It wasn't hard to find ammunition on the beach. We loaded some 60 mm mortar shells, some grenades and several boxes of .30 caliber rifle ammunition. The bandoleers were packed in boxes, I think there were 1,300 rounds in a box. They were darned heavy; they each weighed about 95 pounds. We took the ammunition up to the company and then returned the horse and wagon to the farm.

The carbine was more a personal protection weapon; they could have very well armed us with pistols. It wasn't an assaulting type weapon. I was able to do pretty well with it out to 300 yards back in training. We fired at 100, 200 and 300 yards. That's what made me so attracted to the carbine, the ability to hit something at 300 yards. I considered it to be a reliable weapon; I never had any malfunctions with it whatsoever. I cleaned it periodically, although I didn't clean it every day. When I had some time, I'd run a patch down the bore, but that's about the extent of the cleaning.

On the night of the 10th of July, we dug our foxholes in an apple orchard. A few hours before dusk, the Germans came through our lines with a white flag. I learned later that it was a medical officer. They wanted to know if we could hold a truce for a few hours so they could pick up their dead and wounded. They were given permission to do so and we were told about the truce. Well, that night the Germans threw a terrific attack at us and they knew where everything was. They overran our heavy weapons platoon. I was asleep in my foxhole when the attack started. When the shells started coming in, a shell hit a tree nearby. Whether it was the concussion or a shell fragment, something slammed my carbine against my knee. It was pitch dark and I grabbed my carbine. I could hear voices and they sounded like German voices. I looked out from my foxhole and I could see tracers flying through the air and hear shouting. I went to chamber a round and I couldn't get the operating handle to move. It was jammed tight! I could feel splintered wood. I thought "I'm without a weapon and we're under attack!" The only thing I could do was crawl down into the hole deeper and hope for the best. Come morning, I found that the stock of my carbine was shattered and the operating rod was bent. I don't know if a fragment had hit it or if the concussion broke it from slamming it in my knee. On a battlefield, there was no shortage of weapons around, so I got another carbine.

One day, a jeep and a trailer filled with ammunition came up to us to supply the rifle companies. There were four or five of us unloading the jeep when a German with a machine pistol or what we called a burp gun opened up on us. He was probably no more than 50 to 60 yards from us. He wounded our platoon sergeant and a buddy of mine and damn near hit me. I rolled under the jeep and took my carbine and fired all 15 rounds in the direction I thought the fire was coming. I couldn't see anything; I just sprayed bullets over in that direction. Whether I hit anything or scared him off I don't know, but he didn't fire again.

When we were up near the German border, they needed some replacements for the mortars. Since I had trained with a 60 mm mortar squad while in England, I more or less volunteered to go to the mortar squad. I mostly carried the ammunition, although I did get to fire the mortar a couple of times. For carrying ammo, we had a heavy canvas vest that had pockets in the front and the back for the mortar shells. It could carry 12 rounds. There were five guys in the mortar squad and three of us carried ammunition in those vests. I didn't stay with the mortars too long. I returned to the A&P platoon and stayed with them until the end of the war.

Personal Experiences

*Wayne Stephens (right) in Korea. Left to right: M1 Carbine, BAR, M1 Rifle.*

**Wayne Stephens** *joined the Army in March 1950 when he was 17 years old. He took basic training at Fort Ord, CA and then attended leadership school. Upon completion of the school he became an Instructor there. After a year, he was sent to Korea as a replacement in September 1951 and was assigned to A Company, 9th Infantry Regiment, 2nd Division. He arrived as the battle of the "Punchbowl" was starting and he was wounded his first day on the line. After recuperating from his wound in Japan, he returned to his unit. He served in Korea until June 1952, when he was returned to the US as a staff sergeant and was discharged.*

I remember my first experience with the M1 rifle was when I was a 17 year old private while I was in basic training. I liked it from the first time I handled one and I qualified as an expert rifleman with it. We also trained with the M1 and M2 carbine and the BAR. After basic training, the Army offered me the chance to attend Officer Candidate School, but I turned it down. I was a kid from the hills in Idaho and OCS was out of my world. I did attend a leadership school at Fort Ord and once I completed it, I became an instructor at the school. I served as an instructor for about a year and was then sent overseas to Korea.

When I arrived in Inchon, I was a private first class with a group of replacements that were being rushed to the front. The 2$^{nd}$ Division had suffered 5,000 casualties during the fighting up around Sniper Ridge and Heartbreak Ridge and they were getting ready to take the offensive for the Punchbowl. Since I was a big guy, they made me a BAR man. On the way up to join the company, the Chinese were on both sides of the ridge we were climbing. There was quite a battle going on and my group of five guys was pinned down by a Chinese machine gun. I was wounded in the knee and evacuated to Japan.

A few months later, after I had recovered from my wound, I was sent back to Korea to rejoin the unit. I remember we were at Camp Casey getting some training prior to going up to the line. They asked us what type of weapon we wanted to carry. They had M1s, carbines, BARs and Thompsons. There were a lot of Thompson submachine guns around. They were the weapon of choice for a lot of guys; it gave you a lot of firepower. But the weapon of choice for me was the M1. You could stick a bayonet on it and it made a formidable weapon. It wasn't a long bayonet, but if you missed with the first thrust, you always had a second chance. Even with the butt of the rifle, you could nearly decapitate someone if you hit them right. My normal ammo load was a full cartridge belt and two bandoleers. I'd hang one bandoleer under each arm. Sometimes before a patrol they'd tell us how much ammo they wanted us to carry, but that was the basic load.

When I got back to the unit, they'd taken Heartbreak Ridge and the fighting was more like trench warfare. We did combat patrols and probing patrols and there was a lot of sniping back and forth. We had an area where we could sight our rifles in. We'd hang C-ration cans on the barbed wire and use them for targets. I was pretty good at hitting the cans so they issued me a sniper rifle for a while. It was an M1 with a scope and a flash hider. I would sneak out beyond the MLR in the morning and hide out during the day and return to our lines after dark. I'd find a good place to observe the Chinese positions and wait. In my mind, I can remember getting three confirmed kills while I was sniping. I'd never fire more than one or two shots from my position, then I'd get down on my belly and crawl away. I remember that most of my engagements were at a range of 200 to 300 yards. With the flash hider, someone on the right or left of you wouldn't be able to see the flash. But anyone to your front could see it. I never was fired on while I was out there because I changed positions often. Most of the guys I shot at were enemy snipers who were working into positions to snipe at our troops.

We'd do those probing patrols about 500 to 600 yards forward of our lines to take a prisoner. There were a lot of close and quick firefights on those daylight combat patrols. One of the defects with the M1 was the noise it made when the clip ejected after you fired the last round. The Chinese knew what that sound was and if they were close enough, they'd rush you. Again, that's one of the reasons I liked having that bayonet mounted. But, with the ammo in bandoleers we could reload pretty quickly. Even with that defect, I had a real faith with the rifle. It could get all dirtied up, muddy or full of dust and you could shake it out and it would work. It never failed me; it was a very durable weapon. We did our best to keep them clean. Normally we had two men to a hole and we never cleaned our rifles at the same time. If one rifle was broken down for cleaning, the other was available to fight with if something happened. We'd clean them at every opportunity.

I was in a sandbag bunker one day and a Chinese sniper fired a shot through the parapet and the round nearly hit me in the head. It didn't miss me by much more than an inch. It hit a C-ration can behind me. I could tell the angle the round came from and followed it back to where the sniper must have been. It was only about 100 yards away. It really ticked me off! I think I ended up firing about 20 clips, at a systematic rapid fire, at his position. Some of the other guys along the line opened up too. We fired at every inch of ground that the sniper could have fired from. We didn't receive any more fire from that position, so we either got him or scared him off.

In the platoon, we had a little reserve arsenal of weapons. If we were going out on a night patrol and wanted some automatic weapons, we could go over and get a few M2 carbines or a Thompson. When I became a squad leader, I always liked having someone in the squad carrying the Thompson. Even though we had a BAR, that Thompson could lay down some pretty heavy fire. I never liked the carbine; it wasn't very powerful in my opinion.

*Mr. Stephens currently lives in Montana; he receives a disability pension from gunshot wounds and frozen feet suffered during his combat tour in Korea. A few years ago, he returned to Korea for the first time since the war. He visited a unit of the 9th Infantry Regiment, which is still in the 2nd Division. His small group of veterans got to shoot M16 rifles and the 25mm gun in the Bradley fighting vehicle. He was very impressed with the new weapons. They also were able to go up to the DMZ on a tour with a Republic of Korea Army unit. The group was able to look across the DMZ at Pork Chop Hill. From higher ground, they could also see T-Bone Hill and the Alligator Jaws, major battles of the 2nd Division. He was impressed with the progress and prosperity he witnessed in Korea.*

# US Infantry Weapons In Combat

*Clinton Riddle, England 1943*

> **Clinton Riddle** *was drafted in December 1942. He took his basic training at Camp Wheeler near Macon, GA. Following basic, he was sent as a replacement to Fort Bragg and the 82nd Airborne Division. He was assigned to the Division's Glider Infantry Regiment. He participated in the invasion of Italy, the D-Day invasion, Operation Market Garden in Holland and the Battle of the Bulge. He spent 30 months overseas before returning to the US in 1945.*

I took my basic training at Camp Wheeler, Georgia. It was the Army cook and clerk school. I had six weeks of basic and then six weeks of clerical school. We trained with the M1903 Springfield rifle, the BAR, the carbine and 60 mm mortar

Personal Experiences

I made the next highest score in my company on the firing range with my 03 Springfield. I still have my old rifle scorecard. While I was at Camp Wheeler I was up for OCS and went before the board, but they shipped me out to Fort Bragg before I could go.

When we arrived at Fort Bragg, I remember an old sergeant cursing about them sending him clerks and cooks when he needed machine gunners and mortarman. There went my clerk job. They first transferred me to the MPs, where I was issued a carbine. Later they discovered that I was two inches short, I was only 5'6" and MPs were required to be 5'8". So I was transferred again into the infantry. I was assigned to B Company, 325th Glider Infantry Regiment in the 82nd Airborne Division. They were getting ready to go overseas and they needed cannon fodder real bad. Since I was a last minute replacement, I didn't get any training while I was there.

I had been issued an M1 rifle at Fort Bragg after I was assigned to the infantry. I carried it on a few hikes, but I never went on the firing range with it. I didn't get any infantry training other than going on a few hikes and doing some field exercises in Africa. I carried that rifle into combat having never zeroing it or firing it.

I didn't train with a glider until we got to Africa, where we were preparing for the invasion of Sicily. They took a bulldozer and made a runway and then brought two gliders in to qualify us. My first ride in a glider was 15 minutes long, which qualified me as a gliderman.

During the airborne operation on Sicily, the paratroopers went in first and the Navy accidentally shot down a lot of our C-47s thinking they were enemy planes. They shot down so many of them that we didn't have enough tow planes to pull the gliders. So they took us out on the Mediterranean for two weeks and gave us amphibious training. Eventually, they got enough C-47s where they could fly us over to Sicily. From there, we made an amphibious landing into Salerno, Italy. I had my first combat experiences in Italy. In my opinion, the M1 Garand rifle was the finest rifle to come out of World War Two. The M1 would fire as fast as you could pull the trigger. In training the rate of fire was 32 rounds per minute. I normally carried two bandoleers and a full belt of ammunition.

I remember when our company was issued a bazooka, all the boys were afraid to fire the thing. It was the long stovepipe and didn't break down like some of the later models. The sight system was very poor. You almost had to guess where to point it. I said I would fire it one time if I didn't have to carry it. It wasn't heavy, but it was awkward to carry. One fellow was brave enough to load the bazooka and fired one round. After that, some of the others tried their luck shooting at a target. We eventually had two bazookas in the company. The later models had better sights and were more accurate.

We landed in Normandy on D+1 at about 7:00 in the morning. We used a British Horsa glider for that operation. It was larger than the US glider, it carried 33 troops compared to 13 troops on the American Waco. My glider was the only one in the company that wasn't completely destroyed during the landing. We couldn't land where we were supposed to because of the poles the Germans had set up in the fields to keep gliders from landing. We had to pick out a small garden-like area to land in that was surrounded by hedges and trees. We cut the top out of a tree with the wing when we went in. It jarred us up pretty good and broke the antenna off the radio I was carrying.

We saw a lot of combat in Normandy, it was 33 days and nights without stopping. Even though I carried the radio, I continued to carry the M1. I only carried one ammunition bandoleer to reduce my load a little. I checked my rifle every day. Usually we were on the move until close to sundown. Then we'd stop, dig in and prepare for the next day, so we had time to check our rifles and ammunition. In Normandy, there wasn't too much sand or dust to contend with.

I was acting copilot in the CG4A Waco glider when we went into Holland. They didn't have enough pilots to have two in each glider. The pilot gave me some instruction on what to do if I had to take over. We had a much better landing area in Holland than we did in Normandy. Our pilot chose to land in a plowed field and when the runners caught the plowed ground it stood the glider on it's nose. It threw everything down on top of me and I was thrown against the crash bar. It bruised my ribs and I had to have the medics tape me up. We spent about two months fighting in Holland. At one point, we were surrounded for about three weeks, they couldn't get supplies to us. Every time the road would be opened the Germans would close it again. I ate my first horse meat in Holland.

During training I went to a number of classes to learn the nomenclature of the parts of different weapons, especially the M1. We would tear the weapon down piece by piece and then put it back together. I remember one day in combat, I replaced the bolt on my rifle while advancing on the enemy. I placed the small parts in my pocket and put it together while moving forward.

I often would give my weapon to a buddy when his jammed or something happened to it. There were always a lot of weapons lying around and I would pick up another and get it to operate. I'd carry it for awhile until somebody else needed one. I remember that during an attack on a small village one day, I had 12 different weapons pass through my hands. I was walking down one of the streets in that village carrying a Thompson submachine gun. I had the barrel pointed straight up and I touched the trigger, not being aware it was ready to fire from the open bolt. What a surprise I got! It never bothered me to pass my own weapon on to someone else.

During the Battle of the Bulge, I became a machine gunner. There was a group of our men that had been cut off and surrounded by the Germans. We rode on tanks over to that village to try to break through the Germans to get to our men. They wanted more firepower when we went in there, so they made up an extra machine gun section. They asked me to be the gunner. I had fired a machine gun during training, although I didn't qualify with one. I only carried it for that operation and later went back to carrying an M1. We had lost some of our fellows and we didn't have enough guys to carry the gun, the tripod and the ammunition. I never had any problem with my M1 in that cold winter weather during the Bulge. The light machine guns would freeze up, we would have to fire them every once in a while to keep them in operation.

When the war ended I was in France. I had been transferred to the 17th Airborne, the 194th Glider Infantry. They disbanded that Division and I had enough points to return home. I was discharged on September 19th, 1945.

> **Don Dencker** *was drafted into the Army in June 1943. He took basic training at Fort Hood, TX at the Army's tank destroyer replacement center. He had taken a test before joining the Army, so after basic he was accepted in the Army Specialized Training Program. (ASTP) He was attending an engineering course in Illinois Institute of Technology when the program was canceled. He was transferred to the 96th Division at Camp White Oregon in March of 1944. He was assigned to L Company, 382nd Infantry. He volunteered to be in a mortar crew and trained with the 60 mm mortar. He made amphibious landings on Leyte and Okinawa. When the war ended he was with the division in the Philippines preparing for the invasion of Japan. He was discharged in January 1946.*

When I was at Fort Hood, we trained and qualified with the bolt action Enfield rifle. They were getting a lot of M1s in, but they went to the organized units. The basic training guys trained with the older rifles. After basic, I went to the ASTP training to study engineering in Illinois. When they shut that down in the beginning of March 1944, about 2,000 other ASTP engineering trainees and me went to the 96th Division. We were integrated into the various units of the Division. I'd say that 95 percent of the ASTP guys ended up in infantry regiments. The Division had already formed and was in battle conditioning training. Once I had joined the Division they put us through M1 rifle training and qualified us with the M1. At that time our assistant division commander was Brigadier General Claudius Easley, who was an Olympic marksman and had been captain of the army rifle team in the 30s. Rifle marksmanship was a big thing and that's how the 96th Division became know as the "Deadeyes." We had a lot of expert rifleman when we started.

I volunteered to be a mortarman. I'd had a little mortar training in basic training and I was interested in them. I also thought it would be safer. As it turned out for me, it was safer. The mortar squad consisted of a squad leader, gunner, assistant gunner and two or three ammo carriers, when we were at full strength. There were three mortar squads in each infantry company with one 60 mm mortar in each squad.

When we invaded Leyte, I was an ammo carrier. We had a canvas sack for mortar ammunition that we wore. It had pouches in the front and back. If you loaded them according to the field manual, you could carry six rounds in the back and six rounds in the front. However, we took the rounds out of their cylindrical paperboard containers and carried them loose, which afterwards I thought was kind of a dangerous thing to do. The mortar shells each weighted 3.05 pounds each, if I remember right. We each carried about 20 of them in those sacks. I also carried a carbine, with two or three ammo clips. On that first landing, I had to use my carbine about five minutes after I landed. Our objective off the beach was Hill 120, which the Japanese had decided to defend. Most of the landings didn't have much opposition, but my battalion did. I never had to use the carbine much, but I liked it. It was pretty satisfactory as long as you kept it clean.

*81 mm mortar. Courtesy of the Robert G. Segal collection.*

The division saw a lot of combat on Okinawa. During that campaign, I was an assistant gunner and then the gunner for a long period of time. When I was the gunner I carried the tube, sight and sometimes the base plate. I can't remember how much it all weighed, maybe 45 pounds, it wasn't too bad. It was lighter than carrying the ammo. I carried a .45 caliber pistol then, but I found out the pistol wasn't that good. I took a few shots at some Japs who were about 75 yards away and missed them. Maybe if they hadn't been moving I would have hit them. I picked up another carbine after that.

We fired the mortar a lot, especially on Okinawa. Most of our engagements were at 200 to 400 yards. When we had a squad leader, he'd be the observer; if not, one of the guys in a rifle platoon would observe for us. We basically fired three types of ammunition, high explosive, white phosphorus and illumination. We mostly used the high explosive rounds. The white phosphorus was good for setting fires or making a smoke screen. We'd use the WP for regular fire missions if we ran out of

HE rounds. We also fired a lot of illumination shells. At night, anytime the guys in the front foxholes thought something was moving out ahead of them, they'd call us on the sound powered telephone and request flares. We'd crawl out of our holes and fire for them.

We finished the mopping up on Okinawa on the 30$^{th}$ of June. By the end of July, we were all on a ship heading for the Philippines to receive replacements and train for the invasion of Japan. Then war ended. I'm totally convinced that the dropping of the atom bomb saved us from having to make the invasion of Japan. After the war ended, they started shipping guys home. I didn't have enough points to go home until December. The remainder of the division returned in January and was disbanded in February.

Personal Experiences

*SSG James Ray Deaton, 1945*

> **James Ray Deaton** *enlisted in the Army three months prior to the attack on Pearl Harbor. After briefly being assigned to the 11th Cavalry at the Presidio of Monterey, CA., he took basic training and served with the 17th Infantry Regiment at Fort Ord, CA. Then he was transferred to the 15th Infantry Regiment, 3rd Division at Ft. Lewis, WA. He went overseas with the 3rd Division and fought with them in North Africa and then was transferred once more to the 9th Division. He landed in France shortly after D-Day and remained with the division until he was wounded for the third time near the German border in September 1944. He was sent back to the states and discharged in April 1945.*

I joined the Army on the 24th of September in 1940, I started out in the horse cavalry with the 11th Cavalry Regiment, but the Army decided there wasn't going to be any horse cavalry so they sent me to the infantry. I think the Army had smelled the mouse on Germany and Japan and knew there was a war coming. They trained me on the water-cooled machine gun, the rifle, the BAR and mortar. Back then we had the old 03 rifle and we wore the old World War One flat helmets. I stayed at Fort Ord for a while and then they sent me up to Fort Lewis, Washington where I joined the 15th Infantry. I believe we got new rifles and new helmets while we were there: M1 rifles and M1 helmets. I thought the M1 was great, it was easier to shoot than the 03 and it shot much faster. I was at Fort Lewis when the Japanese attacked Pearl Harbor.

We trained at Fort Lewis for a while and then rode trains across the country to Camp Pickett, Virginia. From there, we shipped out and landed in French North Africa in late 1942. Later we moved on to Tunisia where I was wounded at El Guettar by shrapnel from a tank shell. The 9th Division had gone up and got hit by a German armored unit at Kasserine Pass and took a lot of losses. Their L Company in the 39th Infantry was one of the units that got hit pretty hard by Rommel and they needed trained men quick for replacements. So I went from L Company, 15th Infantry to L Company, 39th Infantry as a replacement.

I went back to England with the 9th Division and then we landed in France on D+3. Our mission was to widen the beachhead; it wasn't very wide when we landed. I was an assistant squad leader in a rifle squad. Our company commander sent our squad on a recon patrol one day and told us not to fire our weapons. I don't know why he told us that. I'd been taught to shoot half your ammunition at the enemy before attacking them. We went walking out there like we owned the whole world and walked into an ambush. The Germans let us walk half way across a field and opened up on us. The first shot hit my rifle and then I was shot through the neck. After I was hit, I laid low until the firing stopped. I was the only one from my squad who survived the ambush.

My wound wasn't too serious and I got back to the company after a few days at the aid station. They made me a squad leader and I remember they gave me a brand new rifle. The rifle I lost in the ambush was one I had carried since coming overseas; when I transferred to the 39th Infantry, it went with me. Once I was the squad leader, I told my squad when we get fired on, each man shoots three clips back at them. You'd be surprised what a difference that would make, 12 men shooting three clips made a lot of noise and put a lot of bullets in the air. In the hedgerows, the ranges were close and that kind of firing made a difference. Firepower is what keeps you alive. I didn't have too many problems getting my guys to fire. I told them that firing was life. If you didn't fire, you'd die or get captured. You had to shoot to live. I didn't like fighting in the hedgerows, it was rough. There were always fields that you had to cross and you never knew what was behind the next hedgerow.

I carried an M1 for the whole time I was overseas and I really liked it. I didn't have any problem with my rifle, even while fighting in the desert. If you could keep it fairly clean, it worked plenty good. I normally carried a belt full of ammo and an extra bandoleer carried across my shoulder. I'll tell you what, begging for ammunition is like bumming for cigarettes. It wasn't very popular. If one person was out, then usually everyone else was running low. Guys didn't like sharing their ammo when they got low. I only ran low twice while I was over there.

I used rifle grenades a few times. I carried hand grenades too, but never did use one. I never got close enough to the enemy to use them. A hand grenade is only good as far as you can throw it. If we were that close, they usually gave up. I did use the rifle grenade, mostly while we were in France. One time they had us pinned down in a ditch with mortars. We tried to get them with rifle grenades, but they were too far away. The Germans ran out of shells and we were able to advance. The rifle grenades were good if the Germans were dug in and you couldn't hit them with a rifle. If you could get close enough to use them, you could stir them up shooting the rifle grenades on top of them. I'd say you needed to be within 100 yards to use them, though.

I walked point in my squad as we moved across France. I was wounded for the third time on September 15th just outside of Aachen, Germany and was evacuated to England. After being wounded that third time, they decided I was used up and they sent me home to recover. I was discharged in April 1945.

# US Infantry Weapons In Combat

> **Clifford Savage** *was drafted and entered the Army in November 1942. He was sent to Camp Van Dorn, MS where he became a member of M Co. 393 Infantry Regiment of the 99th Division. He trained with the Division as a machine gunner for 14 months and went overseas in August 1944. The 99th Division occupied front line positions in the "quiet" sector in the Ardennes Forest. As the infamous German Offensive started the 99th Division, received the first heavy assaults. Mr. Savage was captured with most of his platoon on the first day of the German offensive. He was a prisoner of war until liberated in April 1945. He returned to the US in June and was discharged in November 1945.*

When I joined the 99th Division at Camp Van Dorn, I was chosen to be a machine gunner. They told me I was the best qualified in my squad to be the gunner. The whole time I was in the army I was a machine gunner, from basic training on until I got captured. I was assigned to M Company, which was the machine gun or heavy weapons company. The company had three machine gun platoons, with four squads in each. Each squad had one heavy, water-cooled .30 caliber machine gun. There was a sergeant squad leader, a gunner, an assistant gunner and six ammunition bearers. Normally, they'd attach two machine gun squads to a rifle company.

Because I was a machine gunner, I never did much rifle training. I never even qualified with one. I carried a .45 pistol as a sidearm. Most of the guys in the squad had .45s, although I think I remember some of the ammunition bearers had carbines. We did a lot of training while we were stateside and I trained with the machine gun quite a bit. I remember shooting live ammunition over the heads of our troops while they crawled through the obstacle course.

The machine gun was a very reliable weapon; I don't remember ever having any problems with it. As a gunner, I had to be able to disassemble and assemble the gun blindfolded. We learned to do that early on in our training. I didn't always like being a machine gunner; as the gunner, I had to carry the gun and it was heavy. The assistant gunner carried the tripod and I think each ammunition bearer carried two cans of ammo. In combat, our machine guns were the first thing that the Germans went after. It was pretty dangerous, but we always had rifleman around to support us.

We were on the line for about 32 days before the German attack. We didn't have any problems with the gun in the cold weather. We didn't keep the water jacket filled, because the water would freeze. We kept the water in our living quarters to keep it from freezing. We were supporting K Company on the morning of December

16th when the German attack started. The attack surprised us; it started about 3 or 4 o'clock in the morning. They hit us with tanks, shells, airplanes and bombs. Just about everything. Their infantry appeared right around daylight. We did our best to fight them off. I fired two or three thousand rounds though my machine gun, but ran out of ammo. There were just too many of them, they kept coming. We'd mow one wave down and they'd hit us with another wave. The German soldiers broke through the line below us and then circled around to our rear. Our guns were dug in to fire to our front and we couldn't turn them around. We had rifleman to protect us, but there were too many Germans and they captured all of us. There were 16 men from my company captured.

The Germans treated us pretty good, although they made us help them carry their dead and wounded back to their Siegfried line bunkers. Later they loaded us on boxcars and moved us to a prison camp in Germany. I was a POW for 134 days before being liberated on April 29th, 1945.

*M1917A1 .30 caliber Browning water-cooled machine Gun. Courtesy of the Robert G. Segel collection.*

# US Infantry Weapons In Combat

*Inman Richard (right) in Korea.*

> **Inman Richard** *joined the Army in 1949. He took basic training at Fort Jackson, SC and was then assigned to the 2nd Armored Division at Fort Hood, TX. After the Korean War broke out he was quickly transferred to the 2nd Division at Fort Lewis, WA and was assigned to C Company, 38th Infantry Regiment. Shortly after he arrived at Fort Lewis, the Division shipped out to Korea. They landed at Pusan in August 1950 and were quickly placed in line along the Pusan Perimeter. Mr. Richard spent 13 months in theater before returning to the US. He was discharged after completing his enlistment in 1952.*

I joined the Army in 1949 and went to Fort Jackson, South Carolina for basic training. I don't recall how much weapons training we did there. After basic, I went to the 2nd Armored Division at Fort Hood, Texas. While I was there, I was on special duty most of the time because I played sports. I was home on leave when the Korean War started. When I got back to Fort Hood, they put me on a troop train and sent me to the 2nd Infantry Division at Fort Lewis, Washington. I got there about two weeks before they shipped overseas.

When we got to Korea in August, we went right up to the line along the Naktong River. Our first combat was at Hill 409. I was the second scout in my squad. As second scout, I stayed behind the lead man and covered him and helped him watch. When we first got over there, I carried an M1 rifle. I had shot the M1 during basic training; it was a good weapon. It was real good for distance, a lot more accurate than the carbine. I carried ammunition in my cartridge belt and then had three or four bandoleers slung across my shoulders. There were times in combat when we just had to put a lot of fire out. I can remember shooting an M1 so much that it would get very hot and cosmoline would run out of it. I don't know where in the world the cosmoline came from. A lot of times you had to see who could get the most firepower out. One thing bad about the M1, when it got cold it was hard to load. I needed to use two hands to push the clip into it.

I carried the M1 quite a bit, but then I switched to the carbine. It was one that would shoot fully automatic. Most of the fighting we did was at close range and I liked the firepower of the carbine. You could also carry a lot more ammunition with the carbine and that's one of the reasons I preferred it. I had two 30-round magazines that I taped together, where with the M1 you only had eight shots before you had to reload. I always liked to keep plenty of ammunition. When we first got over there, we had problems getting ammo. Sometimes supplies ran low and they had to ration artillery fire and everything else. After that, I always carried a little extra. We weren't able to clean the weapons everyday; we just cleaned them when the conditions allowed us to. I never had any problems with either the M1 or the carbine as far as reliability.

I carried the BAR for a couple of months. They appointed me the BAR man, so I carried it. I was a small fellow and it was a little heavy, but it was a good weapon. I wore a BAR belt that held 12 twenty-round magazines. The basic ammunition load for the BAR was 260 rounds, 240 rounds in the belt and one magazine in the rifle. Of course I carried more than that, I usually had 400 to 500 rounds. I carried the extra ammunition in bandoleers of M1 clips. I'd take the rounds out of the clips to load in my magazines. My assistant carried a little bit of extra BAR ammunition too, but not a whole lot. He had enough to carry of his own. He mostly supported me by watching my flank.

One time my BAR messed up on me, but it was my own fault. While I was cleaning it, the spring in the gas cylinder piston rod got sprung. We got in a firefight and I found out I could only fire one round at a time. I'd have to cock it after I fired to chamber another round. We were out on a patrol when it happened. We began drawing fire and the rest of the squad pulled back. My assistant BAR man and I were covering the flank and didn't get the word to pull back. I thought we would hold down for a few minutes and I'd see if I could get the BAR to work. Then our guys called artillery in on the enemy positions. There were airbursts exploding at treetop level. When that started coming in we took off across the rice paddy back to where the rest of the squad was. After we got back, it wasn't hard to fix the BAR. Other than that one time, I never had any trouble with it.

In the middle of November, we were above Pyongyang in North Korea. I hadn't been feeling well and I came down off the hill one day for a hot meal. The platoon sergeant looked at me and said "Inman, you've got yellow jaundice." They sent me by ambulance to Pyongyang and then flew me down to Kimpo. From there, they flew me to Japan and I was in the hospital until the first of February. I got out of the hospital and went right back to Korea. They sent me back to the same platoon, but I didn't recognize anyone.

I was over there for 13 months, including the time I was in the hospital in Japan. I came back and went to jump school and then was assigned to the 82$^{nd}$ Airborne at Fort Bragg. My enlistment had been extended for a year due to the war, but with my combat time they let me out early. I only ended up spending 23 days over my regular enlistment.

# Personal Experiences

> **Thor Ronningen,** like many young men at that time, had to wait until he was old enough to enlist. He joined the Iowa National Guard shortly after his 18th birthday. In June 1943, he completed high school and received his draft notice. He was discharged from the Guard and went on active duty in July 1943. He took basic training at Fort Benning, GA and was later accepted in the Army Specialized Training Program. After a few months, the Army closed down the ASTP due to a manpower shortage. He joined "I" Company, 395th Infantry of the 99th Division at Camp Maxey, TX. After extensive training in the States, he deployed overseas, arriving in France in November 1944. He fought with the division during the Battle of the Bulge and was wounded a few months later. He was sent to England to recover from his wound and was returned to the US after VE Day. He was discharged from the Army in September 1945. During the Korean War, he enlisted in the Army Reserve and spent another eight years in uniform.

During basic training, our weapons training was largely with the M1. We also fired the carbine, the BAR, the light .30 caliber machine gun and we even fired the .50 caliber machine gun a few times. After I was assigned to the 99th Division at Camp Maxey, I was selected to go to a sniper course. There wasn't any particular reason I was selected. You had to have qualified with your weapon as at least a marksman or a sharpshooter, but I don't how we were selected. It seems they only chose two or three men from the company to attend the course. The course was about two weeks long at the most. We trained with the 03 Springfield with a Weaver scope. It wasn't a very strong scope from what I remember, I think it was only four power. The 03 was a good weapon. Most of the sniper training was very similar to the marksmanship training we had done, shooting on the known distance range. We did some range estimation training and fired out to 400 or 500 yards, which in most cases was pretty ridiculous. They very perfunctorily covered stalking and hiding during the course. The majority of the course was basic marksmanship.

I never functioned as a sniper in the classical sense. I was more a rifleman in the squad armed with a sniper rifle. Generally, I thought the marksmanship training we got was sufficient. I had wished that on the weekends they'd have had the ranges open, so we could go out and shoot for the fun of it. So often we would end up going into town and stand around the street and do nothing. I think a lot of fellows would have been out shooting instead of being downtown and drinking beer or something. They had the guns, they had the ammunition and they had the ranges. I think we could have become much better marksman and become more familiar with the weapons if they had done that. I appreciated the necessity for the training the way it was, but I would have done a lot more shooting had I been given the opportunity.

# US Infantry Weapons In Combat

*M1903A4 sniper rifle. Photo courtesy of Scott A. Duff.*

In September 1944, we sailed out of Boston Harbor for England. After a brief stay at Camp Marabout in southern England, we sailed into Le Harve Harbor in France. We boarded trucks and traveled 385 miles to the front lines. The 3rd Battalion, 395th Infantry Regiment went "on line" on 9 November 1944 and was the first unit of the 99th Division to be on the front lines.

At 0530 on 16 December, we were hit by one of the heaviest barrages the Germans ever fired. It was terrifying! I was in a hole with two other fellows and was asleep when it started. In addition to the artillery, we were also on the receiving end of "screaming meemies," which were rockets fired in salvos that came in with an ear-spitting scream followed by a terrific explosion. This punishment went on for almost a half-hour as we cowered in our hole and prayed. It was dark and when the barrage stopped, the Germans turned on aircraft searchlights to reflect off the low hanging clouds which they felt would aid their attacking troops. Of course it worked both ways, we could now see the German infantry as they advanced towards our positions in their traditional slow, plodding march tempo. The artillery fire had cut the phone lines and the three of us were all alone. Several times we fired our rifles at what we thought were enemy soldiers. We heard rifles, a BAR and mortars in action, so we knew that some of our men were still alive. Not long after daylight, about 0900, our phone came alive. Some intrepid souls had repaired the lines. The lieutenant assured us that the line had held. What a tremendous relief! The barrage and attack was the start of what became known as the Battle of the Bulge.

On the first or second day of the battle, we got in a pretty good firefight with the Germans. I've got an 03 with a scope mounted on it that covered the breech so you couldn't even load a five-round clip. I would fire one round, work the bolt to eject the spent casing, reach in my pocket for a loose round, place it in the rifle, close the bolt, and fire again. It seemed that everyone else in the world had an automatic or semi-automatic weapon and I had to load one round at a time. It was frustrating. I had a pocket full of loose ammunition. I usually carried about 20 to 30 rounds in my field jacket pockets. I got my ammo from M1 clips. Most of it was ball ammo, but some was armor-piercing and some was tracer. The next day, I went to platoon headquarters and turned in my 03 and replaced it with an M1.

One of my buddies was killed and I got his rifle. I thought the M1 was the finest infantry rifle ever made. They say you're supposed to remember the serial number of your rifle to your dying day, but I don't. Although I do remember it was a five-digit number, where most of the guys had six-digit numbers. So it was an older one.

We got in a debate one day about the reliability of the M1 and I put 12 to 14 clips through mine as fast as I could fire. It fired like a dream, no problems. We would always carry 15 to 20 clips. We had those cloth bandoleers and depending how you felt, you hooked three or four of those around your neck. I didn't keep clips in my ammo belt; it was easier to use the bandoleers. I wore the cartridge belt because you had your canteen, medical packet and bayonet attached to it, but I rarely put clips in it.

We didn't clean the rifles often; we'd run a patch through the bore once in a while. We got scolded very badly about the shape our weapons were in when we got to the rear for a rest. Some of the butt plates were rusty and that type of thing, but who cares. It was the rear echelon guys who were concerned with those things. Nobody paid attention to those guys.

One night a good-sized German patrol came by our position. We fired at them, but they took off down the road. We couldn't see what happened as they passed another position, but from the sounds we knew that a real fight went on. We could hear our BAR go almost constantly with sporadic firing from enemy weapons and some grenades. The next day, we could see what happened. The BAR man opened up on the patrol with his BAR while the two men with him loaded magazines for him as fast as they could. There were 19 dead Germans in the shallow ditch about 20 feet from their position. We could see in the snow where German grenades had gone off near the hole. The BAR man told us he didn't see or hear the grenades in the frenzy of action.

I remember that they used to tell us not to get "trigger-happy." They didn't want us to shoot unless we were sure of our target or don't shoot unless you have a target. All that makes sense if you're hunting ducks or something, but not for combat. I thought it was more important to shoot. My feeling was you snap one off and it may not be very accurate, but it's going to make the guy get his head down. Then you could aim with the second one.

In March 1945, I was wounded when a few guys in my squad were loading their bazooka. The round slid all the way through the tube when it was loaded and hit the ground and exploded. It must have been a faulty round; it should not have gone off like that. There was a sleeve inside the round, like a mortar round. You needed a sudden change of direction for that sleeve to slide back so the firing pin is exposed. The squad was in a barn at the time and many of us were wounded by the blast. I was initially sent to an army hospital in Paris and then evacuated to England. I was still in England when VE Day came. I returned to the US in April and following treatment for my wounds, I was discharged in September 1945.

Personal Experiences

*John Boitano*

> **John Boitano** *was drafted into the Army in July of 1942. He volunteered to be a paratrooper and he was sent to Camp Toccoa, GA, where he joined B Company, 506th Parachute Infantry Regiment. The Regiment later became one of the infantry regiments assigned to the 101st Airborne Division. During the war, he made combat jumps into Normandy and Holland and fought in the Battle of the Bulge. Following the war, he returned to the US and was discharged in September 1945.*

I tried to join the Navy right after the attack on Pearl Harbor, but they wouldn't take me. I'd been drinking the night before and I think I had alcohol in my blood. I had been working as a sheet metal man and thought I could do that in the Navy too. After they turned me down, I figured I'd just wait for them to draft me and they did. I was at the Presidio of Monterey in California when I volunteered for the paratroops. Some captain told us the food was better and we would make an extra $50 a month. That was good, but I wanted the challenge. I also thought it would give me a crack at the Germans sooner.

We took a train across the south and arrived at Toccoa. They were still building the camp when I arrived. I remember that we got new M1 rifles during our training and the battalion went up to a place in Kentucky to do rifle training. I loved that rifle. When I was a kid, I'd always had a rifle. I took good care of my M1; I oiled it and kept it up pretty good. I rubbed on it so much getting it ready for inspection that it got shiny! I discovered when we were in Normandy that it was so shiny you could see it in the dark. I had worn the finish off. There were a lot of rifles lying around, so I got rid of mine and picked up another rifle.

When we made the jump into Normandy on D-Day, I remember being loaded down with so much equipment that I had trouble climbing the four or five steps into the C-47. Also, when you're scared your legs don't want to work right. I didn't have the strength to climb those steps. I was wearing two chutes, a gas mask, four or five knives, my rifle belt, two bandoleers and two or three grenades. My M1 was in a canvas bag that went next to your body and then you put the chutes on around it. The bag clipped to the top of your harness so you couldn't lose it. The rifle was disassembled into three pieces in the bag. I didn't worry about that, I knew it didn't take long to put it back together.

After we landed, there were 13 or 14 of us that grouped together. We were behind enemy lines for two or three days before we made contact with some of the invasion troops. We didn't do much fighting the first day; we were trying to find our buddies. I killed my first German on our second day in Normandy. My lieutenant wanted to have an outpost forward and he sent me out with about 12 guys. We went across this square field surrounded by hedgerows. We had already learned that you didn't walk through the middle of those fields. I was on point as we moved around the field and I saw some blue smoke coming out of the hedges. I couldn't figure out what the blue smoke was from and went over to see what it was. I walked over and there was a Kraut. He was lying down in a deep slit trench and he had this beautiful sniper rifle. It was no ordinary issue rifle. The rifle was on the ground in front of him and that was the mistake he made. He saw us and reached for a grenade on his belt. When he reached, I let him have it. I think I shot him six times! When I shot this guy, I couldn't believe the effect that first round had on him. He almost came out of his hole with that first blast. He came up and looked me right in the eye! That was from the impact of the bullet! His rifle was really nice; I kick myself in the ass to this day for not taking it.

Another time I was out on patrol with the lieutenant, I was like his bodyguard. We saw a Kraut on a road about a block away. The lieutenant says, "Shoot him." I fired and missed. I fired again and heard him "yelp," but he didn't go down. I fired a third time and hit him smack in the middle of his chest. The impact sent him up in the air and he did a complete summersault before he landed in the ditch beside the road. I'm not kidding. The M1 was a powerful weapon.

Personal Experiences

After we were in France for three or four weeks we weren't doing anything. We were living in pup tents waiting for LST to take us back to England. We were bored. A few of us decided to go on up the peninsula to see all the damage at Cherbourg Harbor. We started up there and we got drunk. We each had our rifles with two bandoleers. We were shooting at everything, the mailman, just fooling around, we weren't trying to hit him, fence posts and the electrical stuff on top of the poles. The MPs came from Cherbourg and told us to quiet down, but we ran them off. That happened a few times. I remember that the last MP had a "chicken" on his shoulder. He was full bird colonel and we respected that. So they took our rifles, although by that time we had shot up all our ammunition. They threw us in with the Germans in a POW pen. We lay there all night asleep on the cobblestones, passed out. We thought we'd all catch hell once the report came in on us. A few days later it filtered down and we had to report to the orderly room. Our Regimental Commander, Colonel Sink, had got the report but figured we were just having a good time.

I jumped into Holland with the same heavy load as Normandy. The jump was around noon, we were supposed to take a bridge outside of Eindhoven. I landed in a tree and was hanging in my chute about a foot off the ground. All I had to do is cut myself out and I was all set to go. It was wonderful; I didn't have any jump shock. Most of the time we hit the ground like hell with the T5 chute.

We saw a lot of combat in Holland. I didn't kill as many Germans in Holland; we took a lot of prisoners. We did really well as far as not losing many men, up until the time we went up north near Arnhem to help with the situation up there. Then the crap hit the fan. We trapped some Germans across the river from Arnhem and they had some tremendous artillery support. The artillery chewed us down to nothing. I ended up having the platoon for a month or so after that.

Another time in Holland, I was leading a patrol down this road. We were patrolling to keep the road open for the Limey tanks. Up came a tank from our rear, a little observation type tank. It was a German tank and they were driving down the road throwing concussion grenades at our men along the road. They were trying to get back to their lines. The grenades killed a couple of our men. When I first saw the tank, I thought it was British. I happened to have a new guy in my squad and he had the bazooka. Just as the tank went by me, my guy fired the bazooka into the back end of the tank. There was a big shower of sparks and a terrible noise. I said "Jesus Christ, what are you doing, it's a British tank!" And the kid says, "Look again sarge, that's a Kraut tank." It got another block up the road and then the guys bailed out of it. I was so surprised about what had happened that I never fired a shot at the crew, they got away.

When the Battle of the Bulge started, I still had the platoon. I remember we heard about the German breakthrough about 0300 in the morning one day in the middle of December. That's how it all started for us, we followed the 501$^{st}$ to Bastogne. We didn't shoot very much around Bastogne; most of the fighting was with tanks. We saw some big armor battles. I saw the U.S. Armored Corps beat the hell out of the Krauts during the middle of the Bulge. It was something to see.

I never had any trouble with my M1. I kept it clean and oiled. With my experience with sheet metal, I knew how to care for it. I didn't have any trouble with it while we were in Bastogne in the cold either. I always kept it in tiptop shape and always had it by my side. Later the lieutenant gave me a grenade launcher for my rifle. It was a bad move; I didn't like it at all. You had to remember to load a blank round and then put the grenade on. If you forgot and put a live round in, you'd blow yourself up. I carried it around for a while, but I didn't shoot very many rifle grenades. At that point in the war we were going through Germany and there was very little resistance.

When the war ended, we were in Austria. I got to go up to Hitler's Eagles Nest, but the British had bombed it to ruin. I had 88 points and you only needed 85 to go home. We went to Marseilles and caught a ship to the States. I flew from the East Coast to Camp Beale, California and was discharged.

# Personal Experiences

> **Everett "Bud" Hampton** enlisted in the Marine Corps in the summer of 1942 and took basic training at Parris Island, SC. After basic, he was assigned to the 23rd Marines, which became one of the infantry regiments of the 4th Marine Division. He made amphibious landings on Roi-Namur, Saipan, Tinian and Iwo Jima. Following the Saipan/Tinian operation, he was given a battlefield commission and became a rifle platoon leader. After being wounded on Iwo Jima, he was evacuated to the US to recover. He left the Marine Corps in 1946, but was recalled for duty during the Korean War. He served in Korea for a year serving with the 7th Marines before returning to the US. Mr. Hampton remained in the Marines and retired at the rank of major after 23 years of service.

I enlisted in July of 1942 and went to Parris Island for basic training. My platoon trained and qualified with the 1903 Springfield rifle. I fired expert with both the 03 and the .45 caliber pistol. I was the only one in my platoon to qualify expert and I got to skip pulling any mess duty. I didn't train with any other weapons while I was there.

Later on, when I went to Camp Lejeune, I joined L Company, 3rd Battalion, 23rd Marine Regiment. For some reason or another, they made me a squad leader. I had this old folding stock Reising submachine gun which I used for about a month. Then they discovered that they weren't worth anything and they withdrew all of them. By that time the company had M1 rifles and the carbine. Since I was a squad leader I was issued a carbine. I liked the carbine and I had real good luck with mine. I never had any problems or stoppages with it all during the time I carried it. As I recall I carried the same carbine up until I was wounded on Iwo Jima.

While I was at Camp Lejeune, I went to the Scout/Sniper School. The school was about four weeks long. They taught us sniper techniques and we did additional rifle marksmanship. We used the 03 in the school, some of them had scopes, although I don't recall using a rifle with a scope much there at all. We did a lot of firing at long range; most of our shooting was done at 300 and 500 yards. It wasn't difficult to hit targets at those ranges with the 03. We had one instructor who could outshoot us at 500 yards firing offhand while we fired from a supported prone position. He was a former FBI man who had joined the Marines. He was an expert with all weapons.

Between basic training and the Scout/Sniper School, I had a lot of experience with the 03 and I really liked it. I bought one while I was in the Corps; they were selling them at Camp Lejeune. I bought a real nice one for $25, which was all they were charging for them at the time. I still have the rifle.

## US Infantry Weapons In Combat

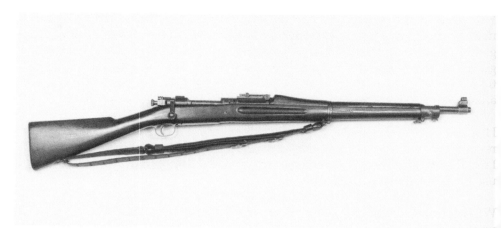

*M1903 rifle. Photo courtesy of Scott A. Duff.*

We took a troop train across the country to Camp Pendleton, California where the 4th Marine Division was formed. We left San Diego and landed in the Marshall Islands. We were the first unit to go directly into combat from the States. We first landed at Roi-Namur, although we didn't see too much combat on that island. We were only there for three days, it was like a training maneuver.

We invaded Saipan in June of 44. Our battalion and company was in the first wave on Saipan. I was a sergeant then, still leading a squad. I carried my carbine with 60 rounds of ammunition and four hand grenades. Like most people who carried a carbine, I took the magazines and taped them together. That way you'd have plenty of ammunition. Once you fired one magazine, you could pull it out, reverse it and put it back in. I carried two of those and that was enough ammunition for me. I didn't have to do much shooting; I spent more time supervising the men in my squad. It was more important to get the BAR teams set up and any of our supporting arms, like the light machine guns, in position. I was the only one in the squad who carried a carbine; the rest had M1s or BARs. Our BAR men always had an assistant who helped carry additional BAR ammo and provided security for them. They were always setup together in the same foxhole. The BARs did good work for us.

We spent 35 days fighting on Saipan, then we rested a few days and went over and landed on Tinian. We went directly from Saipan to Tinian in LVTs, it was just a couple of miles across the bay. Tinian wasn't near as bad as Saipan. We landed on a beach where they didn't expect us and had time to get set up. The first night we had a real big *banzai* attack, they attacked us with tanks and infantry. The Japanese tanks were much smaller than ours were; we took them out with bazookas. I think we clobbered at least a third of their forces that first night. We were on Tinian for nine or ten days.

We had a weapons section in the rifle company. I think there were four or six machine guns and mortars in the section. They would assign a section of machine guns to each front line platoon. Whenever possible, we'd get the heavy machine guns from the weapons company. The heavy machine guns could fire a lot longer than the air-cooled ones. They were really good for defense. During those *banzai* attacks those machine guns were more important than anything else was.

I had my Dad send me a .38 caliber pistol. It was a nickel-plated Smith and Wesson revolver; I think he got it from a policeman. The Marines didn't care that I had it, as I recall quite a few guys had personal side arms. I never used it in combat; I mostly used it as a foxhole weapon.

We landed on Iwo on the 19th of February 1945. Since we had been on the first wave on Saipan, we were in reserve for the invasion of Iwo Jima. We landed on the first day at about 1:00 in the afternoon. When we landed, we were three officers over strength in our company. I was wounded for the first time on the seventh day, but it wasn't too serious. I got a piece of shrapnel in my back. By the eighth day, I was the only officer left. I had the company for two days before they transferred another captain in to take over. On the eleventh day, I was leading a night patrol when we ran across a Jap patrol. We challenged them and they answered our challenge with hand grenades. I was wounded by shrapnel from one of the grenades.

After I was wounded, they sent me to the hospital on Guam and then I went through I don't remember how many hospitals until I got back to the one in Norfolk. Then I was transferred down to Camp Lejeune and I got out in April 1946.

I was recalled during the Korean War in January 1951. They recalled me as a 1st lieutenant and had me attend what they called a "Special Junior Course" at Quantico; it was like refresher training for us. Most of the training was on staff work; there wasn't any field training.

When I got over to Korea, the unit had just got back from the Reservoir Campaign. They were on line south of Seoul below the 38th parallel. I commanded A Company, 1st Battalion, 7th Marines for six months. We didn't see too much combat during that time, a few small skirmishes and manning outposts on the line. After six months with A Company, I was transferred to one of the Marine Air Wings. I served with them until my tour was completed.

# US Infantry Weapons In Combat

> **Hank Hanahoe** *was drafted into the Army in the summer of 1942. He took basic training at Fort Meade, MD and was then sent to Fort Bragg, NC where he joined the 47th Infantry Regiment of the 9th Division. In October 1942, he left the US and went with the division to invade North Africa. He fought across North Africa and then invaded Sicily. Following the campaign in Sicily, the division returned to England and prepared for the invasion of France. He landed in France and fought across Europe until being wounded in the Hurtgen Forest. He returned to his unit just before the end of the war.*

I was drafted and entered the Army in June 1942. I took my basic training at Fort Meade. We trained with the 03, the M1, the carbine and machine guns. I also had demolitions training. After basic, I was sent to Fort Bragg where I joined the 47th Infantry. I was assigned to Headquarters Company and into the A&P platoon, that's the Ammunition and Pioneer platoon. The first squad was ammunition carriers and engineers, the second squad was demolition and the third squad was the same as the first squad, ammunition and engineers. Because of my demolitions training I went to second squad.

In the A&P platoon we were all considered infantrymen, so they gave me a BAR. It was the first time I'd trained with one. I weighed 126 pounds and the BAR weighed 26 pounds with a clip in it. They took me out and let me burn off a clip and that was it. At first I hated the BAR, it was too heavy and I was too light. After I carried it for a while, I got used to it. Later, I changed the spring in it. I put a heavier spring in it and it didn't have such a wallop on my shoulder. It reduced the recoil. If you fired a BAR fully automatic, it would lift you right off the ground. You had to fire bursts. I used to take the bipod off for most of the time, although I'd put it back on if I needed it. When we were in a defensive position, it was good to have the bipod on.

I carried three BAR cartridge belts, there were 12 clips in a belt, 20 rounds to a clip. I wore one around my waist and the other crisscrossed over my shoulders. I didn't have an assistant; I always carried my own ammo. When you were in a firefight you never felt the weight of the ammo. Once I fired a clip I just threw it away; we got more every night. We got the clips in a wooden case already loaded.

I think the extreme range of the BAR was 2,280 yards. I fired at troops running around in the open at 1,500 yards once, but I couldn't see if I hit anything. I'd say the average engagement range was a little over one hundred yards and at that range, it was deadly accurate. I didn't have any trouble hitting anyone at that range. The enemy hated the BAR. I heard that the life expectancy of a BAR man in combat was three minutes. We drew a lot of mortar fire when we opened up. The Germans were good with their mortars and if you didn't move, they'd zero in on you fast. You had to pick several firing positions, because as soon as you opened up, you had to move.

I carried the same BAR through the whole war. That BAR was an old World War One BAR. You could fire single shots and automatic with it. After Saint Lo, I could tell my barrel was burned out. It wasn't shooting very well, it wasn't very accurate, the bullets were turning end over end. After I burned the barrel out of it, I thought I was going to get rid of it and get a rifle. I took it to an ordnance truck to turn it in. The guy at ordnance looked at it and told me that I was lucky, they could pull the barrel and replace it. They put a new barrel on it and gave it back to me.

I never had any problems with my BAR; I kept it clean. I carried a three section cleaning rod on my belt. Somebody always had some bore cleaner and some patches. I used to use a .45 caliber brass brush to clean the chamber.

I got wounded in September 1944 in the Hurtgen Forest. I was hit in the leg by shrapnel and sent to a hospital in France to recover. I got back to the unit just before the war ended. The supply sergeant had kept my BAR for me. The same BAR, I carried that weapon the whole time I was overseas. As I remember, I was the only man with a weapon on the ship coming back to the States. It wasn't until I got off the train at Fort Dix that the Army finally took their BAR back.

*Jack Walentine, Korea, 1950*

**Jack Walentine** *enlisted in the US Army in 1947. He was 16 years old at the time; he got in using his older brother's birth certificate. The Army sent him to Fort Dix, NJ for basic training. Following basic, he attended jump school at Fort Benning and then was assigned to the 188th Infantry Regiment of the 11th Airborne Division in Japan. In 1949, he was transferred to the 25th Division and he remained with them until the outbreak of the Korean War. He served in Korea from July 1950 until being wounded for the fourth time in February 1951. After being wounded in February he was returned to the US. He continued to serve in the active Army and the National Guard until he retired as a sergeant major in 1989.*

I enlisted in October 1947, I was 16 years old and I lied about my age. I had an older brother who had passed away and I used his birth certificate to enlist. They sent me to Fort Dix for basic training; I was there for 14 weeks. The service rifle at that time was the M1 rifle. I remember during our training, we marched out to the range and stayed in tents. We spent four whole days snapping in and shooting. The training wasn't that good; the sergeant and corporal instructing us did not know how to shoot. All they did was rattle off a bunch of instruction and scream and holler at us. If the NCOs didn't know how to shoot, how could you expect them to teach us how to shoot? I'm a lefty, they allowed me to shoot that way, but they had some cockamamie way to insert the eight-round clip with the right hand. It was absurd. I'd shot the M1 long before I went to basic. I had a friend that had been in the Marine Corps in World War Two and he brought an M1 back with him. We went out and shot that thing and he showed me how to shoot with it. He was a southpaw too. I learned how to take it apart and clean it. He even showed me how to scrub the chamber. At Dix, they were more interested in us scrubbing them in hot, soapy water and standing inspection with the damned things.

Back then, I was 5'7" and weighed about 140 pounds tops. I had one platoon sergeant who was a complete idiot. He got me out in front of the entire platoon and called me all sorts of horrible names. One of the things he said was "This man thinks he can shoot from the wrong shoulder and qualify." He wasn't aware I had shot the M1 before. I was one of three in the company to qualify as expert. That sergeant had me on ash and trash detail on Christmas Day for that.

During our training we shot the BAR, which was strictly to show us how to insert the magazine. We shot at paper targets on a very short range. We also shot the M1919A4 and A6 Browning machine guns. That again was strictly for showing us how to open the cover, load it, set the headspace and that was all. I didn't shoot the Thompson, the carbine or any handguns. The only thing I shot for record was the M1 rifle.

After Airborne school, I went to the 82$^{nd}$ Airborne Division. They were reforming the 504$^{th}$ from World War Two. I was only at Fort Bragg for three months and the next thing I know I'm on a ship to Yokohama. I was assigned to the 188$^{th}$ Airborne Infantry Regiment, which was part of the 11$^{th}$ Airborne Division. The 188$^{th}$ had been a Glider Regiment, but by 1948 they were all Airborne Regiments. I had to attend glider school there and was glider rated. About six weeks after that a typhoon came through and all the gliders were left piled up in a ball. Thank God for that! Everyone cheered.

In April 1949, the Army shipped the 11$^{th}$ Airborne back to Fort Campbell, Kentucky. I had only been over in the Far East for 18 months and if you had under two years, they shipped you to another unit. I ended up in the 35$^{th}$ Regiment of the 25$^{th}$ Division. When I got there that division was in shambles, it was in horrible shape. They were very short of men and equipment.

When we were in Japan, each of the rifle companies had 12 or 14 M1C sniper rifles. The rifles were rarely shot. I was on the Far East rifle team in 1948/1949 and we used to use them to shoot on the rifle teams because they were the least shot weapons in the company. When we went to Korea I tried to get my hands on one, but forget it. The scopes were gone and the rifles were lost.

*M1C sniper rifle. Photo courtesy of Springfield Armory National Historic Site, Springfield, MA.*

I was actually getting ready to ship home when the Korean War started. They sent us all from the port back to our regiments. We arrived in Korea on July 14th 1950. I was a corporal and a squad leader. My squad had one BAR and the rest of us had M1 rifles. Not long after that, we went to two BARs. We acquired an extra BAR, but what we needed to acquire were magazines for them. At one time, we were down to two magazines per BAR. The guys would lose them or throw them away in combat. I heard that it was a court-martial offense if you lost your BAR magazines. It was the assistant's job to pick those up. The gunner would hand him the empty and the assistant would hand him a fresh one. We were supposed to be issued ammo in five-round clips for the BARs. We had the thing that fit on top of the magazine that would allow us to strip the clips into the magazines. That was the only way to rapidly reload them. It was impossible to foresee if we would get the five-round clips. As it was, we only got those rarely. We always had to either break the machine gun belts down or get rounds from the M1 rifle clips. All of the 30.06 ammunition that was issued to the infantry squads in Korea was armor piercing. The eight-round clips were AP and the machine gun belts were four of AP and one tracer. Later, in about September or October, we started getting some of the ball ammunition.

We had a platoon sergeant who was a former Marine who had fought through the Islands in World War Two. If it were not for the type of training he insisted on in Japan, we would probably have had far more casualties. He kept us in shape and our weapons were maintained strictly by the manual. He would not allow a weapon to be inspected unless it was properly lubed. Even if the battalion commander wanted to come through on an inspection, he had special permission for the machine guns, the BARs and the M1s to be lubed exactly the way they were supposed to be for combat. If he ever caught you with a worn out chamber brush, it was bad news. We were also required to have rifle grease, the lubriplate grease, in the butt of the rifle. He showed us how to wipe it on the bolt locking lugs and op rod. I saw people go

*Jack Walentine, Korea, 1950*

into combat without a rod, a patch or a chamber brush, but not in our platoon. He also showed us how to use the M1 combination tool to remove a ruptured cartridge. I think I was afraid of him a lot more than I was afraid of the North Koreans.

Something we had to do was zero the elevation knobs on our M1s. Our platoon sergeant could shoot well and he made sure we could shoot well too. You would shoot at a certain range and then loosen the screw on the elevation knob and slip it to the proper range. Then from that time on, the trajectory on those rounds matched the range you dialed in. If you turned the knob to 400 or 450 yards, your beaten zone was right in that area.

The ammunition the American Army shot those first eight to ten weeks was all corrosive, except for the carbines. What happened with the rifles was the chamber would rust in a few hours at the right temperature and humidity. I had that happen to me one time. I fired a shot and the bolt tore the rim of the cartridge off and then shoved a live round right in back of the other cartridge case. There were only a few of us that realized that there was an extractor for that on the combo tool. I was able to clear the jam using the tool. If we were aware that we were going to get in a firefight, our platoon sergeant would make certain that we all scrubbed the chamber of our rifles. Then he would have us rub the cartridge case of the round that was going to be chambered with grease. I know the Army was always emphatic about not oiling ammunition, but he had us do it and it kept the rifles functioning. When the weather got cold, we didn't use the rifle grease. We got some light weapons oil and that's what we used on our rifles and machine guns. And when it got to be 16 degrees below zero, we used that very sparingly.

# US Infantry Weapons In Combat

*Jack Walentine, standing .30 caliber machine gun. Squad members display captured North Korean weapons.*

The M1 was a wonderful piece of equipment. We were in a position in North Korea when the Chinese came in the war. They hit us at 6:00 in the evening, just after dark. By 8:00 the next morning, we had lost 100 guys killed. The M1 that I shot during the night was actually on fire a few times. I have no idea how many rounds I put through it. By the time the sun came up, the rear handguard was gone. The front handguard was half consumed; it looked like a piece of charcoal. The front of the stock, up by the upper band, was completely burned away. Yet that rifle fired all night long. That night the average engagement range was only about 15 feet, so there weren't any accuracy worries. I got rid of it the next day and picked up another rifle. It was easy to exchange rifles there. Especially when the new draftees and reservists came in as replacements, they had new rifles.

Here's a story on the power of the M1 rifle. In the latter part of December in Seoul, there were about six of us on the second floor of a schoolhouse. We heard a lot of rifle and submachine gun fire outside, so we thought let's not be caught on the second floor of the schoolhouse. We walked down the hallway to the stairs with me leading. As I turned to the right to start down the stairs, I was confronted by three Chinese coming up the stairs. We hadn't seen or heard each other and they were right there when I turned to go down the stairs. The guy in front had a long rifle

Personal Experiences

with a bayonet. He wasn't able to drop the rifle low enough to shoot me; his rifle hit my shoulder as he brought it down. Remember I explained that I shot from the wrong shoulder, I'm a lefty. The fact that I was a lefty meant the rifle was on my left side. That rifle came right up and I shot him. The round went completely through him and went through the second soldier. The third guy had a submachine gun, had he been first in line I probably wouldn't be having this conversation with you. But, the power of that rifle knocked the first two guys back on the third guy and they all rolled down the stairwell. That third guy was taken care of by one of the other guys in the squad. The power of that rifle was awesome.

The original fragmentation hand grenades we brought from Japan were World War Two grenades. As soon as you pulled the pin, they would make a loud "pop" and then they would start to smoke. We later received grenades after arriving in Korea that were "popless" and smokeless. After we got those, there were rumors of accidents and soldiers being killed. They would pull the pin and the grenades wouldn't pop or smoke and they'd think they had a dud and wouldn't throw it. I knew of one soldier that thought he had a dud and set the grenade down beside his hole. He was killed when it exploded. The reason it happened was by the time the ammo got from the S-4 section to us up on the hill, it was unpackaged and rolling around the boxes loose. Those new grenades had a very large red and yellow warning tag on the grenade that said, "This grenade is popless and smokeless." But the infantrymen on the hill never saw the warning because the grenades were out of their fiber container when they got to us. That was another example of lack of instruction to the troops.

It was an absolute fallacy that the 2.36-inch rocket would not stop a T34 tank. Here is what happened. The ammo for our particular battalion was stored in an old seaplane base in Japan. It was rusted, it was corroded, and the containers had to be cut off some of the rounds because of all the moisture. The other thing was I have watched soldiers ram a rocket in the back of a launcher without removing the safety pin. The round will not go off with the safety pin installed. People talk of seeing rounds bounce off a tank; it's a HEAT round, it does not bounce off unless it fails to explode. It fails to explode if it's rusted and corroded or the soldier was not trained in removing the safety pin. I watched it happen from 50 feet away as a soldier rammed round after round into the launcher without removing the pins. I was screaming at him, "You dumb SOB, remove the pins!" He throws the rocket launcher down and screams "We can't stop them" and hauls ass. I don't think I ever saw a Russian T34 tank that took a HEAT round hit that did not go through the armor. That round would go through over five inches of homogenous armor. The thickest armor on a T34 was under four inches, although some of the tanks we confronted had an extra steel track pad on the front of the tank. If the rocket hit that pad, it wouldn't penetrate the front armor. One time I got a rocket launcher and found a tank that had been hit and fired a round into the front. The round went clean through the armor and through the back of the driver's seat. Then I shot it from the side and the rocket went completely through the turret. The ammo was old and rotten and the soldiers were not trained. Another problem was most of the rocket launchers weren't bore sighted.

When the 3.5-inch rocket launchers arrived in country, I was sent to receive instruction on it just behind the lines. The launchers and ammo had been flown over to Korea along with sergeants from the arsenals to instruct us. Every rocket launcher that was issued to us had been bore sighted. The ammo was fresh and functional and you had to remove the safety pin or the round would not fit in the back of the launcher. So you could not inadvertently seat and shoot a rocket that was not armed. They showed us by shooting at rocks on the side of a hill how accurate the 3.5 was. It wasn't any more accurate than the 2.36, but it had a larger shaped charge. I went back to my squad and passed the information on to them.

In my squad, each man was forced to carry a cartridge belt of 80 rounds, three bandoleers of 48 rounds each and at least four fragmentation hand grenades. After we received the 3.5 rocket launcher, I gave everyone a rocket round to carry. The rocket weighed about seven pounds and they screamed and hollered about it. The BAR man would carry his 12 magazines in the pouches and one in the weapon. Along with all of that ammunition, I would always try to have at least four or five bandoleers of five shot Springfield clips for my BAR men. Those were hard to find, you had to search for them. We kept them aside for the BARs. Even with all that ammunition, there were times when we ran out.

When we went into Korea, we had the World War Two bayonet. These were the 10-inch ones, the shortened World War One type. In plain English, it was a big son of a bitch. Our platoon sergeant wasn't real fond of bayonets, but he forced us to carry them. He thought having it mounted made the rifle inaccurate. He said if we ever have to fix bayonets, it means we're all out of ammo. I was short a few bayonets in my squad, the guys had thrown them away. They were a pain in the ass, when you sat down they would ram you in the ribs. But after the first time we almost ran out of ammo, everybody found a bayonet and kept it.

Sometimes during an attack, you'd get about 40 to 50 feet from the top of the ridge and you'd think, "Did I shoot four, five or six rounds?" I would stop, open the bolt, pop out what was in the rifle and shove in a fresh eight-round clip. I'd normally do that before that last rush or during a lull in the fighting. It was a common practice; I picked that up from my platoon sergeant.

The average shot if you were in a defensive position was 200 yards tops. And that was during the day. A majority of the fighting was after sunset because they wouldn't have the Air Force to worry about. During the day, when we were fired at by a machine gun, I could see the smoke and dust from its position almost all the time. My eyesight back then was 20/15, which was well above the average eyesight. Between 300 and 350 yards I could see the dust, but couldn't see the

Personal Experiences

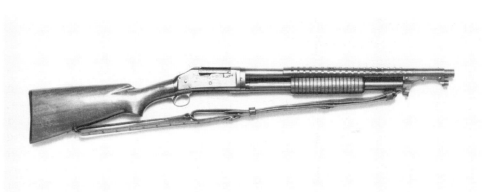

*Winchester M97 trench gun. Photo courtesy of Bruce N. Canfield.*

gun very well. I could also tell where its position was from where the tracers were coming from. I would go off to the flank of the gun, set my sights and from the sitting position I would fire a rapid-fire string through the area where I saw the smoke and dust. I shot into machine gun positions with those large Maxim machine guns with my M1. The armor piercing rounds would go right through the metal shield on the gun. We found guns with bullet holes through the shield and there would be AP slugs in the side of the receiver that stopped the gun from firing.

I carried a .45 pistol for most of the time I was over there. A lot of the guys had Tokarev pistols they had picked up, but I figured that if I was going to carry a pistol, it would be a Colt .45. I picked one up not long after I got to Korea. There were guns all over the place and it wasn't hard to get ammo for it. I used to sleep with it in my hand. I would keep a round in the chamber with the hammer in the half cock position, solely because it was easy to reach, cock and use at a moments notice. That way I only had to finish cocking it to shoot. I only had to use the .45 once.

It was around the end of November 1950, we were about 40 miles south of the Yalu River at the time. The battalion was in reserve, so we weren't on the front line. It was cold and we had a few bonfires going. We had some roving guards pulling security for us. During the night, one of our sergeants got up to piss. He didn't want to walk all the way to the latrine, so he was pissing close to where we were sleeping. He spotted a group of short horses and men passing through our area. He knew that wasn't right and he jumped up on our mess truck which had a ring mounted .50 on it. He opened up on the group of Chinese and the horses. After he started shooting it was utter chaos. I was asleep in my sleeping bag; but when I heard the first shot I opened my eyes. Standing directly over the top of me was a Chinese soldier with a Russian submachine gun. He was kicking my rifle away from my side. I cocked the pistol and fired at him through the sleeping bag three or four times. After the first shot I couldn't see because feathers were flying everywhere. I only hit him one time, in the head, I'm not sure if it was the first shot or the second, third or fourth. The round knocked him over. My sleeping bag was ruined, it had a big 15-inch gash in it. The next day I discovered that the slide of the pistol had left marks on my chest. It's amazing that the pistol functioned in the bag like that.

At one point I got a hold of a Model 97 Shotgun from the MP company and had it for a while. If I was on a listening post at night, I'd carry that shotgun. On a listening post your average shot was maybe eight to ten feet. I used that shotgun several times; it was an excellent piece of equipment.

The Chinese had a lot of submachine guns. After the Chinese came into the war, it wasn't safe to walk a ridgeline with a Thompson submachine gun. It had a distinctive silhouette and the guys would think you were the enemy and shoot you. They had a lot of the Russian submachine guns with the drums. It was a good gun at 40 feet, the thing spit out slugs at about 800 rounds per minute. To be effective, all they had to do is shoot in the general area. They also had bolt action Russian rifles with long bayonets. They had an equal to our BAR; it was a light machine gun with a pancake like drum on the top. That was an excellent automatic rifle.

I never saw an M1 carbine in Korea; we all had M2 carbines. I used to take an M2 carbine if I had to go out on a night patrol. I could carry 300 rounds of carbine ammunition and at night the ranges were short, 15 to 40 feet tops. You hear stories about the Chinese being shot with carbines in their winter clothing and they just brushed it off. I have shot Chinese in all their winter gear with an M2 carbine, and those rounds had gone completely through them, in the front and out the back. I know because I had to search them for maps and documents after I shot them. At 100 to 150 yards that sucker was bad news. I thought it was a lot more powerful than that Russian submachine gun. A wool coat, a parka and a shirt did not stop the Russian slugs either. I liked the shorter 15-round magazines rather than the big banana ones. If you were shooting lying down with the banana magazines, you had to come up an extra four to five inches off the ground. I didn't throw my magazines away; I stuck them in my parka pocket or in the cargo pocket in my pants. Each bandoleer of carbine ammo had a rapid loader that you could use to quickly refill your magazines. If it was a really hot situation I simply hit the magazine release and let it fall.

The 25th Division had the largest amount of the M16 quad .50 half-tracks in Korea. They were an anti-infantry weapon par-excellence. They would bring those up on the line to support us. I would watch them take whole sections out of the Chinese attacks. Whenever those guys came up along side of us, the Chinese would be very unhappy. Most of the time, the Chinese would probe us and spot all our automatic weapons. Then they'd fall back, shift to the place on the line that was the least defended and rush up screaming and hollering and blowing their bugles. A few times we purposely withdrew off the hill when they attacked and right below the crest of the hill we had three M16 half-tracks with their quad

.50s waiting for them. They'd take care of the Chinese when they came over the hill. I think we did that three or four times.

The Chinese would attack in large groups, although I don't think I ever saw a human wave attack. If your infantry company was in a position and three or four companies of Chinese hit you, it may have resembled a human wave. On a small front, that was a lot of people. During an attack like that, I aimed at the center of mass of a group. I could shoot pretty well and when I shot into a group, I bet I got a lot of hits. I think the guys that could shoot inflicted most of the casualties. But, the stuff that stopped them wasn't the rifles or machine guns; it was the 81s, the 4.2s and the 105s.

I was wounded for the fourth time on the 14th of February 1951. We were on the slope of a hill and I was lying on my back with the rifle on my chest. I was inserting a clip and a round from one of those Russian automatic rifles hit the clip in my hand. It set some of the rounds off and I got fragments in my hands, face and eyes. They were not bad wounds; the guys were calling me an SOB because they figured I'd have 90 days in Japan. I caught a ride on an ambulance; it was full, so I was sitting on the back. The ambulance hit a mine and I think I was the only one to get out of it. After that I got an extra shot of morphine, I'm hyper sensitive to the stuff and it almost killed me. It was not the day to buy a lottery ticket for me. That was the end of the war for me. They sent me all the way back to the military hospital at Valley Forge.

# US Infantry Weapons In Combat

> **Gaylen Kittlesen** *volunteered for the draft and was called in March 1943. He joined the 78th Division at Camp Butner, NC and did his basic and advanced training. During the advanced training phase, he volunteered for airborne training and left the 78th Division for jump school at Fort Benning, GA. After completing jump school, he was sent to New Guinea where he joined the 503rd Regimental Combat Team. After fighting on Noemfoor Island, he "volunteered" to join the Alamo Scouts. He served with the Scouts for 18 months until the war ended. He was discharged in November 1945, but after spending some time with National Guard and Reserve units he enlisted in the Army again in 1956. He served in various units before he joined the Special Forces. He did a tour in Vietnam and later participated in the raid on the Son Tay POW camp in North Vietnam. He retired from the Army as a sergeant major in 1978.*

I had volunteered for the draft and went into the Army on March 13th, 1943. I went to Camp Butner, North Carolina for my basic training. I was assigned to one of the regiments of the 78th Infantry Division. The whole division took basic training at the same time. I didn't have a lot of small arms training because I was in a heavy weapons company. When we first started out everyone trained with the M1 rifle. I trained with the .45 pistol and then trained with 81mm mortar and the old water-cooled machine gun. While I was in advanced infantry training one of my buddies said, "Why don't we volunteer for Airborne." I said "Airborne, what are you talking about?" I didn't even know there was any such thing as paratroops. We both volunteered. I passed the physical and he didn't. So I went to Fort Benning from there.

Right after jump school they gave us a 30-day leave and then I went to New Orleans by troop train. I was in New Orleans on New Year's Eve in 1943. Then we departed by ship, stopped in California for a few days and then sailed to New Guinea. I spent about two weeks there doing details and then I was sent to Brisbane, Australia where the 503rd was. The 503rd was an Airborne Regimental Combat Team. I was assigned to C Company in the 2nd Battalion and became a scout. As a scout I was issued a Thompson submachine gun. I had never trained with one before, so they let me go to the range and train with it. We had a range at our camp and we could go out and shoot quite a bit if we wanted to. I did and I was glad I did because I got pretty proficient with the weapon.

Our first combat operation was on Noemfoor Island. The 1st and 3rd Battalions jumped on the Island and had so many injuries on the drop zone that they had the 2nd Battalion land by Higgins boat. We were on the Island for about three weeks.

One day, a lieutenant told me I had volunteered for Alamo Scout school. I hadn't "volunteered" for nothing, but in those days you picked up your pack and went. The Alamo Scouts were a specialized unit organized by General Kruger, the 6th Army Commander. He wasn't satisfied with the intelligence reports he was getting, so he organized the Alamo Scouts. We were given a six-week school in Hollandia on things like small boat handling, the firing of different weapons and map reading. We usually operated in small teams, usually an officer and five or six men. They would send us out on patrols in areas they didn't know anything about to gain intelligence. We carried a different mix of weapons; I was the only one in my team that carried a Thompson. One of the other guys carried a grease gun and the rest carried carbines or M1s. It really wasn't our job to fight; we wanted to gather intelligence. We tried to avoid getting in any fights. Most of the patrols were only for a few days.

I liked the Thompson, although there were a few things I didn't like. It was heavy and the ammunition was heavy, although those .45 slugs would really stop a person. Also, they weren't blued real good and I fought rust all the time. Of course the bluing wore off as you cleaned it and then it would rust more. We had cleaning supplies in the squad and we shared them. The Thompson was a reliable weapon for me. The effective range for it wasn't very damned far. As a scout, most of the time I was on the move, so I never fired from a supported position. I'd say 50 yards was the maximum effective range with it, maybe a little more if you were good with it. I always used it fully automatic, but I developed a three-round burst that I could handle pretty good. It didn't rise too much with a three-round burst. We were on a patrol one time and a Japanese soldier came up the trail, 35 to 40 yards from me. I got him with a three-round burst that flung him over backwards. One round hit him in the chest, one in the throat and one in the forehead. So the burst was fairly well grouped. You almost always fired the Thompson from the hip.

I carried a regular ammunition pouch of magazines; I can't remember how many the pouch held. Those were 20-round stick magazines. Later we got 30-round magazines, but they didn't work out so well because the pouch wasn't made for them. I'd have one of those in the gun and still carry the 20-round ones in the pouch. Towards the end of the war I got a 50-round drum. I don't know how they ever got it for me. I just asked for a drum and thought I'd see what happened and they found one for me. The drum really made the Thompson heavy; I didn't use it a lot. I never got into enough of a fight to use the whole drum.

When the war ended, I was in the Philippines. Our team leader had been wounded and some of the other guys had enough points to go home. I didn't have enough points, so I was assigned to another team. Then I went to Japan for 30 days. We didn't do a damned thing except stay with the Rangers. We drank a lot; the Japanese had plenty to drink. I finally returned to the States in October 1945 and was discharged at Fort Leavenworth in November.

## US Infantry Weapons In Combat

> **Morris Williams** *was drafted in March 1943 and went to Camp Blanding, FL for basic training with the 66th Division. He applied for the Army Specialized Training Program (ASTP) and was accepted in May. He attended school at Bowdoin College in Maine until the ASTP was shut down in February 1944. He was assigned to the 26th Infantry Division as a rifleman. He fought with the Division in France until he was evacuated to England with trenchfoot. Upon recovery he was reclassified and assigned to non-combat duty in Europe. Following occupation duty he returned to the US in March 1946 and was discharged.*

I was drafted in March 1943 and went to the 566th Signal Company in the 66th Infantry Division at Camp Blanding, Florida. The division was being formed at the time and they just put me in the Signal Company. Our weapons training was limited to the carbine. The training in the Signal Company was primarily in communications stuff. But then it was like, you have to know how to shoot a carbine and throw a grenade. I liked the carbine; we fired qualification with it. I later learned that it wasn't the weapon that the Garand was.

I took several tests for the Army Specialized Training Program and in May I was accepted into the program. I went up to Bowdoin College in Brunswick, Maine in late August. I attended school until February 1944 when the Army closed the program down. They shipped a whole bunch of us to the infantry and I was sent to the 26th Division.

The 26th Division was an old Massachusetts National Guard organization, so they were an old outfit. I joined them while they were doing the Tennessee Maneuvers. I was assigned to the first squad, first platoon, C Company, 101st Infantry Regiment as a rifleman. At first we didn't receive any extra training, they treated us like we'd been there forever. They assumed we had already received infantry training. I had my introduction with the M1 rifle at that time; I fired a lot of blanks through one. It was good training for me, I learned how to handle the M1 and get used to it.

After the maneuvers, we went to Fort Jackson, South Carolina and they ran us through a lot of training with the rifle. We received some really good training; we fired it quite a bit and qualified with it. We also trained with the Thompson submachine gun, the .45 Colt, the BAR, the bazooka and with the grenade launcher for the M1. I didn't train with the grenade launcher very much; I only fired one round. I was on KP that day and they took me from KP duty out to the range. I didn't know anything about shooting rifle grenades and I put the rifle to my shoulder and fired a grenade. That really smarted, the old guys running the range got a good laugh out of that. I didn't break anything, but I wouldn't do that again. I trained with the division for about seven months before we went over to France. We were beginning to wonder why we weren't being sent over.

We arrived in France in September 1944 and before long went up to the front. There were a few things that I thought were noteworthy for those of us who went overseas with the division. During training we were taught when you're advancing and being shot at, even if you can't see them, shoot back. That was a very common practice for us, if you knew the direction the fire was coming from you fired in that direction. Most of us guys trained in the division did it, but the replacements tended to hit the ground and not fire their rifles. I think that was probably the most important piece of training I got with the M1 that served me the best in combat. I have read what S.L.A. Marshall wrote about men firing their weapons in combat and I don't think it was true with the well-trained guys who went over with our outfit. I can see where it could easily be true after most of us were gone. The replacements weren't trained as well as us. The other thing we learned was to keep moving. If you went down to ground, never get up in the same place and always keep going, don't try to crawl into the ground. I thought doing those things made a big difference. You didn't make yourself a good target that someone could take good aim at.

I thought the M1 was a good combat weapon. It never jammed or anything like that. It got treated pretty roughly, but it was very dependable. I don't recall ever cleaning mine while I was in combat. We used to throw several bandoleers over our shoulders. I didn't keep clips in my ammunition belt; I just carried the bandoleers. The engagement ranges varied quite a bit. Moving through the open country, the shooting would usually start at a couple of hundred yards. They would usually wait until we were exposed in a field or someplace in the open before they would open up on us. Our main problem was we were constantly moving against prepared positions. Once we closed on them, their burp guns were murder at close range. I don't think our grease guns or Thompsons compared with them.

I was on a BAR team for a while, although I carried a bazooka. We had another fellow who carried extra ammunition for the BAR. Normally there were only two of us, but this one time there were three of us on the team. They must have known something was going on. I only carried the bazooka for two or three days. A German 88 had come up to fire at our troops. I was in front of the company, so I was closest to it. I was able to get a shot off with the bazooka from about 200 yards away. The sights on the bazooka weren't very good and I missed the gun. The Germans only fired a few a rounds and left.

When we first got on the line, we had to stay in our holes all day or we'd draw fire. So we'd just sit there and soak in those holes. We only had regular army shoes with canvas leggings and we never had any dry socks, our feet stayed wet.

*M1A1 bazooka. Hayes Otoupalik collection. Photo courtesy of Bruce N. Canfield.*

Even when we were moving, our unit was always out in the countryside. We didn't go through any small towns where we could take our shoes off and light a fire to dry them. I knew something was happening with my feet and I went to the aid station. The medic told me to keep off my feet and keep them dry for a couple of days. He gave me some clean socks, but I had to put my feet back into those same wet shoes and then go back on the line. A couple of weeks after that, they had to carry me off the line. I was hospitalized on November 20th with trenchfoot. The first combat boots I ever saw was on the ambulance drivers that took me to the hospital.

I was sent to a hospital in England and I was discharged for limited duty in February. Because of my limited duty, I was assigned to one of the replacement units as a clerk typist and a bugler. After the war I didn't have enough points to return to the US right away, so I served in Europe during occupation. I returned home and I was discharged from the Army in March 1946.

Personal Experiences

> **Robert Seiler** enlisted in the Army Air Corps in July 1942 with the hope of becoming a pilot. He was unable to pass the physical for flight training, but remained in the Air Corps as a clerk. In July 1943 he was accepted in the Army Specialized Training Program (ASTP) and attended school in Illinois. When the ASTP was closed in early 1944, all the ASTPer's at his school were assigned to the 96$^{th}$ Infantry Division at Camp White, Oregon. Mr. Seiler became an assistant BAR man in the 382$^{nd}$ Infantry Regiment and fought with the Regiment on Leyte and Okinawa. He was wounded on Okinawa ten days after the invasion and evacuated to the US. He was discharged from the Army in November 1945.

I joined the Army as an Air Corps Cadet in July 1942; I wanted to be a flyer. I was working in the Elgin National Watch factory and I was exempt from military service. About 90 percent of the work we were doing was government work. When I told them I was leaving to join the service, they asked me where I was going and I told them I was joining the Air Corps. They let me go, but they said if I had told them that I was joining the infantry, they wouldn't have let me go. I went into the Air Corps, but as soon as I had the physical they washed me out because I had hay fever. My commanding officer saw my grades from school and he got me into the ASTP. In September 1943, I went off to school in Peoria, Illinois at Bradley Technical College. I was there for about six months and then they closed the program down. Everybody from Bradley, about two or three hundred of us, went to the 96th Division.

The 96$^{th}$ Division was at Camp White when we arrived. When we showed up, they started us out like we just came out of civilian life. All of us from ASTP went through basic training; the rest of the division's soldiers had already been trained. The division had been together for about a year by then. I remember training with the M1 rifle; we did quite a bit of marksmanship training at Camp White. I qualified as expert. I still have my old rifle marksmanship scorebook. It even has the serial number of my rifle in it, during training I had rifle serial number 990712. I don't remember ever training with a machine gun. We had familiarization training with the carbine and the BAR. I don't remember ever taking a carbine apart and I only took a BAR apart a few times. I was assigned as a rifleman to K Company, 382$^{nd}$ Regiment and was designated as an assistant to the BAR-man.

We went overseas to Hawaii and we did jungle training. They had some pretty thick jungles in Hawaii. We also did some dry run amphibious landings on Maui. Then we packed up and ended up landing in Leyte in October of 1944. When I landed on Leyte, I carried an M1 and was wearing a BAR ammunition belt and had a bandoleer or two of ammunition for my rifle. The BAR belt was very heavy and very uncomfortable. Not long after the landing we had problems with the M1s

## US Infantry Weapons In Combat

rusting. By the third morning I'd say 20 percent of them wouldn't fire. We'd been rained on every night and some of them had rusted shut. You couldn't even pull the bolt back. I remember on the third night we had an Amtrak pull up to our position. I took my rifle and pushed the op rod against the tread to break it loose. Looking back, I think we were negligent that we didn't oil our rifles. I know that a lot of guys cured the problem by picking up the oil cans out of Jap rifles. We used the Jap oil and didn't have any more problems.

In combat very seldom did you have the luxury of zeroing in on a target; it was especially like that on Leyte. The foliage was so thick that you always carried your rifle on your hip. You shot from the hip; you wouldn't bother to bring it up to your shoulder. A lot of times you wouldn't even see anything; you'd hear something and fire into an area until one of them fell out of a tree. It was common for Japs to be up in the coconut trees where you couldn't see them.

As an assistant BAR man, I stuck with the BAR man; wherever he went, I was his shadow. Normally he would use the ammo from his belt first and then I would pass him ammo from mine. After we landed on Leyte, he didn't last very long, only about four or five days. We had some short rounds come in and he got hit. So I got his gun and had it for the rest of the time. That was the way it worked: if the BAR man got hit, the assistant took the BAR. I didn't ask for it. I really hadn't trained much with the BAR before that. I did get a lot of combat experience with it on Leyte; it was a very reliable weapon. My BAR fired single shot or fully automatic. Most of the time, I fired it single shot. The BAR man before me had taken the bipod off and thrown it away. As I said, we shot from the hip most of the time, so it didn't matter. After I became the BAR man, I never had an assistant to help carry extra ammo, I just carried the magazines in my ammunition belt.

We were on Leyte until March of 1945, and then we invaded Okinawa on the first of April. An interesting thing happened to me on Okinawa. The first time I got hit, my BAR went flying and I got spun around from a bullet hitting me in the side. I thought I'd lost the gun. A round from a machine gun passed through my side and creased one of my ribs. The aid man put sulfur on it and wrapped it up for me. Then I put my jacket back on, picked my helmet up, found my BAR and we moved on. When I picked my gun up, I found out that another bullet had hit the trigger guard and bent it. I could hardly get my finger in it anymore, but it was still usable. If that bullet hadn't hit the BAR, it would have hit me.

There was one day on Okinawa that we caught the Japs off guard. It was the first real encounter we had with them on Okinawa. I think it was at Kakazu Ridge. They were in a deep gully and they had to climb up the hill on the other side to get away. As they were trying to get up the hill, we sat on the other side and picked them off. They were only about 100 yards from us; we had a turkey shoot. I rested the handguard of my BAR on the ground and fired at them from a prone position.

I had a tracer round every eight or ten rounds, so I could tell where the rounds were going. You'd see a few of them moving and we'd fire at them and then we'd see a couple more moving and fire at them. We kept knocking them off. One of the other platoon BAR men was there too and we had a heyday. Our barrels had turned cherry red by the time they stopped going up the hill. The whole encounter lasted about 15 minutes.

The first week on Okinawa was real simple because they were waiting for us. Once we got in the hills, we went from the frying pan into the fire. I got hit on the 10$^{th}$ of April, which was pretty early in the fight. I was wounded in the leg by shrapnel from an artillery shell. They evacuated me off the island; I felt guilty that the other guys had to stay. I got one of the first planes, a C-54, off Okinawa to Guam. From there they put me on a ship and sent me back to the States.

> **Lawrence Moore** *enlisted in the Marines in September 1948 and was sent to Parris Island for basic training. Following his initial training, he was sent to the Marine Detachment on the Island of Adak in the Aleutians. He spent 18 months on the island before being transferred to the security detachment on Mare Island in San Francisco Bay. With the Korean War underway, he transferred down to Camp Pendleton, CA for intensive infantry training and then was sent to Korea as a replacement. He was assigned to D Company, 2nd Battalion, 1st Marine Regiment. He served in Korea for about a year before returning to the States. He remained in the Marines until he was medically discharged after 16 years of service.*

I enlisted in the Marines in September 1948 and went to Parris Island for boot camp. At Parris Island, we had basic weapon training with the M1 rifle and the hand grenade. They worked with us for about a week at the rifle range teaching us about the sights, figuring the windage and snapping in. After that week of training, they had us fire our weapons for record. They showed us some of the other weapons, but we didn't get into them. We spent most of our time just learning how to be a Marine.

After boot camp, I went on a troop train to San Francisco and then volunteered for duty in Alaska. I went to Adak Island, which is one of the Aleutian Islands. Our Marine Guard Company did rifle company type training and I trained with .30 caliber machine guns. We had a very good sergeant that trained us with the M1919A4 machine gun. The weather up there was rotten; we did gun drills on the ground in an empty Quonset hut. The squad was broken down to seven men; the squad leader, the gunner, the assistant gunner and four ammo carriers. We'd all lie down in a column and the instructor would say "On this line, action." That's when the gunner and assistant gunner would leap up and run forward. The gunner carried the tripod and the assistant gunner carried the machine gun. The gunner would open the tripod and the assistant put the gun into position. By that time the ammo carriers had come up along the left and dropped off their ammo and then returned to the flanks of the gun to help protect the gun. The four ammo carriers each had two cans of ammo and they carried a carbine for self-protection. The ammo cans had 250 rounds and weighed 15 pounds each. On those drills, we could get the gun in action in around five seconds. It depended on how far we had to run from where we were down to where we had to set the gun up. I started out as an ammo carrier, but I worked up to an assistant gunner. We would have a drill called "fall out one" and that would mean the gunner was shot and the assistant had to take over for him. Everyone would leap frog up one position in the squad.

I trained with the .45 pistol and the carbine while in Alaska. The .45 was a great weapon. It was difficult to learn how to use, but it was a very good weapon at close range. I thought the carbine was too light. It was OK for in close, but in my opinion it was too light of a weapon.

After spending 18 months in Alaska, they let me have a little stateside duty before they sent me to Korea. I went to Mare Island near San Francisco and pulled guard duty for a few months before I went down to Camp Pendleton. We had extensive training while we were there. We did machine gun drills and practiced taking the gun apart and putting it back together. We also trained with the water-cooled M1917 machine gun. It was a very good weapon, but it was meant to be used for a different purpose than the air-cooled gun. The water-cooled guns bolstered our lines in Korea and did a good job. After a few months of training, I went over to Korea as a replacement with the ninth draft of replacements. At that time I was a corporal and my MOS was 0335, which was a machine gunner.

I got over to Korea in June 1951. Once we got there, we were separated out to the different regiments and battalions where we were needed. We replaced Marines who had been wounded or whose time was up to go home. There were experienced combat veterans in every unit and we just filled in. It was a good way to work it instead of taking a brand new green unit and putting them in the line. I went to D Company, 2nd Battalion, 1st Marines. We were up in defensive positions up around the 38th parallel; we dug in World War One style and went on patrols.

When I first got there, I don't know why, but they made me a BAR man. I had trained with the BAR during our training at Camp Pendleton. We learned how to take them apart, put them together and fire them. I went on patrols in enemy country carrying the BAR and that was a hairy feeling. I only carried it for a little while before I went back to machine guns, I never fired it at the enemy. It was a bulky weapon and the magazines in the BAR belt hurt your belly when you hit the ground. Carrying the BAR was a pain in the ass to me; I didn't like it.

Most of the fighting during my time there was from fixed positions, except Hill 749. We had an awful hard battle in September called Hill 749. Other Marines had gone up that hill and tried to take it and couldn't. I was climbing up that damned hill with a machine gun on my shoulder and a .45 in my other hand. The first enemy I shot was with the .45 as I went up that hill. The .45 was a very good weapon to stop an enemy at close range. It was my first close combat experience. We made it to the top of the hill and held it. I violated the rules and set the gun up on the topographical crest of the hill. Even though I was just the assistant gunner, I chose where the gun was to go. It was a good firing position. The military crest of the hill was where you were supposed to set your gun up, but the Marine unit who had been up the

## US Infantry Weapons In Combat

*SGT Lawrence Moore's machine gun squad, Korea, 1951*

hill before us had been wiped out after setting up on the military crest. The North Koreans counterattacked us several times, but they were pretty much decimated by the time we got through with them. We hit them with everything: air strikes, artillery, mortars and our fire. I started up that hill as the assistant gunner and became the squad leader by the end of the battle.

When I became squad leader, my personal weapon was a carbine. I never had to use it because the machine gun was there to do the job. We were in defensive positions. The carbine was there to use, but I never had to use it.

Personal Experiences

The machine gun was designed to give overhead fire to friendly troops as they advanced. On Hill 749 we applied what is called the gunners rule: up to 900 yards, which is a point of sight that you can fire into until friendly troops hit that area. Then you can apply the leaders rule, which was 1,500 yards, and continue to give them support. It was an involved process; you had to know what you were doing so you didn't shoot your own troops. We had trained in those techniques and we used them in battle.

As a squad leader, you tied your machine gun in with the other gun in the section. There were two machine guns in a section. The machine gun section leader had to know the terrain and how best to employ the guns. Once the machine guns were placed in defensive positions, the rifle platoon leader tied his men in and around the machine guns. That's the way it worked. You tried to cover all avenues of advance.

The machine gun was a good weapon; it was reliable as long as you kept it clean. Our machine gun held up well, we never had a stoppage in combat. Our weapons were well cared for. The gunner and the assistant gunner took care of the gun. During the Korean War, there were a civilian group of Koreans who wore blue uniforms and they brought up our ammunition, food and water to us. So we were getting resupplied with ammo as we used it. We didn't have to go far to get more.

I spent about a year in Korea and returned to the US. I became a drill instructor at Parris Island and then became a weapons instructor at Camp Geiger. After the Marines leave boot camp, they go to Camp Geiger to receive advanced weapons training. I stayed in the Corps for 16 years before I was medically retired in 1965.

> **Harry Hagstad** *served with B Company, 394th Infantry Regiment, 99th Division during World War Two. After seeing my request for information on the M1 in the 99th Division Association's "The Checkerboard" newsletter, he wrote me the following letter.*

Dear Mark,

When the Garand was first manufactured it was made as quality weapons have always been made, the components were forged. Later, as demand increased, everyone got into the act and a weapon of lower quality was turned out. The components were stamped out. It was a cheaper rifle. I'm not disparaging it, it did the job, but there was a difference.

During basic training I was issued a rifle that belonged in the first category. I later learned that the tip off was the serial number. Mine was 994041, a six-digit number. The lower quality rifles had seven-digit serial numbers.

When we were about to ship out, we were given a choice; we could turn in the rifles we had beat up during basic and advanced infantry training and get a brand new one, or keep the old one. Just before we received that offer we had gone out to the rifle range to zero our weapons in for 500 yards. Our normal qualifying ranges were 200 and 300 yards. We were shooting from sandbags. I elevated my sights the number of clicks that should respond to a 500-yard range and squeezed off my first shot. We were only given three shots to zero in our weapons. As luck would have it, (I am not an "expert" rifleman) I made a bullseye. What really impressed me was what followed. I didn't change the setting and the next two rounds were also bullseyes. Needless to say, I didn't turn in my piece for a new one. M1 rifle serial number 994041 served me well.

Sincerely,

Harry Hagstad
B Company, 394th Inf.

Personal Experiences

Tom Shoen (left, center) Camp MacKall, North Carolina 1943 holding M1A1 Carbine.

> **Thomas Shoen, Jr.** was drafted into the Army in 1943 on his 19$^{th}$ birthday. He reported to Fort McArthur, CA and volunteered for paratrooper training. He was assigned to the 11$^{th}$ Airborne Division and sent to Camp MacKall, NC. Mr. Shoen received jump training at Fort Benning and qualified as a paratrooper on June 10, 1943. After additional training in the US, the 11$^{th}$ left the US in May 1944, setting sail for New Guinea. The 11$^{th}$ Airborne Division entered combat in November 1944 with the invasion of the island of Leyte in support of the liberation of the Philippine Islands. Mr. Shoen was wounded on Leyte in December 1944. He returned to combat on the island of Luzon in February 1945 where he made two combat jumps and participated in the liberation of Manila. He returned to the US and was discharged in December 1945.

I enlisted in the Army right after Pearl Harbor. I was only 17 and lied about my age; I wanted to go fight the Japs or the Germans. My mother found out where I was and turned me in. She brought me back home and made me finish high school.

I was drafted on February 7th 1943, my 19th birthday. We were sent home for one week to tie up our affairs. On February 15th 1943, I reported to Fort McArthur and was sworn into the Army. While at McArthur, they asked for volunteers to become paratroopers, so two of my buddies and me volunteered. Two of us were assigned to the 11th Airborne Division and the other guy to the 101st Airborne. We were transported from California to Toccoa, Georgia by train. I was only at Toccoa for one day. This was where we were assigned to units. I was assigned to the 2nd Platoon, Company C, 127th Airborne Engineer Battalion. We were transported by truck to Camp MacKall in North Carolina. That winter at MacKall was very cold with many ice storms. Growing up in southern California, it was the first time I ever saw snow or ice. Those tarpaper-covered barracks sure let a lot of cold wind blow through.

We got our M1 rifles during our second month at Camp MacKall. They were new rifles in the cosmoline. We spent all day cleaning them and learning the nomenclature of the parts. The M1 Garand was the first weapon I qualified with; I liked that rifle a lot. It sure would shoot and it never malfunctioned if you maintained it properly. I qualified expert with it. In fact, every man in the 127th qualified expert. We were told beforehand that anyone who qualified expert would get a 10-day furlough. The way it worked was A Company scored for B Company and Headquarters Company scored for C Company. Then we switched, B scored for A and C for HQ. We all qualified as experts! Colonel Davis, our battalion CO, said that we were the only battalion that had accomplished that. I went to New York City on my furlough, because 10 days wasn't enough time to get home to California and back.

We also qualified with the M1 Carbine. Later, when we started jump training, we were issued folding stock carbines. The only other weapon that I officially qualified with was the .45 pistol; now that was some gun. It did a real good job for me later on. Some guys qualified with the BAR and some with the Thompson. I never qualified with either, but I shot them both.

*M1A1 carbine, issued to paratroopers. Shown with stock in the unfolded, open position. Photo courtesy of Scott A. Duff.*

In training, we mostly jumped with the folding stock paratrooper carbine. You could either just sling it around your neck and go or you could put it under your reserve chute, sandwiched in next to your body. But when the chute opened, the gun would come up and the pistol grip hit you under the chin. It hurt pretty good! I recently heard that they had a canvas "holster" for the folding stock carbine. They may have had those in Europe, I don't know, but I never saw one in the Philippines. I also saw a carbine a few years ago that had an adjustable rear sight and a bayonet lug. We never had those either.

As engineers, our primary job was mostly to blow things up, demolition and that sort of thing; that and clearing mines. We also would walk in front of the tanks so they wouldn't run over a mine. The mines weren't too tough to spot, so it wasn't as dangerous as it sounds. But when you were out there you just knew that every Jap rifle in the jungle was aimed at you and that you'd be the first one to get shot. You'd stay out there for about 10 or 15 minutes at a time, then you'd rotate back behind the tank and someone else would take a turn out front. But that was almost as bad, because now one of your buddies might get shot. It was tough on the nerves being out in front of one of those Shermans!

Company C was the only fully jump qualified engineer company in the 11th. General Swing wanted everybody to cross-train between parachuting and gliders. I made a couple of landings in a glider while we were still in North Carolina, one with a little bulldozer on board the glider. I never wanted to do that again! I'd take a parachute any day. Company C was attached to the 511th Parachute Infantry Regiment during most of our time in the Philippines. We often fought as infantry and saw a lot of action. I was in six major battles. During the taking of Manila, we were on the line for 31 days straight. The 127th and the 511th took shifts in the foxholes to give each other a chance to get some sleep.

When we shipped overseas, our equipment, including weapons, were packaged for shipment on the ships with us; we didn't carry them on board. A lot of us engineers worked as stevedores in New Guinea unloading our equipment. Most airborne engineers were issued either a standard carbine or the folding stock paratrooper carbine, but I didn't like them too much. They were no good in the Philippines where we fought. The heavy jungle would deflect or even stop the bullets and they just didn't hit hard enough. If you hit a Jap, he just might get back up! I saw them take three or four rounds from a carbine and just keep coming. I got rid of my carbine for the first Garand I could find. I sure liked that M1 rifle; when you shot them with a Garand, they stayed down. I never had any problems with the M1s I used. They always worked; they were a heck of a rifle. I liked the .45 pistol too; I carried one whenever I could. They weren't issued to us, but we found ways to get them. When you shot a Jap with a .45, he sure didn't get up after that.

On the evening of December 6th 1944, we were hit by the only Japanese parachute assault on US troops during the entire war. We were at San Pablo Airstrip on

*Paratroopers with M1 rifles in Griswold bags behind their reserve parachutes. Left to right: Frank Penesi, Dan Abbomonte, LeRoy Wade, Co. C, 127 Airborne Engineers Battalion, 11th Airborne Division, Camp MacKall, North Carolina, October 1943. Photo courtesy of LeRoy Wade.*

northern Leyte. I had just finished cleaning up my mess kit after dinner when we saw the planes coming over and the parachutes opening. It took us a few minutes to realize what was going on. We fought through the night and I was wounded in the morning of the next day, December 7th, while we were retaking the airstrip. I was hit in both legs and the right arm by shrapnel from a hand grenade that was rolled at me. I used my Garand to kill the Jap that rolled that grenade. They evacuated me by ship to New Guinea. I was on the operating table for three hours and they removed 33 pieces of shrapnel from me. I received a Purple Heart while in the hospital in New Guinea.

I returned to my unit on February 22nd 1945. They had moved on to Luzon by then. My first combat jump was on Tagaytay Ridge on southern Luzon in the Philippines on February 23rd. It was one day after I got back from New Guinea after recovering from being wounded. My second jump was on June 23rd in northern Luzon, south of Aparri, Operation Gypsy Task Force. I was armed with a Garand rifle on both jumps. I carried my M1 disassembled and in a canvas case, I think it was called a Griswold bag. You assembled the rifle after you landed. I carried the bag sandwiched behind my reserve chute. We had bayonets, but I always carried a trench knife too. I kept one shoved down in my boot, tied to my lower leg. I never went anywhere without one.

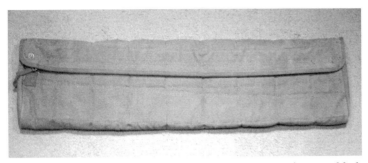

Griswold bag issued to airborne troops for carrying a disassembled M1 rifle during a parachute jump. Photo courtesy of Scott A. Duff.

I sure was glad when the war ended. If it weren't for the atomic bomb, I probably wouldn't be here. I fought in six battles, I doubt I would have survived the seventh one; it saved my life and the lives of many of my buddies. When the war ended, we were in northern Luzon. They flew us to Okinawa first and re-outfitted us, new uniforms and so on. It was the first time I ever landed in an airplane. I'd made 17 takeoffs without a landing! The 11th were the first US troops to set foot on Japan. Our company landed near Yokohama on August 28th 1945. As engineers, in preparation for General MacArthur's arrival, one of our first jobs was to check the roads and bridges along his planned travel route for mines and explosives. Later, they moved the 127th to Sendai, Japan for occupation duty.

I left Japan by ship in December 1945. It only took seven days to get home. That was a lot better than on the way over when it had taken us 31 days to get to New Guinea because of zigzagging to dodge Jap submarines. After arriving back in the States, I was discharged on December 17th 1945.

The thought of losing the war never entered our minds. It wasn't "if" we would win, it was "when" we would win. We were trained to believe that we couldn't be beat and that we could do anything. It probably served us well after we came home from the war. We still thought that we could do anything.

*Jim Haahr, Germany, 1945*

**Jim Haahr** *joined the Army in mid-1943 and took infantry basic training at Camp Roberts, CA. Following that, he went to engineering school in Maine as part of the Army Specialized Training Program (ASTP). When the ASTP program was terminated, he was assigned to the 26th Infantry Division which was training in Tennessee. The division deployed overseas, arriving in France in September 1944. Mr. Haahr fought with the division through Germany until the end of the war. Starting out as a private first class, by the end of the war he had been promoted to tech sergeant. He was wounded twice during the war and served in Czechoslovakia and Austria during occupation. He returned to the US in December of 1945.*

I took infantry basic training at Camp Roberts, California in May of 1943. We used the Enfield rifle for most of our training. We drilled with it and carried it on training exercises. We also trained with the light machine gun and 60 mm mortars. We did no training with the bazooka or the carbine. Toward the end of our training, we trained with the M1 rifle and qualified with it. I also had some sniper training with the Springfield 03 equipped with a scope. Not everybody did that training. Some of us who had received an expert rating with the rifle got a little bit of training in sniper work with the 03. Not that we were going to be assigned into a particular sniper unit, but simply to receive some extra training. It wasn't a long course, just five or six days. We did some additional marksmanship training and then some training on hiding, estimating ranges and movement, things like that.

Following basic, I went into the ASTP and went to college in Brunswick, Maine to study basic engineering until the program was cancelled in February 1944. The whole group from my school was assigned to the 26th Division. I was assigned to C Company, 101st Infantry Regiment as a rifleman. They were in the middle of the Tennessee Maneuvers when we joined them and we just melded in with the cadre and started training with them. It was good for us coming straight out of the ASTP.

We landed in France in September 1944. The 26th Division was the first division to land in France directly from the States without stopping in England. We took over front line positions from the 4th Armored Division on October 7th, facing the 11th Panzer Division.

As a rifleman I thought the M1 was a great rifle; I never had any problems with it at all. During that time in France, the weather was very bad. There was almost constant rain, there was mud and it was cold. It was a difficult job to keep the weapon clean while living in that weather in a two-man foxhole. You couldn't keep your rifle under your poncho or raincoat; you had to have it out and ready. I couldn't strip it, but I wiped it down a couple of times a day. I did my best to keep the canvas pouch over the barrel to keep it clean.

We were in purely defensive positions; Patton was out of gas. I didn't fire that rifle until the 22nd of October. I didn't have anything to fire at until then, we had no engagements with the enemy. Our problem was artillery: 88s, mortars and screaming meemies. We attacked with Patton's 3rd Army on November 8th and I was wounded on the 10th. I was sent to a convalescence hospital in the UK until I returned to my company in late January.

In general, when we attacked, we employed marching fire. We'd advance on line with the weapon at our hip, firing as we moved. It was unaimed fire. There was no prescribed rate of fire as I recall. I just tried to have some balance between the amount of ammo I was carrying and the rate I was expending it. I sure as hell didn't want to run out. I usually carried one cloth bandoleer and a full cartridge belt. I think marching fire was effective in keeping people down.

Later in the war, we did a lot of house-to-house fighting. I thought the M1 was fine in that type of fighting. We used a lot of hand grenades and some guys used rifle grenades from their M1s. I wasn't equipped to fire rifle grenades. We also used the bazooka against houses when we thought there might be snipers or if we knew there were Germans in them. I never used the bazooka in an anti-tank role, but it was very effective on houses. It would blow a good hole in a wall. We'd also shoot them through the window so they would explode in the room. The only weapons I used in combat were the Garand, the bazooka and hand grenades.

One night in Germany, we were told to expect an attack, so we left the basement of the house we were in. I was lying out in a courtyard; the Germans were about 100 yards away in a park. I felt this punch on my helmet. I looked off to one side and there was one of those little yellow and black German rifle grenades. It had hit me on the helmet and it bounced off without exploding. That was something! I think they were firing at one of our heavy machine guns that we had set up in the kitchen of the house we had been in. It had been doing a lot of firing and the Germans were firing back with machine guns and rifle grenades. I was lucky!

Another time, we were clearing through some houses. I was alone and I went down some steps into a basement, which I shouldn't have done. I had my rifle pointed ahead of me. I swung it around a corner and there was a German officer sitting at a table. His hands were outstretched on the table and ahead of his hands was a Luger, which he had obviously pushed forward. I pointed my rifle at him and he said in very good English, " Don't shoot, the war is over." I took his Luger and got him out of there and turned him over to some others on the street. After that, I was working down the block and was about to go around a corner. I stopped and took a peek first and there were two Germans pressed up against the side of a building. I pulled out a grenade and threw it around the corner, then pulled back and waited for it to go off. After it exploded, I swung my upper body around the corner with my M1 at the ready. One German was lying there, but the other one was gone.

During the war, I had picked up a Walther P38, a Luger and a Mauser 98 rifle, all of which I sent back home by mail. I just took the Mauser apart and sent it home. Those were the days where you could ship those things in the mail. I used to keep them in my duffel bag; I didn't want that stuff on me if I was taken prisoner.

After the war ended, we were in Czechoslovakia. We were on one side of the Enns River and a Russian Division was on the other. They had a lot of Siberian troops and you had to be a little careful with them. They'd get pretty loaded on vodka and they'd start firing and they didn't care which direction they fired. When we changed guards on the bridge, I used to talk to a Russian lieutenant who had lived in Brooklyn before the war.

The 26th Division was pulled back to France in late 1945 and was sent home as a division, landing in various debarkation points. I spent Christmas 1945 at sea, debarked at Newport News, went to Camp McCoy, Wisconsin and was discharged on January 10, 1946.

# US Infantry Weapons In Combat

> **Terry Tennant** *enlisted in the Army in September 1948. He took infantry basic training at Fort Devens, MA with the newly reformed 7th Infantry Regiment of the 3rd Division. He spent several years at Fort Devens in the 7th before the unit was sent to Korea. His first combat experience came after the division landed in Wonsan, North Korea in late 1950. He fought in Korea with the Heavy Mortar Company until July 1951 and then he returned to the US. He was discharged from the Army in September 1951.*

I enlisted in September 1948. I had grown up with a bunch of guys and we decided that when we turned eighteen that we'd join one of the services. I voted for the Air Force and one of the other guys voted for the Navy, but the three other guys wanted to go in the Army. So we all went into the Army. We were sent to Fort Devens, Massachusetts and that's when they reactivated the 7th Infantry Regiment. We were used to fill it out as they were forming the regiment. They had a cadre of men come up from Fort Benning and we had our basic training.

I remember the first weapon we trained with was the M1 rifle. Although we were a peacetime army, we trained on a lot of stuff. We did training with the old 2.36-inch rocket launcher, the .30 caliber air-cooled machine gun, the .30 caliber water-cooled machine gun, the .50 caliber machine gun, the .45 Colt automatic, the M1 and M2 carbine, the BAR and the 60 and 81 mm mortars. I was assigned to the Heavy Mortar Company, so I also trained with the 4.2-inch mortar. I still remember the serial number from the rifle I was issued in the Mortar Company. They told me never to forget it and I never did. It was 393899; it was like new when I got it. I really liked the Fort Devens area and I volunteered to stay there.

We were training the National Guard in the summer of 1950 when we heard about the Korean War. I'd never heard of Korea, so I had no idea where it was. I remember we fell out for retreat ceremony one night and the first sergeant told everyone to stay put afterwards. He got out a list and started reading off a roster of men and he read everybody's name below the rank of sergeant. I was a sergeant at that time. All those men were told to pack up their stuff and be ready to load up on trucks at midnight. I found out years later that just about all those men were sent over as replacements to the 24th Division and were killed, wounded or taken prisoner within four days. The rest of us loaded up our equipment and we took a troop train to Camp Stoneman, California for a few days. Then we went up to San Francisco and loaded on a ship to go across the Pacific.

We landed in Japan and they filled us up with replacements and gave us six weeks to train and be ready to fight in Korea. I had five Koreans who spoke no English, two Puerto Ricans who only spoke Spanish and five reservists and National Guard troops. None of them knew anything about the 4.2-inch mortar. Considering what we were up against with the language barrier and the limited time to train, we did a marvelous job getting ready.

Once in Korea, we were often split up into Battalion Combat Teams. We had three platoons of mortars, with four guns in each platoon. Each one of our platoons would go with one of the combat teams. I was a staff sergeant and a squad leader; each squad had one gun. I acted as forward observer some of the time. We had two or three of us that rotated being an observer. We would go forward for a week and then one of the others would relieve us and we'd spend time with our squads. At various times when I was an observer, I had the whole company under my direction, all 12 guns at my command. Each gun could fire 20 rounds a minute. The shells weighed 25 pounds, the same size as a 105 mm howitzer. When you can call fire in at 20 rounds a minute from 12 guns, you can really blacken an area in a few seconds.

In my squad, the squad leader had an M1, but the rest of the guys had carbines. I think they were M2 carbines, I remember they had the selector switch and they would go full automatic. We started off with the smaller 15-round magazine for them and then we got some that were bigger, about double in size. The guys would tape two or three of them together. I hardly used my M1 because I had picked up a .45 caliber grease gun. The 187th Airborne had made a jump out in front of us one time and they lost a whole lot of people. They brought out three jeep trailer loads of weapons and I grabbed one of those grease guns. I took three magazines and taped them together and that's what I carried most of the time. I could hang it around my neck and it didn't bother me. I just left my M1 cradled beside the seat in the three-quarter ton truck most of the time.

*M3A1 submachine gun with 30-round magazine and stock extended. Often referred to as the grease gun. Garand Stand collection. Photo courtesy of Bruce N. Canfield.*

I never did use the grease gun in combat. The only time I ever shot at a target and saw somebody fall was with the M1. I was always busy with other jobs, so I didn't have time to do much shooting. When I was with the rifle companies on the OP's I had plenty of opportunities, but I would be busy calling for fire. I didn't have a whole lot of time to be drawing a bead and pulling a trigger.

My first experience of using my rifle in combat was up north. We were trying to keep this road blocked off to keep the Chinese from cutting the Marines off worse than they were already. We were with a group moving to reinforce one of our battalions and we got separated from the group because a bridge gave way and we couldn't cross. We were out there with a few trucks and a tracked vehicle with twin 40s and a half-track with quad .50s. We didn't shut the trucks off all night because it was so cold we were afraid they wouldn't start again. It was so damned cold I thought I was going to freeze to death. I didn't sleep at all that night, I walked in circles around one of the trucks all night. In the middle of the night, a Chinese patrol came from the hills above us and we got fired on from up above. I fired my M1 a couple of times at where the fire had come from. The rifle wouldn't cycle at first. After I fired, I would have to push the op rod with the heel of my hand to close the bolt. After I had fired three or four times it started to warm up and fire the way it was supposed to. Later, some Chinese came around this finger about 200 yards down the road and fired on us. One of my Koreans was hit in the back. I brought my M1 up, drew a bead on one of them, pulled the trigger and fired. He grabbed his hip and rolled over. I don't know if I killed him or not, but I sure wounded him.

During the evacuation of Hungnam, North Korea in the winter of 1950, the 3rd Division was the last unit to leave. The Marines left on the 13th of December, but we were there until the 24th of December facing the Chinese. The perimeter got smaller and smaller. I left around noon on December 24th with my company. At that time we were the closest thing to artillery left in the perimeter; they had already loaded all the big guns. We were set up right on the beach, right next to the water. At the given time, these Marine tracked vehicles came up and we broke our mortars down and threw them into the vehicle. They did a 180 and went back out into the water and we were gone.

I was in Korea from November 1950 to July 1951. I was supposed to be discharged in September 1950, but Harry Truman extended everyone's enlistment by one year so September 1951 was going to be when I was discharged. They offered me an advancement in rank if I would re-up right there in Korea. But I thought after what I'd just been through, a guy would have to be an idiot to do that.

Personal Experiences

> **Henry Turner** was drafted in May 1943. He took basic training at Camp Shelby, MS as part of the 69th Division as it was being formed. However, he was sent overseas as an infantry replacement. He was assigned to the 29th Division in France shortly after the D-Day invasion. He was wounded in August 1944 and evacuated to a field hospital to recover from his wounds. When he returned to the regiment he became a personnel clerk at the regimental headquarters and served with the regimental personnel section until the end of the war. He later served for 12 years in the National Guard.

At Camp Shelby, I was cadre for the 69th Division when it was started. We trained with the M1 and I thought it was a heck of a nice rifle, but I have a bad right eye and I had to shoot left handed. It was a hell of a thing to try to reload the M1 in rapid fire like that. We trained with everything except the machine gun. I fired a bazooka, carbine, pistol and BAR. When I finished training I was sent overseas as an infantry replacement. They needed replacements in England just before D-Day. I joined the 29th Division just after D-Day in France.

I was assigned to C Company, 116th Infantry Regiment in the 29th Division. I explained to them that I was basically a company clerk. They said, "Fine, this is a BAR, you can use this instead." That gun was too heavy, the ammunition was too heavy and I was too young and too lightweight to carry it. So, I got rid of it in a hurry. I thought it was impractical for anyone to have to carry that thing and it's ammunition. We carried two magazines in each pouch on the BAR belt; it must have been about 16 magazines. The gun was damned heavy and the bipod on the barrel swinging loose made it uncomfortable to carry. They didn't have a problem with me getting rid of it. I just threw it away and picked up an M1. Then I got rid of the M1, I thought it was too cumbersome to carry as well.

I became the company commander's bodyguard, which is not a TO&E slot at all, but it gave me the right to carry the carbine. So I carried that and I had a .45 pistol that I got from a friend of mine who was killed. I always wore that because it was a good thing to sleep with. In a foxhole, you could sleep comfortably with the pistol across your chest and shoot anybody who came in at you. As the CO's bodyguard, I watched out for him to make sure he didn't get shot and I sometimes carried his radio.

I really liked the carbine. We were in the hedgerow country and the hedgerows weren't that far apart. With the range we were fighting at, the carbine was good enough. I don't know that we ever had to reach out to three or four hundred yards with a rifle. Normally, I carried two magazines in a pouch on my belt and one in the rifle. We never had prolonged firefights that used a lot of ammunition. That was enough ammunition for what we got into. Every night we had ammunition brought up to us and you could always find ammunition around if you needed it. I never saw anybody that had to go through a couple of bandoleers and a cartridge belt of ammunition with an M1.

I think if I ever did any serious damage, I did it with a hand grenade. There were times up close from one hedgerow to another, when a hand grenade was handy. I always carried two hand grenades. I traveled pretty light. You couldn't carry a lot of junk with as much running and marching as we did.

I never had any trouble with the carbine. We were always on the line for at least ten days at a time and usually longer than that. I don't think I cleaned it until we came off the line. I think with all the weapons our infantry had you could bury them in the dirt, dig them up and continue to shoot them. They just never malfunctioned that I know of because they were dirty, wet or anything else.

The issue weapon for the tankers was the Thompson submachine gun. We didn't have them in the infantry. One of our lieutenants made a trade with one of the guys on a tank and got himself a Thompson. Later, he was badly wounded and asked me to take care of his Thompson until he got back from the hospital. His wounds were severe and I knew he wouldn't be returning, but I carried that Thompson for two or three days. It was uncomfortable to carry, the magazines were too long and the balance was bad. I finally threw that damned thing away, it wasn't an infantryman's weapon. The ammunition was heavy too; I carried one magazine in the gun and two in a pouch.

I carried a grease gun for a while. The gun and the ammunition was heavy and the cyclic rate was too slow. I found a German burp gun outside of Saint Lo and thought I'd give it a try. I got in one firefight with it and took friendly fire. After that, I thought I'd better get rid of it. It had a very distinctive sound. The German burp gun was better than any of our guns; I liked everything about it. I also tried a British Sten gun; it was fun to play with. I carried it until I ran out of ammunition. I always went back to carrying the carbine.

I had a chance to use a bazooka once. I didn't want to, but the company commander told me to. So I went up and took a shot at a tank and hit the turret where it turned, right where we were supposed to hit it. Unfortunately, the guy who loaded me forgot to pull the safety on the warhead and it bounced off the tank. I don't know what kind of tank it was, it was a big tank with an 88 mm gun. I think if the round had exploded, it would have at least damaged the turret.

Personal Experiences

I was wounded on the 8th of August just as we were getting out of hedgerow country. I was evacuated to a field hospital, but when I found out that the unit was moving out, I went AWOL and hitched a ride back. When I returned to my outfit, the regiment was totally cut off fighting at Brest, so they kept me at headquarters. I pitched in to help out at Regimental HQ, they were swamped with the number of final statements required for the many combat deaths. I proved sufficiently valuable that they kept me with the personnel section. By the end of the war, I was the personnel sergeant major of the regiment and brought the regiment back to the United States to be deactivated.

# US Infantry Weapons In Combat

*T.C. Mataxis in Europe, 1945.*

**T.C. Mataxis** *had a very long and interesting career in the Army. In June of 1940, he joined the Army a week after completing his ROTC course in college. He attended the Infantry Officer's Course at Fort Benning, GA and then served in a variety of positions in several Infantry Divisions. He attended the Command and Staff Course in 1943 and was assigned to the 70th Infantry Division. The 70th Division was initially sent overseas piecemeal and its infantry regiments were sent out to reinforce other units during the German Norwind Offensive in January 1945. Major Mataxis was given command of the 2nd Battalion, 276th Infantry after the commander had been relieved. He commanded that battalion for the rest of the war. During the Korean War, he served as XO and then commanded the 17th Infantry Regiment for a year. In Vietnam, he served both as a military advisor and with the 101st Airborne Division. In 1970, he returned to Vietnam for two more years. He was the Assistant Division Commander and then Commanding General of the 23rd Infantry Division. Brigadier General Mataxis retired from the Army in 1972 after 32 years of service. He offers a unique perspective on the use of US infantry weapons from his combat experiences.*

Personal Experiences

I attended the Officers Infantry School at Fort Benning in early 1941. The first course second lieutenants take is the Officers Heavy Weapons Course. It was the first reserve officers course they'd given since World War One. It was a composite course; they were testing the training schedule with us. After we finished, they started Basic Officer Course Number One. We had a lot of weapons training in the course. My experience in ROTC and the regular army had been with the M1903 Springfield rifle. At the course, we were introduced to the new M1 rifle. They told us that we would be responsible to teach the sergeants back in our unit about the M1. Most of them had no experience with the M1 and we would have to teach them how to fieldstrip it and fire it. We qualified with the M1 and I thought it was terrific, much better than the 03. A lot of our old sergeants didn't think it was as accurate as the 03, but I think for the average shooter it was. We also trained on the BAR. They had a new version of the BAR; it had a smaller handgrip and a bipod on the front of the barrel. Quite a few of the guys who had trained with the older BAR with the longer handgrip would burn their hands on the barrel after firing it. We also trained on the new light machine gun. I had trained with the old heavy water-cooled machine guns, but this was a new lighter air-cooled version of that weapon. We did not have the 60 mm mortar in the army at that time, but we trained with a French 60 mm mortar. Our 60 mm company mortar was an exact copy of this mortar. We also trained on the British three-inch Stokes mortar. Later the US produced the 81 mm mortar, which became the standard battalion level mortar.

The 70th Division was among the last infantry divisions formed. During our training, we were stripped of over 6,000 people to fill the combat casualties from Europe and the Pacific. We never finished our combined training. In the Fall of 1944, the Army needed more troops overseas and we were sent to Europe to the 7th Army to finish our training. As soon as we landed in December, they stripped us of a number of our rifleman to fill the units that had been shot up in the Bulge. Then Operation Norwind came around the first of January; the Germans attacked and tried to pinch off a corps in France. They started throwing us in by battalion and regiment to fill the 15-mile gap the Germans had tore in our lines. From there, we went up to Saarbrrucken and took it. Then we were transferred from the 7th Army to the 3rd Army until the war was over.

I normally carried a carbine and .45 in a shoulder holster under my field jacket. During Norwind, we were fighting in the Vorge Mountains, attached to the 45th Division. I was the battalion exec at the time and the battalion was stuck on a ridge. I was called back to the rear by the regimental commander. The commanding general of the 45th Division had relieved my battalion commander, so I took over command of the battalion. I was told that the 45th Division commander had told the regimental commander that if we didn't get that next hill by the next morning, he would be relieved. Of course the regimental commander told me that if he got relieved, I'd be relieved too.

I went back up to the hill and aligned the troops. I took one company and gave my S-3 the other one. We started the attack off moving through snow that was about knee deep. When we got over the top of the hill, German machine guns on the back slope opened up. They surprised us; before, we'd only been getting fire from the ridge ahead of us. I dove into the snow and lost my carbine. The machine gunners would sweep back and forth over the fields and then they would start going up and down to catch the guys who had hit the ground. These were those MG42s with the high rate of fire. I figured I needed to get out of the area and I looked down ahead of me and saw some bushes about 50 yards away. I got my .45 out and ran for those bushes to get away from the machine gun fire. I jumped into the bushes and fell into a German machine gun position. I used my .45 and killed three of them and captured a couple. When it was all over, the slide of the pistol was locked back and I was pointing it, still trying to fire.

After that, we got the troops together and took that next hill after dark. Once we got to the top of the hill, there was a German company marching down the road in front of us. We had one heavy machine gun that we had dragged up with us. We waited until they got in front of us and we opened fire on them. As a result of that, we were cut off for two days on top of the hill.

We learned a lesson at that time about machine guns. I sent one of my good sergeants out, you know, the guy who goes out and gets things for you. I told him to get us a light machine gun to go with every heavy machine gun we had. So when we were advancing, we used the light machine guns and left the heavy machine guns on the trucks. Then when we went into defensive positions, I had the heavy machine guns brought up. We would have one heavy and one light machine gun in every position. I also did the same thing with the light machine guns in the rifle companies. I put an extra BAR with each one of our light machine guns. I never asked the sergeant where he got the extra guns.

In the winter conditions we were fighting in, sometimes the water in the jacket of the heavy machine guns would freeze. We would try to fire short bursts to warm them up. If you fired too long of a burst, the gun would overheat. Short bursts would melt the ice. If the light machine guns froze, the guys would piss on them.

At that time, the Germans really outgunned us. They had the MG42 machine gun and we opposed German units armed with the new MP44. It was an outstanding weapon. That's why I got the extra machine guns, but we depended very heavily on our artillery fire when we ran into something. We'd stop, call artillery and shoot the hell out of them.

During that operation, we ran up against units from the 6th SS Mountain Division, which had come down from Finland. They would come skiing over the slopes, hit the ground and open up on our columns with their MG42s. One of our sergeants came up with an idea. He got a 60 mm mortar and filled a helmet with dirt and would fire the mortar without the base plate. We'd have that in the lead squad and when they saw the Germans skiers coming down the slopes, they'd fire the mortar at them. When the Germans saw the mortar fire coming in their direction, they wouldn't stop, they'd continue skiing. Firing the mortar that way wasn't accurate, but it served its purpose in this case.

A few weeks later, we took over some defensive positions from the 103rd Division. We were facing bunkers and outposts on the Ziegfried line. The Germans used to have their supplies come up from the rear at night by horse and wagon. During the night our forward people could hear the squeaking of the wagons. I got four .50

M2 .50 caliber Browning machine gun. Courtesy of the Robert G. Segel collection.

caliber machine guns that I took off our mess trucks. I gave them to one of my old World War One era sergeants. He was one of those guys who would be good for 30 days or so and then he would get drunk and get busted. He had a clinometer from World War One; he had been in a machine gun battalion back then. They would use indirect machine gun fire on the trenches. You could put the clinometer on the barrel of the gun and use it to adjust the guns for indirect fire. I had him form four machine gun crews for the .50s. When he got the word that the outposts could hear something coming up the road, they would use the .50s for indirect fire into that area. Later we picked up some POWs. They told us they had foxholes dug every 100 yards along that road so if they heard artillery coming, they would jump into a hole. But they couldn't hear the machine guns fire and didn't know they were under fire until the bullets started bouncing around them. Those .50s caused a lot of apprehension for them.

I got to Korea in 1952/53; I was XO and then commanded the 17th Regiment in the 7th Infantry Division. At that time, most of the fighting was for the outposts. What the Chinese were doing at places like Pork Chop Hill, T-Bone and others, was attacking and trying to inflict casualties on us. We were trying to defend those hills and outposts and keep our casualties down as much as possible. We were at the point in the spring of 1953 where a regimental commander couldn't use more than a rifle platoon without getting permission from the division commander. He had to go all the way back to the army commander for permission. The war was very unpopular by that time and trying to keep the casualties down was very important. This was after the big fight for Pork Chop Hill in April 1953.

With the trench type warfare, there was a lot of sniping. We had a special training course in the regiment to select the best guys to be snipers. They used M1 sniper rifles and I thought they did a good job. If nothing else, it kept the other guy on the other side very cautious.

# Personal Experiences

*Gerald Cosgrove, photo taken after the Korean War.*

**Gerald Cosgrove** *enlisted in the Marine Corps in November 1942. After taking boot camp on Parris Island, he went to Camp Lejeune, NC where he joined the 2nd Battalion. As the 4th Marine Division was formed, the 2nd Battalion became 2nd Battalion, 24th Marine Regiment. The division deployed to the Pacific and invaded the Islands of Roi-Namur in the Marshall's, Saipan and Tinian and finally, Iwo Jima. Mr. Cosgrove was wounded on Saipan five days after the invasion. After recovering, he rejoined his unit and participated in the assault on Iwo Jima. He was wounded 14 days after the landing and was evacuated to a Navy hospital in Hawaii. After returning to the mainland and serving at the Brooklyn Navy Yard, he was discharged in December 1945. He was recalled to duty during the Korean War and served six months with an infantry unit in the Mediterranean.*

Back in late 1942 at Parris Island, the bolt action Springfield 03 was the issue rifle for us. The M1 Garand didn't come around until 1943. We started our training with the 03; we mainly did close order drill and things of that nature with it. We did fire it a couple of times, but when it was time to qualify we got M1s. We all qualified with the M1 and after qualification, the M1 wound up being our rifle for the rest of training. The 03 was a very accurate rifle once you got your windage down. But of course you had to work the bolt every time, you didn't have semiautomatic fire. Therefore the M1 had more of an advantage over the 03. Not having fired the 03 that many times, it would be very unfair to compare both rifles as far as accuracy is concerned. I did hear many guys say that they thought the 03 was more accurate.

I finished with boot camp at Camp Lejeune, after I had fired on the range there for qualification. At first I did 30 days mess duty and then I was assigned to the 2$^{nd}$ Battalion. That wound up turning into the 2$^{nd}$ Battalion, 24$^{th}$ Marines. I was a rifleman in 2$^{nd}$ squad, 2$^{nd}$ platoon in Easy Company. We went across the country to Camp Pendleton and the 4$^{th}$ Division was formed there.

Our first combat was in the Marshall Islands at Roi-Namur. There were two Islands: Roi and Namur. Roi had the airfield and Namur had the supply and ammunition dumps. We invaded Namur. I was in the first wave and we saw a lot of fighting. When we landed, I was carrying my M1 with a full cartridge belt and two bandoleers of ammunition. There wasn't any resistance when we first landed, but there was shortly after. What happened was we landed on the back end of the island and they had expected us to come in the other way. We secured the island after about 26 hours of fighting.

We landed on Saipan and I got wounded on the fifth day. The fighting on Saipan was pretty open. Until we got to Iwo, nothing was real close. I would say most of the fighting took place at a couple of hundred yards. Unless you came up on somebody coming up out of a pillbox, then it would be a close, quick engagement. On the fifth day, I got hit in the knee with shrapnel. I didn't know it until the next morning, my knee wouldn't bend and it was all swollen. I was evacuated from Saipan and they sent me to a hospital on Guadalcanal. I missed the Tinian operation. I rejoined the division in Hawaii and went back to the same outfit.

In combat, the Marine marksmanship training we had received didn't apply all the time. If you were watching someone approach you, then you zeroed in, let your breath out and squeezed a shot off. But if you were in a massive fight where they were running at you in waves, you were just shooting at random. You'd be aiming towards the mass; you wouldn't be picking out one individual. I would pick out groups. If there were three of them running at me, I wouldn't know which one I was going to hit, but I would be aiming at the three of them. You'd shoot pretty fast if they were coming at you in a wave. There were times where we'd see them coming on one of their *banzai* attacks from a couple of hundred yards away and we would pour some heavy fire on them. They really were suicide attacks. On Saipan they were never able to close in on us. We had some close combat on Iwo.

My unit was in reserve for the Iwo landing. We landed in the afternoon, right after the Japs opened fire. I was a squad leader then, I had 12 men under my command when we landed and after eight days, I only had three left. The combat on Iwo was much different than Saipan. Except for one *banzai* attack one night, I don't think I saw more than 50 Japs. They were always hidden; they were popping up here and popping up there.

The M1 was a good combat weapon, I never had any problems with mine in that volcanic sand. But they had problems with the BAR, the sand would get into the bolt and lock it up. I had a BAR man who was about to throw his BAR away, he was sick and tired of trying to get it to work. It would only fire single shots. I got on his ass and told him to put it in the jeep, we needed the firepower at night. So from about the second day on he would leave it in the jeep during the day and the driver would bring it up to us at night. During the day he carried an M1.

It was difficult to break a weapon down for cleaning; you had to take a chance. If you were with your foxhole buddy, he would be on double alert and you did what you had to do as quickly as you could do it. Then maybe he did the same with his weapon. That bolt closing action of the M1 during loading sometimes made it hard to operate your weapon at night. If you were lying in your foxhole at night trying to reload and the clip popped out, you'd have to put another one in. It wasn't the easiest thing in the world lying in the mud or sand. During that one *banzai* attack, I fired 10 to 15 clips really fast. My rifle got so hot that cosmoline ran down from the upper handguard over my hand. It made the rifle difficult to hold. You would have to be in a pretty severe firefight for it to get that hot.

On Iwo, I always filled my cartridge belt and tried to carry two or three bandoleers. I would use a lot of ammunition during the day and a lot of nights I would need another bandoleer or two. I always tried to maintain a full cartridge belt; I mostly worked out of the bandoleers. You could throw the bandoleer away when it was empty. There was a couple of times when I had to use ammo from the cartridge belt. There was that one night on Iwo when we had that big *banzai* attack. On occasion if we ran low, we could send someone back for more ammunition. I don't recall ever using any armor-piercing ammunition; we were issued the standard ball ammunition. I usually carried three grenades and sometimes I would get a few extras. There were times when the demolition man wasn't able to be there to do his job of closing up a hole, then we would lob a grenade or two in the hole and fire into it. Or if we could, we'd have the flame thrower man come up and seal the hole.

My squad was good, but I guess every sergeant says that. They knew to keep a rifleman on the outside flank of the BAR. After they were in position, all I would do is worm around on my stomach as quick as I could to see that they had a good field of fire. I can honestly say that I very seldom had to correct my guys. Our assistant BAR men sometimes carried the carbine because they were carrying all the extra BAR ammunition. They carried as many magazines as they possibly could.

I was on Iwo for 14 days before I was hit. The Japanese had these big rockets. You could even see them in the air, they were so big. One landed maybe 10 to 15 yards behind me and blew me up through the air. I was deaf for about 36 hours and it gave me a severe concussion. I spent a few days at a hospital on the beach and then they evacuated me to a ship. I ended up at the Naval hospital at Pearl Harbor and then returned home in September 1945.

Personal Experiences

> **John Nothnagle** *enlisted in the Army in December 1943. He went to infantry basic training at Camp Blanding, FL. and then attended radio school at Fort Benning, GA. Upon completion of his training, he was assigned to the Signal Company in the 70th Division at Fort Leavenworth, KS. He arrived in France in January 1945 and served with the division until the end of the war.*

I enlisted in December 1943, but I didn't enter service until February 1944. I was sent to infantry basic training at Camp Blanding, Florida. At Camp Blanding, most of our weapons training was almost exclusively with the M1 rifle. We did practice a little with the bolt action M1903 Springfield. We used the Springfield to practice shooting rifle grenades. The M1 couldn't shoot rifle grenades because it was gas operated. We were impressed with the kick of the 03 when we launched grenades. We were instructed to put the butt on the ground and not to hold it to our shoulder. We also received a little training with the M1 carbine. I thought the M1 was an excellent weapon and I thought I shot very well with it. I qualified as a sharpshooter.

After basic training, they sent me to the infantry school at Fort Benning to learn radio communications. For most of the time there, I learned to take and receive International Code, which was like Morse Code. When I finished there, I was sent to the 570th Signal Company of the 70th Infantry Division at Fort Leonard Wood, Missouri. I traded my infantry blue piping for the orange of the Signal Corps.

We went overseas in January 1945. The signal company, the artillery, quartermaster and units like that were referred to as 'special troops" and we were the last units to go overseas. The signal company had three platoons: a wire platoon, a message center platoon and a radio platoon. I was in the radio platoon and we were organized in three man teams. We were parceled out to support regiments or battalions. The radios were mounted in three-quarter ton trucks, so that's how we traveled. We generally weren't attached to units for very long. Usually it wasn't more than three or four days at a time.

I was carrying an M1 when we first went overseas and for a while after. I never fired my M1 in anger; I just never had a target. Then at one point we were called in and told to turn in our rifles. We were equipped with the M3 submachine gun, the famous grease gun. It was quite heavy, although I'll say that it wasn't as cumbersome as the rifle. We'd sling it over our back and it wasn't too bad. It wasn't an effective weapon; it was a very slow firing piece compared with other submachine guns. It also had the unfortunate propensity of dropping its magazine when it fired. When you fired it, the motion of the weapon would cause the heavy magazine to drop out. We learned to hold the magazine when we fired so it wouldn't drop out. We practiced with them after they issued them to us. I only carried two or three magazines for it. I kept one in the gun and kept the others on the truck. The truck was our home.

I did fire the grease gun once in anger. On that occasion, I had been transferred to the wire section and I was stringing wire in a small village in Lorraine. A sniper took a shot at me from a barn like building across the road, only about 60 feet away. I heard the round pass by my head. I turned around and I knew exactly where he had fired from, there was an upper window. I fired about a 10 to 15 round burst from my grease gun that shattered the window and window frame. It was a good burst and the magazine held. About two minutes later, the shooter appeared with his hands over his head. It was a kid; he was one of those boys the Germans mustered in towards the end of the war. He wasn't a very good shot and I was happy he wasn't. I took him prisoner.

When the war ended, I was in Erlangen, Germany, just north of Nuremberg. The 70th Division was deactivated and I was transferred to the 3rd Division. I remained with the 3rd Division until I had enough points to go home. I returned to the US in May 1946.

# Personal Experiences

> **Marion Throne** *enlisted in the US Army in 1936 and served in a horse cavalry unit at Fort Clark, TX. Colonel George Patton was his regimental commander. He was transferred to the 7th Infantry Regiment of the 3rd Division at the Vancouver barracks at Fort Lewis, WA in 1939. He went overseas and fought in North Africa and Italy. He was captured in 1944 at the Anzio beachhead and spent the rest of the war as a POW. After the war ended he remained in the Army and served in Japan with the 24th Infantry Division. He was reassigned to the 2nd Division in 1950 and served with the division in Korea. He retired from the Army in 1956 after 20 years of service.*

I enlisted in the Army in 1936 and served with the 5th Cavalry at Fort Clark, Texas near Del Rio. Back in those days, you enlisted for the unit you wanted to go to. Each organization got its own recruits and you stayed with that same unit until your enlistment was up. You went into a platoon and a squad and the platoon sergeant trained you. Back then we had the 03 Springfield; my rifle was serial number 7527. It was a real low number and it had lots of pits in it. I went to what they called a rifle troop; we had light machine guns and BARs. We trained with the rifle, but our primary weapon was the .45 pistol. We had the rifle as a backup. Back then we had to qualify with our weapons every year and if you didn't qualify, you couldn't stay. They'd send you to the quartermaster or the medical corps. I made expert with the 03, it was pretty accurate at long ranges.

We qualified with the .45 while riding a horse. We had a course where you'd shoot two shots to the right and two shots to the left and then one overhead. Five shots was all we ever carried in a clip, we never carried seven. Then we would reload with the horse at a gallop and then fire another five rounds. It wasn't hard to learn to shoot from a horse.

I saw my first M1 rifles in 1936 or 1937. They gave us six of them, but we weren't allowed to fire them. We had to carry them on our horses for a week and get them real dirty and dusty. They told us not to clean them. I suppose it was a test to see if they would fire in combat conditions after they'd been in the dirt and the weather. After the week, ordnance came and picked them up. We never knew how they did on the tests.

I transferred to Fort Lewis in 1939 and was assigned to D Company, 7th Infantry Regiment, which was part of the 3rd Division. When I got up there, the division had units spread all over. It was hardly a division. They seemed to anticipate that the war was coming on and they started to consolidate the units in 1940. I made corporal around then and helped train the draftees that were coming into the division.

I can't remember when we first got our M1s, although I'm pretty sure that we got some before we went overseas. On our first beach landing, in North Africa, I carried a Thompson submachine gun. In those days, most of the officers and NCOs carried submachine guns for all beach landings and river crossings. I didn't carry the Thompson for too long. I carried one on the North Africa landing and I think I had one for a while in Sicily too. I liked the Thompson; the only thing was the ammo. When I got off the boat in North Africa, I was carrying 600 rounds of ammo and it was heavy. All of my ammo was in clips; they were the ones that held 20 rounds. I fired all of it the first day except for a few clips. It wasn't a very accurate weapon; you just sprayed with it. They were really good in villages. We'd form a team and one man would kick the door open and then you'd spray the room with the Thompson. You didn't have time to aim, if there was anyone in there you just hoped you got him. We'd used them quite a bit that way; they were good for clearing bunkers as well.

Later, they took the submachine guns from all of us and they gave us .45 pistols and carbines. We had never heard of the carbine before we got overseas. I did use the carbine in combat a little, but I didn't care for it. The carbines were supposed to replace the .45s, but they didn't prove to be successful. It was short ranged and had a small bullet. Every chance we had, we got a rifle instead. We didn't like going into combat without a rifle; those little carbines didn't get it.

I was carrying an M1 when we invaded Anzio. I used to know the serial number; it was a six-digit number. I think it was serial number 144628, but it's been a long time. The M1 was a good, reliable rifle and you could fire those eight rounds really fast. There was one thing with the M1 and I don't know if this was a fault with the rifle or from it getting dirty: when you loaded a clip and let the bolt go forward, you always wanted to check it and hit the operating rod handle with your hand. If you didn't, the bolt might not be fully closed and then you'd have a misfire. That happened to me once when I was on an outpost at Anzio. I had crawled on top of a haystack when the Germans counterattacked us. I spotted two Germans with a light machine gun trying to move around our flank to get in a position behind our lines. I waited until they got about 50 yards from the haystack and I thought I better get them while I can. I raised my rifle and pulled the trigger and the round didn't go off! I hadn't hit the op rod handle with my hand! I was dumbfounded; the Germans were so close that they heard the rifle click. They looked up and saw me and they took off. I was so dumbfounded that I never did fire at them. It was just such a surprise. I couldn't believe that I was so stupid to not tap the operating rod. Overall, the M1 was a good rifle; not all of them would do that. On some of them, the bolt would close all the way. Once you fired the first round, you wouldn't have to worry about it.

At Anzio, my battalion was doing a reconnaissance in force. We didn't have any support or heavy weapons with us. When we ran into a large number of Germans there was no way we could fight through them. We got cut off and our other units couldn't break through to us. We had to surrender and I became a POW. That was the end of the war for me.

After the war, I served with the 21st Infantry Regiment of the 24th Division in Japan for a few years. My enlistment was up and I was transferred back to the States. I left Japan by ship and three days later, the North Koreans crossed the 38th Parallel. Our ship docked in Washington and I was assigned to the 2nd Division because they needed men.

I went to the Heavy Mortar Company in the 38th Regiment. They had 4.2-inch mortars; I hadn't had any experience with them before then. The infantry didn't get the 4.2 mortars until after the end of World War Two. In Korea they couldn't get artillery in some of those mountains, so they gave each regiment three platoons of 4.2s. There were 12 tubes, about the same as an artillery battalion. Each battalion got four tubes and they were pretty powerful and accurate weapons. We mostly hauled them in three-quarter ton weapons carriers, although sometimes we carried them.

I saw a lot of combat in Korea. I carried a .45 and I kept an M1 in my jeep. Once in a while, we'd get tangled up with a small arms fight if we were on an outpost. But most of the time we were busy shooting the mortars. It was an all-together different war than World War Two. I spent a year in Korea, then I rotated out.

*Ray Aebischer*

**Ray Aebischer** *was drafted in 1942 and he volunteered for airborne duty while at the induction center. He was sent to Camp Toccoa, GA to train with the 506$^{th}$ Parachute Infantry Regiment, which was being formed. He became a member of Company F. The 506$^{th}$ became part of the 101$^{st}$ Airborne Division and deployed overseas with the division in 1943. Mr. Aebischer made combat jumps into Normandy on D-Day and Holland during Operation Market Garden in September 1944. He was wounded in Holland and evacuated to England, where he spent several months recuperating from shrapnel wounds. He was able to rejoin his unit in Bastogne during the Battle of the Bulge and fought with the 101$^{st}$ through the rest of the war. Following WW2, he briefly left the Army, but re-enlisted and attended OCS. In 1953, he was sent to Korea and spent 16 months assigned to the 17$^{th}$ Infantry Regiment in the 7$^{th}$ Division. Mr. Aebischer spent 21 years in the Army and retired as a lieutenant colonel.*

Personal Experiences

I was drafted in July of 1942. I received greetings from Franklin Roosevelt, along with millions of others, telling me that I had been selected. I was living in California at the time and when I got to the Presidio of Monterey for induction, I volunteered for airborne duty. I knew little or nothing about paratroops, I'd just heard they existed.

They put me on a train to Toccoa, Georgia, where the 506th was being formed. The 506th was one of the parachute infantry regiments that was later attached to the 101st Airborne Division. Except for the first sergeant and the platoon sergeants, the rest of us were raw recruits. If you want to know what our training was like, read *Band of Brothers* by Stephen Ambrose. He describes it perfectly.

We were issued brand new M1 rifles packed in cosmoline, right out of the manufacturer's box. There wasn't a firing range at Toccoa, so we were trucked to Clemson, South Carolina to use the range at the college. They had a very good known distance range there. We received our marksmanship training and fired qualification at Clemson. During our training, we also trained with the light machine gun, the BAR, the carbine, 60 mm mortars, the .45 cal pistol and the 2.36-inch rocket launcher. I carried the M1 through basic training, but before going to Fort Benning for jump school, I became the squad machine gunner. We had M1919A4 .30 caliber air-cooled light machine guns.

We shipped over to England around August 1943. We trained constantly until the D-Day invasion. We had a lot of maneuvers and made a few jumps. Most of it was typical infantry training. For the D-Day jump, I packed my equipment in an equipment bag that attached to my leg with a strap. The bag contained my machine

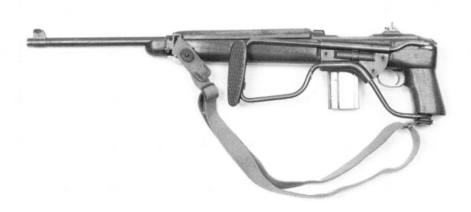

*M1A1 carbine, issued to Paratroopers. Shown with the stock folded, closed position. Photo courtesy of Scott A. Duff.*

gun, an M1A1 folding stock carbine, a machete, some hand grenades, a land mine, clothing items, rations and a little bit of ammo. I didn't carry too much ammo for the machine gun because some of the other fellows carried that. The bag must have weighed close to 100 pounds. When I jumped, the opening shock from the chute opening tore the bag loose from my leg. I landed in France with nothing but a trench knife stuck in my boot. I teamed up with some others during the night and picked up a German rifle in the morning. Eventually, I found another machine gun and used it in the fighting.

Our units got back together that morning and we finally went on with our mission. We never really completed our original mission, but we were able to secure some of the flanks for the troops coming ashore. We linked up with some of the ground troops around noon that day. During the battle we were covering the flank of one of our positions, the platoon was lying along a hedgerow. I observed a column of Germans coming towards us down the road. I was able to use my machine gun with great effect to halt the German advance. After six weeks in France, they relieved us and sent us back to England.

In England, we went back to training again. Then we made the jump into Holland during Operation Market Garden. On September 17th, we jumped into a landing zone near Zon, which was just north of Eindhoven. By then I was a corporal and an assistant squad leader, I carried a Tommy gun. The Tommy gun gave you a lot of firepower, but I didn't like it too much. It was heavy and it jammed too easy, you couldn't depend on it. It would work OK, but if it got a little bit of dirt in it, it would jam. It was difficult to keep a weapon clean when you're crawling around in the mud and dirt. I'd take an M1 over it any time; you could always depend on it, dirty or not. I only lasted six days in Holland before I was wounded by a mortar round and was airlifted back to England. I spent the next three months recuperating.

I rejoined F Company on January 2nd, 1945 at Bastogne. They weren't encircled any more, but there was still a lot of fighting around the town. We spent another month fighting there. I don't recall what type of weapon I used when I returned, I think I carried a rifle or a carbine. We never experienced any problems with the weapons in the winter weather that I can recall. I remained with the 101st until the end of the war. We were in Austria when the war ended. We were on the high seas in August 1945 going home. We were going to do some further training and then go to Japan. But, you know what happened, the war ended.

I got out of the Army for a while, but enlisted again in 1947 and attended OCS. In 1952, I got sent to Korea and was assigned to the 17th Infantry Regiment in the 7th Division. I started as an infantry platoon leader. By then the war was pretty static, we were all dug in along the 38th Parallel. We did some patrols and I hate to say it, but we made some foolish attacks on enemy positions. We'd lose men taking hills and just retreat back off of them. I normally carried a .45 caliber pistol, but didn't use it in action. Except for the attacks, most of the combat was artillery exchanges. I was only in the platoon for about three weeks, then I was sent to the regimental S-3 to work as an assistant S-3. I ended up spending 16 months in Korea.

*Of interest, In 1999, a Frenchman contacted Mr. Aebischer and told him he had found some equipment with his name and serial number on it. He had found the carbine, web belt, first-aid pack and machete that he had lost the night he made the Normandy jump.*

# US Infantry Weapons In Combat

> **Robert Young** *joined the Army in January 1949 and was sent to Fort Dix, NJ for basic. Once he completed his basic training he was assigned as a rifleman to K Company, 38th Infantry Regiment in the 2nd Infantry Division. The division deployed overseas to Korea in the summer of 1950. He was wounded in September while fighting in South Korea and sent to Japan to recover. He returned to his unit in November and was wounded for a second time while fighting the Chinese during the division's retreat from Kunu-ri. The Army evacuated him to Japan for treatment and then returned him to the US. He was discharged in January 1952 after spending six months in the hospital.*

I took my basic training at Fort Dix, New Jersey. We only had eight weeks of basic, it's usually a 16-week course. I think they knew something might be happening, although I don't know. We trained a lot with the M1 rifle and a little with the carbine. I didn't train with any other weapons, although some guys trained with the .45 pistol and the .30 caliber machine gun. Other than with the rifle, I don't recall doing much weapons training while we were there. We did more weapons training during advanced infantry training after we were assigned to our units.

After basic training, I was sent to Fort Lewis, Washington where I was assigned to K Company, 38th Regiment in the 2nd Division. While I was at Fort Lewis, I went to SCR-300 radio school and I was trained as a wireman for the field phones. I learned how to lay wire and make the proper splices to repair wire. Other than that, I was strictly infantry, but they wanted a few people to know a little about other things. I also remember I was given some training on the air-cooled .30 caliber machine gun. They had two machine guns in our weapons platoon. Something else we did was training with rifle grenades. They taught us to put the butt of the rifle down on the ground and angle it so the grenade went to where you wanted it to go. We had a couple of tough fellows fire them from the shoulder. I felt we had quite a lot of good training at Fort Lewis, but you never had the training you needed because you never knew where you were going.

After the Korean War started, we left the US by troop ship in early August 1950. We landed in Korea at the port of Pusan on the 19th of August. They took us right up to the line on the Pusan perimeter. The situation was really bad when we arrived. If more troops hadn't arrived, they probably would have been driven into the sea. Initially I was a rifleman and carried the M1. In my squad, I was what they called the "number two" man. Actually you were the first man out; it was like being the scout. Then they needed a radio operator and since I had radio training, I ended up carrying the radio. Because the SCR-300 radio was so heavy, I switched to carrying a carbine. The carbine was a nice light weapon; it shot really fast. We would tape two 30-round clips together and you could flip them around real fast. I liked the carbine, but it wasn't a long range weapon. I always thought it was better to wound the enemy than to kill them. It takes two or three men to take care of a wounded man.

I was wounded on the 5th of September and evacuated to Japan. My brother, who was in A Company, was wounded the day after I was. I saw him in Japan; he had a knee wound and was being sent back to the US. I returned to Korea in November.

I landed at Inchon and then took a train back to my outfit. They were up in North Korea at that time. I went back to the same unit I had been in before I was wounded. I went back to being a rifleman and carrying an M1. While we were up in North Korea, we didn't have much extra equipment. We just had our rifles, bayonets and cartridge belts. It got really cold and we were still wearing regular leather boots and wool overcoats. We called the overcoats "horse blankets." You couldn't move very well in them and when it got wet, it was very heavy. It was no wonder we had so many men get frostbite. I felt we weren't supplied very well. I normally wore a cartridge belt with the pockets for the clips. I know some of the guys carried bandoleers too. Sometimes we had to be careful how much we shot to conserve our ammunition. We usually carried two or three grenades clipped on to our pockets, but we had to use them carefully too because you didn't know when you'd get any more.

I really liked the M1. It shot real well and I thought it was really accurate. I don't ever remember having problems with it. Although fighting in the snow, if your rifle was warm from being fired and you had to dive down in the snow, you had to be careful that the melted snow didn't get in the action or it would freeze. We cleaned our rifles whenever we had the chance, but we didn't dare field strip them. We'd just run a rod down the barrel and clean them out the best we could. Even that was hard to do up north when it was so cold, your fingers just couldn't handle it. Most of the time, that rifle would keep on shooting.

You could really shoot an M1 fast if you had to. There was one time where we knew the general area the enemy was in. We happened to have a lot of ammunition on hand. I can remember we fired into the area, trying to keep the enemy from advancing. We'd drive those clips into the rifle and fire as fast as we could. On that occasion, our fire kept the enemy from advancing.

I fought North Koreans when I first started fighting in the south and then North Koreans and Chinese when we were fighting up north. Life didn't seem important to them at all. They would blow bugles, holler and hoot and come at us in waves. The second wave would pick up weapons from the ones who were shot from the first wave. The Chinese used a lot of bolt action rifles, but they had a lot of Thompson submachine guns too.

During the retreat from Kunu-Ri, we came to a Chinese roadblock. We had the regimental tank company with us and we were trying to fight our way through the roadblock. The Chinese were in the hills above us throwing everything down on us. I was on the road, shooting up at any Chinese on the skyline or coming down at us. We were quite low on ammunition by then. I heard a grenade land right next to me; I got up and started to run, but was wounded by the blast. My buddies first dragged me underneath a tank for protection and then they put me on a litter, on the back of a jeep. The Chinese were right on top of us. Lying on the litter I could look right up and see them. It was tough; I didn't have a rifle or anything. A bullet killed the guy in the litter next to me. It was very cold, around 25 below zero. I wasn't able to move after being wounded and I got frostbite on my feet. They finally broke through the roadblock and I was eventually sent to a MASH unit. They put my leg in a cast and I was evacuated to Japan.

From Japan, they flew me back to the US. We flew from Japan to Midway Island, then to Hawaii and from there nonstop to San Antonio, Texas. Back then they would try to send you to a hospital close to your home, so I was sent to a hospital in Waltham, Massachusetts. After about six months in the hospital I was sent down to Fort Benning. I was discharged from there on 22 January 1952; I served three years and 19 days. The Army had extended our enlistments by a year. I was supposed to serve for another six months, but my combat time got me out early.

Personal Experiences

> **Radford Carroll** *served with E Company, 383rd Infantry Regiment with the 99th Division during World War Two. He saw my request for interviews in the 99th Division Association's newsletter ("The Checkerboard") and wrote me the following letter:*

I did use the M1 in World War Two in the 99th Division. It was a very reliable weapon, best in the world at the time. But as I relate in the following story, it could not overcome the handicap of poor ammunition. The story is from the Battle of the Bulge; a German scout had jumped into an outpost foxhole.

I quickly fired a couple of shots at the scout's position, and then emptied the rest of the clip into the edge of the facing woods where I could see some flickering movements. I fired several more clips of rifle ammunition at movements in the woods before I noticed that the German scout had poked his head up and fired again. I was surprised because he was in such an exposed position. I had expected him to stay low. His last shot had gone directly between the two guys in the next foxhole. I rested my rifle on a branch of the hedgerow and took careful aim at the left edge of the dirt heap that marked the scout's foxhole.

Our book told us to always fire around the right-hand side of any object, and I was sure that the German book was just as arbitrary. Sure enough the scout slid his head and shoulder right into my sights after about a minute of waiting. I used the target shooting mode of very carefully squeezing the trigger and, as the rifle discharged I saw the German flop over backward.

I know that, according to the literature, people are supposed to be overcome with remorse when they kill someone. I felt like I had won first prize, I was exuberant. There was the feeling that I had done my duty and any more that I did thereafter would just be dividends.

In any event, remorse would have been premature. Just as the people next to me were extending their congratulations, I saw a white object attached to a stick being waved from the scout's foxhole. My first feeling was one of disgust and betrayal — I thought I had killed him and here he was, obviously wounded and wanting out, but still alive.

After a little thought, I shouted for the scout to come out and surrender, using the few words of German that I knew. My plan was to get whatever food he might have in his pack. The scout did come out of the hole, but suddenly wheeled and ran, with his right arm dangling, for the woods where the Germans were.

Just as the German turned to run, I snapped a quick shot at him but missed what should have been an easy shot. The scout ran into a little dip in the ground where I could not see, but I knew he would have to come into view before getting to the woods. Again I rested my rifle on the hedgerow, set the sights at the point where he would come into view, took up the trigger slack and waited. Sure enough he came right into the sights, running directly away — an easy shot, and as cool as on the target range I squeezed off the trigger. A good marksman, and I was one, knows where his shot will go as the trigger releases (this is known as 'calling the shot'), and I knew that the shot would go just between his shoulder blades.

Then a genuine miracle happened; my rifle did not fire. The semiautomatic rifle uses the power of the shot to eject the spent cartridge case and load a new cartridge. If the spent cartridge case is not ejected, the rifle jams in an obvious manner. In this instance, the spent case was ejected, but the next cartridge was not loaded so I was trying to shoot with an unloaded rifle. This had never happened to me before, and never happened again. I quickly jacked another shell into the chamber and fired a couple of wild shots just as the scout reached the woods, but with his luck I am sure that I did not hit him.

I was bitterly disappointed at the moment, but much later I began to realize that my luck was also operating. The scout was wounded and out of action. His care would cost the Germans more effort than if he were dead, so my country was better served by him being wounded. My killing him under those conditions would approach murder, and a merciful providence had spared me that. I wonder if that scout ever suspected just how lucky he was.

There is an explanation for the miracle. The cartridge, by some manufacturing freak, contained only a portion of its gunpowder, a squib load. When I took the easy snapshot at the German, I missed because the bullet dropped to the ground before it got to him. The gas pressure was so low the bolt was driven back far enough to eject the cartridge case but not far enough to load the next round into the chamber, so I had an unloaded gun with no indication that it was unloaded.

Because I can explain the mechanism of the miracle does not deny that there was one. The probability of a partially loaded cartridge coming through the automated machinery is extremely low. Maybe one in 10,000. The probability of that cartridge being used to spoil two sure death shots at a wounded man is so remote that I couldn't even start to calculate the odds. Isn't that what a miracle is, something that's so unlikely as to defy belief?

After the scout vanished into the woods, I found that a gap in the trees allowed me to see Germans in the woods running across the gap. Whenever one would run across the gap, about a yard wide, I would trigger about 4 or 5 shots as fast as I could into the bushes wherein they had vanished. I must have used about half my available ammunition this way.

I never knew if I hit anyone, and there was no time for aimed shots, the Germans were across the gap faster than my reaction time — they knew the gap was under fire and they crossed it at a dead run. This is the way that most soldiers are hit by rifle fire in combat, not by aimed shots but by filling the area with shots. Not by bullets with someone's name on them, but bullets addressed to 'whom it may concern'.

I think it was at that time that I realized that my rifle had a red-with-rust bayonet on it and the bayonet was sticking through the hedge visible for anyone to see. I took the bayonet off, and vowed never again to put it on the rifle, if I had a choice. Sometime later a German ran across a hill on the other side of the gully. He was in clear view, but I could not estimate his distance easily. I must have fired 16 shots at him, changing the lead and range by guess. He never gave any indication that he was being shot at, just kept trotting at the same speed until he reached cover. It was very frustrating.

There was another German with a really loud mouth concealed in a hedgerow near us. He was shouting in a deep bass voice, apparently to the people in the woods, presumably giving directions and information as to our location. One fellow in the foxhole to my right estimated where the voice was coming from, and I did the same so between us we got a fix on his position. Then we both emptied our rifles into the position. I have no idea whether or not we hit the man, but he kept quiet after that.

There was a disturbing thing happening. About half the people in my platoon were not firing at the enemy. They were hunkered down in their foxholes trying to ignore the entire situation. The ones who were firing were popping up and down like a jack in the box.

I would not allow my own fear to keep me down in the foxhole; I was afraid that the Germans would walk up and shoot me while I couldn't see. I knew that if I didn't shoot at them they would come up. Moreover, from my hunting experience, I knew that a movement like the popping up and down attracted attention, the last thing I wanted from the Germans. So I kept my head up and moved as smoothly as I could when I had to reload my rifle.

I also got a change of weapons, I had been complaining about how awkward it was to carry both a rifle and a bazooka, so I finally got a submachine gun. The .45 caliber M3 machine gun was about as heavy as the rifle, but it was much smaller and could be slung crosswise. The M3 was made of stamped sheet metal with a metal extendable stock, a very cheaply made device. It had its merits but also had some serious defects. The major defects were that the springs were not correctly tempered. Unless the bolt springs were stretched every so often the gun would not function. The magazine was designed to hold 30 bullets, but if 30 bullets were loaded the magazine springs would not have enough force to lift the bullets, so I had to load only 20. Even then I had to empty the magazine every so often and stretch the springs again. Also, the .45 caliber ammunition was heavy and had a slow muzzle velocity. The bullets hit with a big impact, but they had a short range and were not very penetrating.

We had been firing some at the German positions, although there wasn't much hope of hitting anything. Nearly all the automatic weapons were not working because the snow was getting into the chambers and preventing the bolts from fully closing. My little submachine gun had a chamber cover on it so I could open the cover, fire a burst and then close the cover. It was about as effective as throwing rocks at that distance, but it was something to do.

Personal Experiences

*Sergeant Paul Cain at Camp McClellan.*

**Paul Cain** *was drafted into the Army prior to Pearl Harbor in 1940 shortly after the draft law was approved. He served as a company clerk in several units before he was sent to Fort Benning, GA to attend Officers Candidate School. After completing OCS, he was assigned to the 24th Division in Hawaii as a brand new second lieutenant, becoming a platoon leader in K Company, 34th Infantry Regiment. He saw extensive combat across the pacific theater, fighting in New Guinea, Biak and the Philippine Islands. During action on Leyte, he became the commander of "Item" Co. and fought with that company through the Philippine campaign. They were in a rest area receiving new replacements and training for the invasion of Japan when the atomic bomb was dropped. When the war ended, he had participated in five amphibious landings. He was discharged from active duty in 1946, but remained in the reserves. His perspective is from the platoon leader/company commander position.*

## US Infantry Weapons In Combat

I was drafted in 1940, about 12 months before Pearl Harbor. I was sent to Camp Cross, South Carolina and when they found out I could type, they made me a clerk. I spent that winter in South Carolina and then I was sent to another unit at Fort McClellan, Alabama. I was running the company mess when my company commander recommended me for OCS. I think he did that because there was another man he wanted to run his mess hall and he would make room for him by sending me away. I had my first real weapons training while I was in OCS. I remember qualifying with the M1 rifle and firing the carbine and both the heavy and light machine guns. I think I pretty much trained on all the current infantry weapons.

After I completed OCS, I was sent to Hawaii to join the 24th Infantry Division in 1943. We experienced our first combat on New Guinea, although we didn't see much action there, we mostly did patrols. I remember when we first landed in New Guinea, everyone was loaded down with grenades and machetes to chop through the jungle and everything you could imagine. We were even carrying gas masks. We had to march inland two miles through the mud. The guys started unloading stuff because they couldn't keep up. They threw away the gas masks, the machetes and the extra ammunition. We just didn't know how much we really needed. We learned pretty quickly that you don't load the men down with more than they can handle. There's usually supply coming in right behind us and we could almost always get what we needed. In combat, you have to be able to move fast. We learned what equipment we needed and distributed the loads within the platoon. I liked for each squad to have at least one machete. I wanted a couple of incendiary grenades in each squad. We would come across piles of Japanese ammo in the jungle and you could drop an incendiary on the pile and it would take care of it. The squad leaders would make sure we had the stuff we would need.

I carried a carbine; it was a very good weapon. I remember the M1 and the carbine were both good. I've seen them get dunked in the water or dragged through the mud and they'd still work very well. If you got in hard combat and your weapon didn't work, you threw it away and picked up one that worked. I generally only carried one extra clip of ammo. If we thought we were going to get into some heavy combat, I'd carry more. It was the same with the men. I'd let the squad leaders determine how much they needed to carry based on the situation. I carried a .45 along with my carbine towards the end of the war. One of our planes was shot down near one of our positions and the pilot was killed in the crash. I got his .45 and the only thing I can say about that thing is it wore a sore in my side from carrying it. I had qualified with the pistol during training, but to me it wasn't a good weapon. I'd rather have a carbine over it any day.

On the third day after we landed on Leyte in the Philippines, the battalion commander relieved the company commander in I Company and he sent me to take over. We fought through several of the Philippine islands and saw heavy combat on Corregidor. We made an amphibious assault the same time as the 503rd Airborne jumped in. They hit them high and we hit them low. It was the heaviest combat of the war for me. I can remember one day when my company killed 50 Japs in about three hours. It was the only time when we almost ran out of ammunition, it got real scarce. We did run out of grenades. We had been on top of a hill and all night the Japs were crawling up the hill to try to infiltrate our lines. My men kept dropping grenades down the hill. For about ten days, it was heavy fighting night and day.

I thought our weapons were superior to the Japanese weapons. In that type of combat, the engagement ranges varied from zero to 100 yards. Most of the riflemen stuck with the M1 because it had more range than the carbine. It was better in the jungle because the round was more powerful. The BARs were very effective too. It took a rugged individual to carry the BAR through the jungle or anywhere. It was a heavy weapon and the ammunition was heavy. We could have had extra BARs if we had wanted them, but it was hard to find men to carry them. If you had extra BARs, it was great. It gave you the firepower of a light machine gun and it was more maneuverable. The Japs would zero in on them because it was an automatic weapon. Of course, we did the same to their automatic weapons. We used rifle grenades a few times, but very little. It was another one of those extra pieces of equipment that initially they wanted every man to carry. But, we really didn't use them that often. They weren't very effective. If we got in a situation where we thought we needed one, we could send for one. Every company had two jeeps and a trailer. We kept our extra ammo in the trailer and there were rifle grenades if we needed them. It was the same with the bazooka or flamethrower, if we needed one we could go and get it.

I remember when we were moving into Subic Bay in the Philippines. There was a bridge across the Subic River as you entered the town of Subic. My second platoon had moved up on a hill with a cemetery on the top, that overlooked the bridge. The bridge was probably about 150 yards or so below the hill. We didn't know at the time, but the Japs had the bridge set to blow. A Japanese soldier ran onto the bridge to light the fuse on the explosives they had planted. One of my soldiers spotted him, wheeled his rifle up and killed him with one shot from his M1 before he could light the fuse. It was a good shot. My guys had told me the story, but at the time there was a lot going on. I never did find out who made that shot.

One of the biggest things was we had great logistics and fire support. Every time we got in a firefight, I could get artillery or mortar fire right away. Once on Corregidor, we were on a hill and there was another knoll about 50 to 60 yards away covered with brush. Some Japs got up there and started sniping at us and they killed one of my men. I looked at that hill and thought we could throw mortars at them, but that wouldn't get it. I thought if we could get some napalm on that hill, it would burn the brush off. So I called the Naval Liaison Officer at Battalion Headquarters and asked for him to get a napalm strike for us. He called me right back and told me the planes would be over in a few minutes. I directed the pass, they came with three planes, each with a napalm can under each wing. That took care of the Japs on that hill. It burned the brush and the Japs took off in every direction. Our men had a field day, at that range they cut them down. The Japanese never had any support like that.

Personal Experiences

> **Richard Finkbone** *enlisted in the Army two weeks after he graduated from high school in June 1942. He received radar training and then became an instructor in the radar school at Drew Field in Florida. He entered the Army Specialized Training Program (ASTP) and attended engineering school in Mississippi. When the program was closed, he was assigned to the 94th Infantry Division at Camp McCain, MS. The division arrived in France in September 1944 and fought across France and Germany. Mr. Finkbone was wounded three times during combat; his third wound caused him to be evacuated to the US for treatment. He was discharged from the Army in December 1945.*

A few weeks after high school was out, I enlisted. I had tried to join the Marines, but they said I was colorblind so I ended up in the Army. I took two weeks of basic training at Camp Crowder, Missouri; it was Signal Corps training. We didn't do any weapons training. After that I was sent to Camp Murphy, Florida for radar school. That was when radar was highly secret, we were hidden back in the swamps. Then I was stationed at Drew Field teaching radar operation and maintenance. I applied for and was accepted into the ASTP and got about six months of the program under my belt at the University of Mississippi. Then the program closed and they put me in the 94th Division.

The 94th Division had already formed when I arrived at Camp McCain. I was assigned to E Company, 302nd Infantry Regiment. They had already received all their infantry training. I joined the outfit and started on the job training. I got the full treatment of infantry training. I trained mostly with the M1, which I thought it was one of the best weapons to come out of World War Two. I also received some good cross training with some of the other weapons. We got a little training on the BAR, the Thompson, the light machine gun and the bazooka. The BAR was highly respected by the Germans, but I never carried one in combat. The ammo for it was very heavy. One of the great things about the BAR was it was really accurate. For a period of time I became the company communications sergeant because of my signal corps training.

The division landed on Utah beach in September 1944 and we moved right up on the line. When we landed in France I was still the commo sergeant, but as we pushed through to the Ziegfied Line we got very short of men. After all the losses the division had suffered, they needed all the hands they could get. So I became an assistant squad leader in one of the infantry squads.

In Germany, on the edge of the Zeigfied line, there were some partially blown pillboxes that our company was ordered to take. Even though I was a straight

## US Infantry Weapons In Combat

infantryman at that time, I was carrying an SCR-300 radio along with my M1. We had moved out about 1,000 yards in front of our lines to get to our objective. Our squad took our objective with no problems; we didn't even have to fire a shot. But the Germans almost immediately repelled the other companies and we were stuck out there all by ourselves for the night. After dark, the Germans sent patrols out to counterattack us. They were carrying land mines on their belts and every time they'd move we'd hear this clink of metal. When we heard the clink, we'd throw a hand grenade at the sound. I used the radio to call artillery all night long. There was at least one shell coming in every five minutes. When we got low on hand grenades, we'd throw rocks. They would hear the rock hit the ground, think it was

Hand Grenades, left to right: Mk I offensive, Mk II fragmentation, Mk 1A1 dummy training. Hayes Otoupalik collection. Photo courtesy of Bruce N. Canfield.

a hand grenade, move and make more noise. Then once we were sure where they were, we'd throw a hand grenade at where we heard the noise. Fortunately we didn't run out of rifle ammunition, we had been carrying enough. We didn't have to fire our rifles too often; we mostly used the grenades. Finally, our artillery laid down a really heavy barrage just before dawn and we pulled out. When we got back to our lines, we checked the position out with binoculars and there were dead Germans stacked up all over the place. There was at least a company of them that our grenades and the artillery had cut to ribbons.

One of the fellows told us about this one great big German he shot during the night. He said the guy was a monster! This big German came in towards our pillbox and this fellow emptied the whole clip from his M1 into him. Even after that, he still kept on coming until he finally dropped dead just in front of him.

The M1 saved my life in a very unusual way other than the fact that it was a great weapon and one of an infantryman's best friends. Our company jumped off just prior to dawn to take the town of Sinz, Germany. The ground was covered with two feet of snow and it was tough going. We took a wooded area not far from the town with some difficulty. After entering the woods and securing our positions we started to receive German artillery fire. The artillery was creating tree bursts due to the dense stand of trees. I was leading my squad in the woods carrying my M1 in front of my body at a 45-degree angle when a tree burst exploded just over my head. The shell rained shrapnel all around us. A large piece of the shrapnel (about the size of a baseball) struck the stock of my M1 and broke it into two pieces. The shrapnel would have hit me somewhere between the chest and the stomach if it were not for the thick and sturdy stock on my M1. I picked up another M1 from one of my buddies who wasn't as fortunate as me. We then continued our attack towards Sinz, which we took the next day.

During that attack, we had to cross 1,500 yards of open terrain and we used marching fire to do it. As soon as we stepped out of the woods we started firing. We moved forward firing from the hip and it kept the German's heads down until we got on top of them. It worked very well. You would fire a lot of ammunition doing it, but you carried a couple of bandoleers of clips. They sent a resupply of ammo once we got into town.

In early March, I was on an outpost that was overrun by a German patrol. I was wounded in the arm by a machine gun bullet and taken prisoner. I was only a prisoner for about 12 hours, the German patrol was wiped out before they could get back to their lines and I was freed. Because of my wound, I was evacuated to an Army hospital in Paris and then sent back to the US for treatment. I was in a hospital in New York City when the war ended. I was discharged from the Army in early December 1945. I'd seen quite a bit of combat; I'd spent 180 days on the line. I had been wounded three times, twice by shrapnel and once by the bullet in my arm.

## US Infantry Weapons In Combat

> **Win Scott** *joined the Marines in 1948 and took his basic training at Parris Island, SC. After basic, he served with several different infantry units on Guam. Following that assignment, he was transferred to a naval base in Japan until the Korean War started. He was sent to Korea as an infantry replacement just after the landing at Inchon. He became a member of the C Company, 1st Battalion, 5th Marines. During fighting in North Korea, he was wounded up near the Chosin Reservoir and evacuated to Japan. After recovering from his wounds, he was returned to the US. He served four years in the Marine Corps and was discharged.*

During boot camp, our basic weapon was the M1 rifle. We also trained with the pistol, the carbine, machine guns and a little on the mortar. We trained on the different weapons because they didn't know where we would be assigned or what job we would be assigned to. I remember my first impression of the M1: "I thought it was heavy." When I first qualified with it, I only weighed 138 pounds and it would knock me back pretty good. That was my first impression of it, but it wasn't my last. I shot pretty well with it. The first time I only qualified as marksman, but we had to qualify every year and as I got older I did better with it. I was able to qualify as sharpshooter and then expert. We also qualified with the .45 caliber pistol.

When I first got to Korea, I was an ammo carrier in a machine gun crew. It was the standard air-cooled M1919A4 machine gun. I carried two 250-round cans of ammo for the machine gun. If we anticipated that there would be heavy fighting, we sometimes carried four ammo cans. We had a harness that we could hang two cans from and then we'd carry the other two. All that, plus I carried an M2 carbine and sometimes a pistol. I carried two 30-round magazines for the carbine and a few smaller 15-round magazines. With all of that, I was pretty laden down. We had four ammo carriers for the gun, each with at least 500 rounds. That was a lot of ammo. The gunner would carry the tripod and the assistant gunner would carry the gun. That was the standard procedure. When we went into action, the gunner would throw the tripod down and the assistant gunner would come up and put the gun in the pindle and the first ammo carrier would drop down and put a belt in and the gun would be ready.

We did have .30 caliber heavies with us, but they were a brute to carry. They were easier to use once you got them set up, but they were tough to drag around. The tripod alone weighed 56 pounds. If you had a defensive position, that's what you wanted. They had a little longer range and you could fire them longer without burning the barrel out. If you couldn't get a .50 caliber machine gun, that's what you'd wish for. They had seven pints of water in the water jacket. Up north, you needed anti-freeze in them. However, if you wanted coffee water, you just fired a few rounds through them and you'd have hot water. We didn't have as many of those guns in the rifle companies; the weapons company had most of them.

We landed at Hungnam up in North Korea in October and started moving up to the Chosin Reservoir. As we got further north, we started finding a lot of Chinese. When we got into the Chinese, it was a different ballgame; they were a pretty tough enemy. The Chinese would get close in at night, they'd get within 30 to 40 yards of us and lay in the snow and wait for a signal. They would use a cymbal, a whistle or a bugle for the signal and they would make a frontal assault. They generally knew where our lines extended to and they would come in close with their weapons. They were shooting at us with American, German and Russian weapons. They had everything. They had those burp guns that would carry 71 rounds in them. It was a super good weapon for what they wanted. At close range, those things were tough; they threw a lot of lead. Although I'd seen guys get hit seven or eight times from one of them and it didn't stop them. The Chinese also threw fragmentation and concussion grenades and German potato mashers. Some of their men weren't even armed; they would follow the others and picked up weapons from the dead.

The Chinese also had a lot of Thompson submachine guns that they used against us. There would be weapons all over and you could pick one up if you wanted one. The Thompsons were heavy and cumbersome, but they would throw out a lot of firepower. They were excellent at close range; those big slugs would knock a guy over. The problem was getting the ammo and it wasn't worth the trouble. The Thompson didn't fire as well in the real, real cold. The M1 was the best one and we didn't have much trouble with the machine gun. The carbine wasn't good in cold weather; we didn't like it. I wouldn't give you ten cents for the carbine. I did not have any confidence in that weapon. First of all, if you could get it to fire you couldn't stop anybody with it. We had a lot of close combat and a carbine hit didn't seem to faze them much unless you hit them in a vital spot. The M1 would knock them flat.

We were called out one night at about 10 o'clock. It was one of the coldest nights on record. I don't know how cold it was, but it was miserably cold, some 20 degrees below zero. They told us the 7th Marines were in trouble up on one of the ridges. It was difficult getting up to them; we had never seen the terrain and it was dark. By the time we got up there, it was a melee; there was no control of anything. So we grabbed a hole and set up our gun. After that, I lost track of time; we did a lot of fighting. Normally it would stop at daylight, but the Chinese attacked us six different times during the night and then attacked us all day long.

If you could see them and you hit them far enough out with the machine gun, stuff would fly like when you hit a bird with a shotgun. It was because they had quilted, cotton-padded uniforms.

I can remember throwing hand grenades that were World War One issue; they were painted yellow and dated 1917. We kept fighting them, but they went around us and behind us. We had tremendous casualties, but we held the position. I can remember the end of the machine gun barrel was greenish yellow. The explosion from the Chinese grenades had stained it. To this day, I can distinctly remember that barrel and the smell of the cordite. But I can't recall the sound of any of those grenades exploding. I would have liked to have taken the jacket of that barrel and kept it as a souvenir.

During the battle, a wireman came up the hill with a roll of wire on his back and an M1 cradled in his arms. He saw our machine gun position and asked if anyone had a pistol. Obviously we weren't going to give him a pistol, but I told him I had a carbine that wouldn't work. He threw me the M1 and he took my carbine. Not long after that the machine gun barrel burned out. If you fired one of them too much and too hard you'd burn the barrel out, but we didn't have a choice that day. We held that hole by fighting with that M1. We took belted machine gun ammunition and put it in clips and continued to fight. It was tough pulling those rounds out of the belt and reloading them into the clips in the cold, but we didn't have much choice. The clips were hard to find, we didn't find many near our position. The Chinese got so close that some of the guys used pistols. The trouble with the pistol was it was hard to use because of the cold. As big as a .45 is, when you had mittens on, it was hard to shoot it. If you took your hand out of a glove to use the pistol, it would freeze.

Late that afternoon, they told us to pull off that hill and bring the dead with us. There wasn't anyone for me to carry and I didn't want to leave the machine gun there. I thought I could take the gun down and get a new barrel for it. I sure didn't want to leave it for the Chinese. I slung the M1 over my shoulder crisscross so I could carry the machine gun over my right shoulder. As I was going down the hill, we started taking some incoming from a 120 mm mortar. I got hit from the blast of one of the mortar rounds. Another Marine found me and got me a corpsman and they took me down the hill. I had been hit in the back by a mortar fragment. It took a while, but they got me down to the airstrip at Hagaru-Ri and flew me out. I figured out that the mortar fragment that hit me went through the stock of the M1 that I had slung over my back. The wound is right where the stock was on my back. If I had been carrying that carbine, it would have gone clean through me. I think that M1 saved my life twice that day. Besides saving my life with its firepower on the hill, it slowed that mortar fragment down.

I was too badly wounded to return to Korea. I had the fragment in my back and my hand had been wounded too. After recovering in a hospital in Japan, I went back to the US in April. It had been almost three years since I had been back in the States. They tried to station you as close as possible to where you lived. I had joined the Corps from Connecticut, so they stationed me at the New London submarine base. I was a good assignment; I stayed there until I left the Corps.

Personal Experiences

> **David Clymer** *was drafted in late 1943, leaving home in December for Camp Shelby, MS. He spent 26 weeks training there with the 65th Division and was then reassigned to the 26th "Yankee" Division. The division shipped out for Europe in late summer, arriving on Utah Beach in September 1944. He fought in four major campaigns, including the Battle of the Bulge and spent 166 days on the front lines. When the war ended in Europe, he was in Czechoslovakia with his unit. He returned to the US in early 1946.*

When I was at Camp Shelby I trained on the BAR, the 60 mm mortar, the .30 and .50 caliber machine guns. I also attended demolition and minelayers school. I was in a rifle company and I carried an M1. The M1 was a hard hitting weapon. We'd set up targets out to 800 yards on the range. When you missed they'd wave a pair of red "maggies" at you. I never qualified with the M1, although I fired it lots of times.

After I joined the 26th Division, I was issued a carbine. That was the first time I had ever seen one. I qualified with it and shot "sharpshooter." I carried that same carbine through the whole war. I qualified expert with the 60 mm mortar and I made 100 percent on the mortar test. Being an old country boy, I was good at guessing distances and adjusting the rounds on target. They wanted squad leaders for the infantry platoons and they offered me buck sergeant stripes, but I refused them. I knew what I'd wind up doing, leading a squad and I didn't want that. So they put me in the anti-tank company of the 1st Battalion, 101st Infantry Regiment.

The 57 mm anti-tank gun had a crew of eleven men. There was a squad leader, the gunner, an assistant gunner and the rest of the men were ammo bearers. We fired the gun quite a bit, but we didn't knock out any tanks. We had to set the guns up to give us shots to the side or rear of those Tiger tanks. The 57 mm round would bounce off the front armor of one. Sometimes we used the guns on buildings. A lot of the time we'd be set up to guard the Regimental Headquarters, but the Germans tanks never got that far behind our lines.

One time, our captain pointed out a hill nearly a mile away and handed me eight 15- round clips for my carbine. He told me to get on the hill and fire over the town while the rest of the company slipped around and came from the opposite side. I fired those rounds just as fast as I could, the gun barrel got so hot that you could barely put your hand on it.

The carbine was reliable at close ranges, but I'd say it was only good out to three hundred yards. I'd shot at Germans with it that far away and I'd see them duck, but I couldn't be sure if I hit them. Over there in the wintertime we had freezing rain, snow, sleet and it would be very muddy. You did have to clean it every chance you got. In that weather, you had to take good care of your weapon.

Another time we were on one side of the river and the Germans were on the other side, about 1,200 yards away in pillboxes. Once in a while I'd borrow an M1 and go up to the attic of one of the houses and fire at the Germans. You could see where the bullet hit, the dust would fly up and the German would hit the ground. It was too far away to hit anyone.

I also worked with a buddy as a bazooka team. I hadn't trained with the bazooka before that. I was his loader, but we switched off. We didn't get any tanks with the bazooka either. Most of the time the tanks didn't come in close enough, they'd back off. One time one got real close, but he backed off before we could do any shooting at him.

When the war ended, I was in Czechoslovakia. The division was sent home, but I was five points shy of having enough points to go home with them. I was transferred to another unit and all I did was pull guard duty on the motor pool. I returned to the US with the 94th Division in January 1946.

Personal Experiences

Donald Van Roosen, with Thompson submachine gun.

**Donald Van Roosen** *volunteered for the US Army in April 1943. He took basic training at the infantry replacement training center at Camp Wheeler, GA. Following his training, he was sent to England as an infantry replacement and assigned to H Company, 115th Infantry Regiment, 29th Division. He landed with the regiment on Omaha Beach on D-Day. He was wounded four times as he fought through France and Germany with the division. He received a battlefield commission and commanded a weapons platoon in G Company until the end of the war. He returned to the US in September of 1945 and was discharged. He later served with the Army Reserve for 23 years.*

At Camp Wheeler we trained with the .45, the carbine, the M1 and the heavy .30 caliber machine gun. I actually qualified with all of those weapons; if you didn't qualify they would recycle you until you did. The attitude of the camp commander was to turn out well-trained people. They had the time to do it and that's what they did. I qualified as either sharpshooter or expert with all of those weapons. We also trained with the 2.36-inch bazooka while I was there.

I went over to England in December 1943. At first I was sent to a replacement depot near Cardiff and from there we were shipped out to all the assault divisions to bring them up to 110 percent strength. When I first joined the 29th, I was assigned to an 81 mm mortar squad for a little while, but I was transferred to the heavy machine gun section. We trained all the way up until a few weeks before D-Day. Although I was only an ammo bearer, I trained extensively with the gun. We had the first exams for the Expert Infantry Badge in early May. Each member of the squad was tested on range estimation, setting up the gun and practical knowledge on the use of the gun.

On D-Day, I landed with the 115th in mid-morning. Originally we were supposed to land to the west where the 116th Regiment landed. But things were piled up on that part of the beach, the barricades hadn't been blown yet and no one could move off the beach. The Navy took us down and landed us on Easy Red Beach beside the 18th Regiment of the 1st Division. We got off the boat in chest high water and waded in. The boat that brought us in was sunk right after we got off. I was the number five man in a heavy machine gun squad. I carried ashore two 100-round cans of .30 caliber machine gun ammunition, a bazooka with five rounds of ammunition and a carbine. It was something over 100 pounds of equipment. The ammo cans had straps that I had crisscrossed over my shoulders and on top of that on one side, I had the carbine and the other the bazooka. If the water had been deeper when we got off the boat, I would have drowned. We got onto the beach and moved right up the cliffs and started inland towards our objective.

We used our machine guns quite a bit. We got our heavies up very close to the action, as close as the light .30s. We tried to get as much firepower forward as we could because we were significantly behind the Germans in firepower. They had five automatic weapons for every one that we had. They could throw a lot of lead at us. I was impressed with what the Germans could do with their air-cooled MG34s and MG42s. Our guns were pitiful compared to those. The heavy .30 was very cumbersome. You had to keep them filled with water and the damned things were heavy. We never had the occasion to use it for sustained fire, which was its greatest asset.

I had an incident on D+3. I was sitting with the gun in a roadway between two hedgerows. It was the only field of fire we could get. At 2:00 in the morning, some Germans who were fleeing the beachhead attacked us from the rear. I started firing down the road and after 10 or 15 rounds, the gun jammed. I wasn't the gunner, so I didn't have the proper tools to fix the jam. It could be a difficult weapon to operate and maintain. You had to know what you were doing to get the right headspace and get the gun to the point where it would set up and fire well. I had to abandon the gun and two Germans ran down, took the machine gun and ran off with it.

Although I was in a weapons company, we participated in patrol activities and a lot of other things. I used the carbine quite a bit in combat. I didn't like it, I thought it was too light a weapon. I had hit people with the carbine and they kept coming. The early carbines only had a leaf sight and they were very inaccurate. There were a lot of production problems too; I had one with a front sight that rotated right off. I couldn't figure why I couldn't hit anything and I noticed that the sight had rotated ten degrees off the vertical.

I traded weapons with a guy from the 2nd Armor Division. They liked the .45 automatic because they could always get out of the tank with it if they got hit. They might not have the time to pull out their submachine gun. Our gunner and assistant gunner were issued pistols, so we could always get them. So I traded a pistol to a tanker for a Thompson submachine gun and carried one for most of the time I was in combat. I carried a Thompson while I was an NCO and after I received my commission. I tended to have my people up forward to support the rifleman and the Thompson was good for the sort of close in work I used it for. I wouldn't want to fire it at ranges any farther than 35 to 40 yards; it was very powerful within those ranges. If you hit them anywhere, it would spin them around and drop them. I kept it clean as a matter of practice and I never had any problems with it.

Because I used my Thompson a lot, I carried a lot of ammunition for it. I found that the Germans had a very good pouch for their MP40s that would carry five clips, so I got one of those. Because I had run out of ammo on several occasions, I would also carry several boxes of .45 ammo. The ammo was very, very heavy. I had to carry a lot because sometimes it was hard to find. Everybody had carbine or rifle ammunition, but they didn't always have .45 ammo. During my time in combat, I carried three different Thompsons. I went to the hospital after being wounded and lost the first one. I lost the second one when I was captured and I ended up with a third one. They weren't hard to come by if you wanted one.

I got captured from being too far forward while we were fighting in Brittany. We were up in support of a rifle platoon and we got surrounded. No reinforcements came during the day and that night they closed in on us and captured us. We were fighting German paratroopers from the 2nd Parachute Division and they were good soldiers. We were taken into one of the sub pens. While we were being held in the pens, we were bombed by our own bombers, which was a terrible experience. The Germans were cut off and surrounded and they eventually surrendered. I was only a POW for a week.

After I became a lieutenant, I was a platoon leader for a weapons platoon in "George" Company. We had two light air-cooled .30 caliber machine guns and two 60 mm mortars. I thought the air-cooled .30 was a better weapon than the heavy water-cooled .30. It was lighter and it was more reliable as far as I was concerned. The heavies were older guns, I think they were from World War One. They just weren't as reliable.

When the war ended, we were up on the Elbe River due west of Berlin. I had a lot of points, but I was delayed going home because I was in the hospital after being wounded. I rejoined the division while it was in Bremen. There was some talk about being sent to the Pacific, but that didn't work out. I finally got home in September, which was a few months later than I should have with all the points I had.

Personal Experiences

> **John "Red" Lawrence** *enlisted in the Marine Corps in February 1942 and went to boot camp at Parris Island, SC. Following boot camp, he was assigned to several units in the States for training before being sent overseas. He joined the 22nd Marines on the island of Samoa in November 1942 and saw his first combat in the Marshall Islands in February 1943. Later, he fought in the campaigns to take Guam and Okinawa. He was wounded for the fourth time on Okinawa in May 1945, which ended the war for him. He was evacuated back to the US for medical treatment. Because of his wound, he was unable to remain in the Corps and was discharged in late 1945.*

I joined the Marine Corps in February 1942 and went to boot camp at Parris Island, South Carolina. The only weapons we trained with in boot camp were the 03 and the bayonet. We went up to the range at Quantico for a week to do marksmanship training. I remember I didn't qualify with the 03 when we fired for record. Very few of us did. On the day we fired for record, it was raining so hard you could hardly see the targets. Of course the war was on and we had to keep on going. I didn't qualify with a rifle until after I left Parris Island.

I went overseas in November 1942 and was assigned to the 22nd Marines on Samoa. I started out in B Company, 1st Battalion, but during training, I got jungle rot pretty bad and had to go into the hospital. I was in the hospital for about a week and I was reassigned to Fox Company when I was released. I stayed with that company through the war.

I think we got M1 rifles when we were on Samoa. They were used rifles; we never got anything brand new. We got everything the Army didn't want. After we got the M1s, we did a lot of firing with them during training. I liked the 03 a lot better than I did the M1, I think 90 percent of the guys did at first. It was a little lighter than the M1 and I liked the way it handled. I liked the bolt action too. I'd say the accuracy of the two was about the same; there wasn't that much difference. When I first qualified, I was only a marksman, but I got a lot better. The next time I qualified, I qualified as a sharpshooter and the next time, I was about two points under expert. After training on Samoa, we went to Hawaii for further training.

Our first combat operation was in the Marshall Islands, on Engebi. It was one of the islands in the Eniwetok chain. The 22nd Regiment as a whole landed on about nine to ten different islands of that chain during the campaign. It was a cleanup operation, but there were Japs on all those islands. They were small islands; we took a few of them in just three days. I was wounded on Parry Island by shrapnel.

It wasn't bad, just enough to earn a Purple Heart. I spent a day or so in the hospital tent and went back to the unit. When you got wounded, they took everything from you before they sent you to the hospital. When you got back to the unit, you went to supply and they issued you a rifle, a bayonet, a Ka-Bar and a cartridge belt. The rifles were all battlefield pickups, they weren't new rifles.

We were in the Marshalls for about two months. From there, we went to Guadalcanal for advanced training. While we were there, we formed the First Provisional Marine Brigade. We were attached to the 3rd Marine Division for the invasion of Guam in July 1944.

We saw quite a bit of combat on Guam. I was wounded a couple of weeks after we landed. We were right outside the old Marine barracks and that was the first time I'd fought with a fixed bayonet. The Japs overran us during a big *banzai* attack and they called for fixed bayonets. That was the first time I had to use a bayonet.

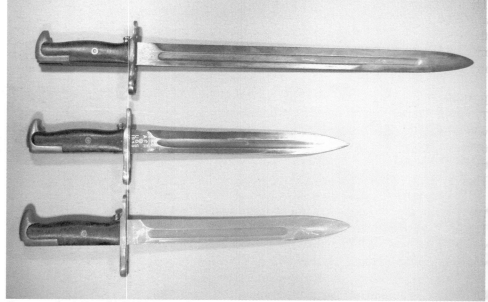

Bayonets for M1 and M1903. Top to bottom: M1905 bayonet with 16-inch blade, 16-inch shortened to 10-inch, M1 bayonet manufactured with 10-inch blade.
Photo courtesy of Scott A. Duff.

It was one of those situations where we had to fight with them. We had trained with the bayonet and we were confident using them. It was times like that when I felt our training really paid off.

On Guam, I was wounded by a piece of shrapnel in my foot. I was put on a stretcher to carry me back and the Japs shot all my stretcher-bearers. I rolled off the stretcher into a slit trench. I was lying there looking for my rifle. To this day, I can't understand what ever happened to my rifle. I looked up and here comes this Jap coming down at me. He tried to bayonet me. I reached up and grabbed a hold of the bayonet. He sliced me across the forehead and cut the insides of both my hands. Just about then, somebody shot the Jap. To this day, I'm still trying to find out who it was. I know it was a corpsman because it was a shot from a .45. That's what saved me. After all that, they put me in a jeep and got me down to the hospital near the beach. They kept me in the hospital on Guam for a month or so. I got back to my unit while they were still on Guam.

We had problems with the M1s jamming. Sometimes after the last shot, the clip wouldn't fly out. There were a lot of guys that had trouble like that. I think it was because of the climate. We cleaned our rifles as much as possible, but we couldn't take the time out to fieldstrip them while we were on the line. The only time you had to do that is when you got a break or some relief, but that seldom happened. The M1 was a good combat weapon, but it was important to keep the weapons clean and oiled in the jungle. I usually carried anywhere from two to three bandoleers all the time and ammunition in my cartridge belt. I carried my bayonet and Ka-Bar on my belt. We had the 16-inch long bayonets; I didn't see a shortened bayonet during my service. We used that long bayonet the whole way through the war.

In the squad, besides the M1, some guys had Thompsons and some had BARs. There was one BAR in each fire team. The officers mostly carried carbines, along with their .45s. The enlisted men didn't carry carbines, unless something happened to your rifle and you picked one up. Most of the guys didn't like carbines. You had to be right on top of a guy to make sure you killed him, they weren't very deadly. They wouldn't shoot straight. I wouldn't give you a dime for a dozen of them.

We had the firepower, but we didn't always have the ammunition to go with it. That was the trouble, a lot of times they couldn't get the ammunition up to us. If you take two bandoleers and a belt of ammo and fire steady, it's not going to last very long. Sometimes we would run out of ammo.

During training, they taught us to shoot in the prone position, the sitting position and the kneeling position. When you got in combat, you shot when you figured you were in the best position. I shot lying on my belly, I shot while on my side, I shot standing up and I shot running. You couldn't say "I'm going to kneel down so I can shoot better." By the time you thought of what you were going to do, it was too late. It was instinctive firing. The only time you really took your time in aiming was if there was somebody tied up in a tree or something. Then you wanted to make sure. I know I've shot them down out of the coconut trees where they were tied up there with a rope and their weight would break the rope when they fell. They had quite a few guys in the trees, that's how a lot of our guys got shot. They would wait for us to pass and shoot us in the back.

I thought the Japs were well trained. I'll tell you, if they had had our weapons it would have been tough. It was tough anyway! They must have been able to shoot OK because they got me three times. A lot of times they were sakied up. On Guam, we knew we were going to get it. We could hear them that night howling and carrying on. They kept hollering "Marine you die"! They always waited until early in the morning to hit us. The fighting on every island was different. Guam was like Guadalcanal; it was mountainous and heavily jungled. Okinawa was more open, but they had more caves.

After the Guam operation, we became part of the 6th Marine Division for the invasion of Okinawa. We landed on Okinawa on D-Day; it was Easter Sunday morning, April 1st 1945. We landed and didn't hear a shot being fired. It wasn't until the second day that we started getting some sniper fire. Some of the natives told us all the Japs were on the southern end of the Island. Most of fighting I was in was at Junction 15, Shuri Castle and Sugar Loaf Hill. That was one of the worst battles of the operation. I was hit on May the 14th on Sugar Loaf Hill. We tried to take that Hill three times and that last time none of us made it. I got a bullet straight through my knee and that wrapped me up. They took me back and laid me on the beach for a while. They were getting ready to load the boat to take us out to the hospital ship and the Japs blew the hospital ship up. The next morning they put us on a plane and as the plane was taking off, I could see tracers passing right outside the wing.

From Okinawa, I was sent back to the hospital on Guam. When we got there I didn't know where I was at; I didn't recognize the place. They had a pretty nice hospital there by then. They told me I was on Guam at Naval Hospital 101 right outside the old Marine barracks. It was where I'd been wounded the second time

I stayed in the hospital on Guam for about three weeks and then they sent me stateside. I ended up in the hospital in Philadelphia. I had signed up as a career Marine, but my wounds were so bad that I couldn't stay in. I was discharged in October 1945.

Personal Experiences

> **Robert Cashion** *was drafted into the US Army in February 1952. He took basic training at Fort Dix, NJ followed by an eight-week leadership course. Upon completion of his training, he was sent to Korea as an infantry replacement. He was assigned to the 31st Infantry Regiment of the 7th Division and took part in heavy fighting in the Pork Chop Hill area. He served in Korea for a year and was discharged after returning to the US in late 1953.*

During basic training at Fort Dix, I trained with everything from the 4.2-inch mortar down. I trained and qualified with the 4.2, the 81 mm and 60 mm mortars, the 57 mm and 75 mm recoilless rifles, the grease gun, the M1, the BAR and the pistol. I didn't train with the carbine while I was there. When I left basic training, I had a Heavy Weapons MOS. I took 15 days of leave and then went to Fort Lawton, Washington and boarded a troop ship. We landed in Japan and I spent about 24 hours in Yokohama before I was shipped over to Pusan.

After arriving in Pusan, we rode a train up north to the front. Before we got on the train, I was issued an M1 and ammo, I guess because there was a guerrilla problem behind the front lines. When I got up to the MLR, I was assigned to G Company, 31st Infantry and went to the 4th platoon. The 4th platoon was a weapons platoon and I was assigned to the 57 mm recoilless rifle. Normally, we only used those while we were on the MLR. If we were on the attack, we'd leave it behind. We weren't allowed to shoot it unless we had orders to fire. I did that once and I almost got court-martialed.

I would go down to the artillery forward observer bunker and watch the enemy positions. I saw a few guys come up and silhouette themselves on the hill. They fired a few shots and were gone. I got my 57 out and zeroed it in on that position; it was about 500 to 600 yards away. I left it set up all night, covered with a poncho. The next morning, I borrowed a set of binoculars from the FO and sat there and waited for those guys to come up again. I saw them and got off a round before they could fire a shot. I don't know if I hit them or not, but they didn't fire that day. The 57 was very accurate if you bore-sighted it right. That was the only time I fired the 57 over there. The company commander came by and asked who had fired the shot. I told him I had and he threatened to court-martial me. They didn't want anybody shooting without orders, but nobody had told me. The next day, the enemy was back at that position and firing again.

I continued to carry the M1, although the one I got in Pusan got tore up. My first night on the line, I was put out on the backside of a listening post. There was a big attack on our positions and our artillery was shelling the area. The next morning, we were moving through the communications trench. There were a lot of bodies and equipment in the trench and somehow a concussion grenade went off. The blast picked me up and threw me down and broke the stock on my rifle. They told me to leave it in the trench and I got another rifle when I got back to the company.

Our section of the line was up around Old Baldy, Pork Chop Hill and the Arsenal. We saw a lot of combat; they attacked us and we attacked them. The M1 was a good rifle, but it didn't shoot fast enough. It wasn't like the grease gun or the souped up carbine we had. The grease gun fired slowly, but the carbine put enough out where they weren't going to stick their heads up. The carbine was a popular weapon; most of the NCOs carried them. The North Koreans had those burp guns and they were superior to the M1 as far as firepower goes. One thing I noticed with that burp gun, it didn't climb up and to the right when it was fired like a BAR or a grease gun. You could take a burp gun, set a gallon can out there and hold it like a pistol and put every round in that can. It didn't climb. When they fired it, they would hold it by the sling and spray with it.

I normally carried a cartridge belt of ammo and wore a flak jacket. Most of the fighting was at night. If something moved, you shot at it or if you thought something moved, you shot at it. Sometimes we used flares at night and then we'd be able to see them. The engagement ranges were pretty short.

I spent about seven months in G Company and then I was transferred to the intelligence and reconnaissance (I&R) platoon. In the I&R platoon we mostly took people out to the listening posts forward of our lines. We'd take them out to make sure they went to the right place. I didn't see any combat while I was with the I&R platoon; we just did the patrols putting the LPs out. After a few months with them, I asked for a transfer to work in the motor pool. I didn't like making those patrols into no-man's land. The lieutenant who ran the motor pool knew me and he arranged for me to work there my last few months in Korea.

Once I'd done my year, I was returned to the US and was discharged from Fort Knox, Kentucky, in October 1953. I had been in the Army for less than two years They told me I was being discharged for the "convenience of the government."

Personal Experiences

> **Earle Slyder** *volunteered for the draft in January 1943 and was inducted on the 9th of April 1943. He took his initial basic training at an Air Corps facility in Kearns, UT. He qualified for the Army Specialized Training Program and studied civil engineering in Arkansas. When the program closed, he was assigned to F Company, 395th Infantry Regiment, 99th Infantry Division. He had his baptism of fire during the Battle of the Bulge and then fought into Germany with the division. He was wounded on the 9th of April 1945, two years from the day he was inducted. After recovering from his wound, he rejoined his outfit and served until the end of the war.*

I took my basic with an Air Corps basic training unit. I really hated it. I was an 18-year-old patriot ready to do or die for Uncle Sam and they sent me to the Air Corps. Those of us training at Kearns weren't going to be fighter pilots, we were going to be MPs or truck drivers, some sort of backup job. I was scheduled to become a x-ray technician! We did very little weapons training there. I qualified with an Enfield rifle, which was the damnedest rifle I'd ever got my hands on. There was something a little different about the stock, when you fired that thing it would spin you around on your belt buckle. Once I finished my training there, I qualified for the Army Specialized Training Program and was sent to the University of Arkansas to attend school. Nine months later when they closed down ASTP, I was sent to the 99th Infantry Division at Camp Maxey, Texas.

When my group arrived they distributed us all out to the different rifle units, and then they suddenly realized that we all had a different quality of basic training. They left us in our units, but they pulled us out daily to train with what they called the 99th Provisional Training Regiment. They gave us a real fast, I think it was six to eight weeks, of infantry basic training. For some guys it was a rerun and for some of us it was new. I had my first experience with the M1 during that training; I'd never seen one before that. We trained with the whole scope of weapons. We trained with carbines, pistols and shotguns. They trained us how to lead with the shotguns. They had model airplanes on wires and they'd race them by us and we'd shoot at them. I suppose it was some kind of anti aircraft training. Then we threw grenades, observed mortars and got a little bit of a hands-on with machine guns. Some of the guys got very intimate with the BAR, although I never did. I shot the BAR once or twice for familiarization. We did a whole lot of bayonet training too.

The company was looking for people to carry the BAR and they were giving me some pretty hard looks. At the same time, they were asking for volunteers for sniper training. I looked at that 25-pound BAR and looked at the eight-pound sniper rifle and I volunteered for sniper training.

In the sniper course, they taught us the basics on what to do and what not to do. The first thing they did was teach us how to creep, crawl and sneak around without getting spotted. We were issued M1903A4s with a four-power Weaver scope. Once we had them zeroed, we were told if under any circumstance we missed a target at 100 yards, we were out. Every day, the nine of us in the battalion were issued a big wooden crate of ammo. The order was go to the range and when the box is empty you can come back. So we would go out on the range and shoot all day long. The 03 was a beautiful rifle, I really loved it. It was very accurate. We trained on the regular known distance range out to 500 yards. On the unknown distance range we estimated the furthest target was at 800 yards. Most of us could hit the bull four out of five times at 500 yards. When we qualified on the unknown distance range, they had the targets set up like machine gun nests. There were three silhouette target groups and they gave us five rounds for each. We had to have one hole in each silhouette. The targets were scattered all over at different ranges. We had to estimate the range and windage and fire at them. The targets would drop when you hit them. They didn't care where you hit them as long as you hit them. Your score would be based on how many bullets you had left over after you hit all the targets.

We arrived in France in November 1944 and took the Yellow Ball Express to Belgium. When we first got there, our company was detached from the division to help out a cavalry outfit that was north of us. We did usual things: scouting, trying to catch some prisoners, standing guard duty and trading shots with the Krauts. We got back with our regiment on December the 15th. We were scheduled to hit some pillboxes the next morning. I was assigned to use a flame thrower during the attack. As it was, that morning the Germans started their attack and a runner from battalion came up and told us to grab our gear and get ready to move. I shucked out of the flame thrower and got my own gear. We moved down to battalion and they loaded us up on trucks and we started to take off. One of our planes flew over and then came down and strafed right along side of us. We'd been around long enough to know that our own Air Corps would shoot at us sometimes. We were cussing them out when all of a sudden we saw all the black helmets over where they had strafed. We bailed out of the trucks and that's how the Battle of the Bulge started for us.

When things started, I was carrying a belt full of ammunition and a bandoleer. I carried the ammo in eight-round Garand clips. That's the way the ammo was issued to us. Whenever I had the opportunity I would load my rifle with six rounds: one round in the chamber and five in the magazine. In a fight, I would also put one round between each finger in my left hand so I could just click them right in. Most of the ammo we got was ball ammunition. During the fighting over the next few days, we just about ran out of ammunition. We were surrounded on the third day of the Bulge and we stripped the ammo from the machine guns and handed it out to the rifleman. They broke through to us and got us more ammo. After that session was over, none of us carried anything less than a full belt, two bandoleers, plus a clip.

I wasn't so much a sniper than a rifleman in the squad armed with a sniper rifle, although I had one lieutenant who acted like I was his personal hit man. If some Kraut had the audacity to shoot at him, he'd say "Slyder, get that guy!"

They never seemed to know what to do with me, except that one lieutenant. The engagement ranges were much closer than the ranges I had been trained to shoot. You were lucky to see a guy who was moving at 200 yards, and if you could see him at 200 yards, he was making a lot of mistakes. Or else we'd see them way far away, out at 1,000 yards. One time we were up in the Elsenborn Ridge, we had a ten-man outpost. The adjacent company was going to move forward and we were going to supply covering fire for them. So they were anticipating nine rifles and a machine gun to be firing for them. When it came time to do it everything was frozen, except my rifle. So I was trying to sound like nine rifles and a machine gun! The guys were urinating on their rifles trying to unfreeze them.

I got to take a shot at a German ski trooper one time. He was skiing down a ridge about 700 yards from my position. I think I lead him too much with the first round. He started windmilling his arms, so it must have been close. I got him with the second shot and spun him around.

We crossed the Ludendorff Bridge at Remagen into Germany not long after it was captured. I believe the 99th Division was the first infantry division to cross the bridge after it was captured. I had to outrun a Messerschmitt crossing the bridge. He came down to strafe while I was crossing. There wasn't anywhere to go on that bridge. We got strafed often enough to keep our attention. We got strafed as much by our Air Force as we did from the Krauts. We got even with them after the war was over. Anytime we found someone with something that identified them as being with the Air Corps, we hit him.

While we were moving into Germany, we had taken this little town. I was foraging for some food. I saw a German command car coming down the hill. At first I thought some of the guys had found the car, then all of a sudden I noticed that the helmets were black in the car. I got out in the middle of the road and yelled, "Halt"! There were four Germans in the car and every one of them did something different. The driver stepped on the gas, the guy next to him in the front dropped to the floorboard, one of the guys in the back started shooting at me and the other one threw his hands in the air. I shot the driver and the car spun around and hit the corner of a house. The other three guys bailed out and went over a wall. I hit one of them as they went over the wall because I heard him screech. That one guy with the pistol kept shooting at me. Then I told them if they didn't come out, I'd shoot them with a bazooka. They didn't know if I had a bazooka or not, so they surrendered. Some of our guys came down off the hill and took charge of the Germans. I was bleeding all over the place; the guy had shot me in the foot and in the wrist. He was a lousy shot. I didn't know I had been shot until they had given up. It was kind of embarrassing, I have a rifle that will shoot up to 800 yards and I let someone get within 20 feet of me!

That was pretty much it for me. By the time I got back to the unit the war was about over. When I got back, they gave my rifle back to me. When I got hit, the supply sergeant took my rifle and kept it for me. They had us out in some sort of formation when they announced that the war was over. The first sergeant said something to the effect, "Before the company is dismissed, Slyder turn your rifle in." I guess they thought that if I kept the sniper rifle, I'd try to steal it. So I turned it in and was issued an M1.

> **John Shirley** *was drafted into the Army in April 1943. He took his basic training at Camp Cooke, CA, where Vandenberg Air Force base is now. Once he completed his basic training, he was promoted to corporal and sent to Fort Sill, OK. After six months, he was promoted to sergeant and transferred overseas as a replacement. He was assigned to "Item" Company, 15th Regiment, 3rd Infantry Division while they were on the Anzio Beachhead. He fought with the division in Italy and made the amphibious landing in the South of France. He was wounded in the fight for the Colmar Pocket in France. A few months later, he returned to his unit just before the war ended. Mr. Shirley received a battlefield commission and served as a company commander during the occupation of Germany.*

I took my training at Camp Cooke, California; it was armored infantry basic training. It was like regular infantry training, but we learned to drive jeeps, trucks and half-tracks. I think that was the only difference. I qualified with the Thompson and the M1 and fired the pistol. I don't remember firing a carbine. We learned how to fire light machine guns and mortars too. I thought the M1 was a good rifle, I'd never experienced any rifle except for a .22 before that. The M1 was easy to disassemble and to keep clean. I qualified expert with it.

After basic, I was sent to the 166th Infantry at Fort Sill, Oklahoma. They were school troops for the artillery OCS. I was there for about six months and then I was sent overseas. I had made buck sergeant by then. I joined I Company, 15th Infantry Regiment, 3rd Infantry Division while they were on the Anzio Beachhead. I got there late, I think it was the end of March, the big counterattacks by the Germans were over by then. Things were kind of static at that time.

My first combat experience was during the breakout. I got assigned to a special unit for the assault. It was called the Battle Sled Team. They had these steel sleds big enough for one man that was dragged behind a tank. The sleds had protection on the front and sides, but nothing on the top. There were six of them hooked together and each tank would drag two rows of six sleds. Each regiment had a sled team with five tanks, each towing 12 sleds with a total of 60 men. We were armed with satchel charges, bangalore torpedoes or flame throwers, not the usual weapons carried by the infantry. We even traded our M1s in for Tommy guns. We trained with those sleds for about three weeks.

When the attack first started we were in reserve, but when the attack bogged down they called us forward. It was a real mess up front. They got us forward, but the

Germans knew about the sleds and directed heavy fire on us. A few of us managed to crawl forward and get into the German trenches. As I was working through the trench, I came upon a German rifleman firing towards the Americans and shot him in the back with my Tommy gun. I continued on and as I went around the corner of the trench there was a German light machine gunner. I fired at him, but after two or three rounds the magazine was empty. I rushed forward and hit him on his helmet and the stock broke off the Tommy gun. I kicked his helmet off and hit him again, although I think my bullets probably killed him. I looked over his machine gun and could see GIs advancing. I was concerned that they know a GI was in the German trench. Even though the stock was broken off the Tommy gun it was still usable, so I reloaded it and was trying to figure out what to do next. There were a lot of Germans in the next trench line, about 60 feet away. Then all of a sudden, the Germans flew a white flag and surrendered. There were about 30 of them, they'd had a tough morning and they'd had enough. Once that resistance collapsed, the attack really got going. I escorted the prisoners to the rear. I got my M1 back and returned to my unit.

I carried the M1 for the rest of the war. I didn't want to carry a Tommy gun or carbine in combat. I liked the Tommy gun, but it was heavy and short ranged. Some of our scouts carried them. I thought the M1 was a better weapon to have.

After Rome was captured, we started training for the invasion of Southern France. When we made the landing in Southern France, we had a dry landing. The got us right up on the beach; I don't remember taking any fire on the beach. I was carrying an M1 with a full cartridge belt of ammo and a few bandoleers. We usually carried at least one bandoleer of ammo. As I mentioned, I thought the M1 was a good rifle. If you kept it half way clean, it worked pretty good.

We did get into a firefight once we got on to the coastal road just off the beach. My squad had two men killed and four wounded attacking a hill not far from the beach. We moved through France pretty quickly at first. I think we advanced 400 miles in less than a month and then it took four months to advance another 60 miles.

One time on a patrol in Southern France, we picked up a French Colonial and he had an Enfield rifle with only 13 rounds of ammo. We engaged some Germans and he would take aim and fire each shot so carefully. We would fire so much faster, probably with less accuracy. We found that the unit that could put out more fire, especially marching fire, had the advantage. A lot of times we couldn't see the Germans, but we'd shoot in the area where we thought they were. With the M1 being semiautomatic, we could deliver a lot of firepower. We learned how to reload the clips fast.

Our engagement ranges varied a lot. Sometimes it might be 60 to 70 yards and sometimes a couple of hundred yards. The M1 was pretty accurate out to 200 or

300 yards. Most of the time, the Germans had a firepower advantage on us. They had 17 of those MG34/42 light machine guns in a rifle company. We only had nine BARs and two light machine guns. German rifle companies used twice the amount of small arms ammo than we did in a day. We really relied on our artillery, mortars, tanks and tank destroyers for support. It's very hard to get men to move in combat under heavy fire, they won't move unless they think they have a chance.

I didn't care for the carbine. I wouldn't carry one and a lot of the officers chose to carry the M1 instead. You wanted to be able to fire out to two or three hundred yards accurately and the carbine wouldn't do that. The BAR was a good weapon, although I only used it one time in combat. The BAR man and I were covering the platoon while it was withdrawing from an engagement. I took the BAR and returned fire on a German machine gun and it stopped firing. We then went back along the road, walking backwards and firing the BAR to cover ourselves. That machine gun never fired again. That was the only time I used one in combat and it worked fine. The German machine guns were better, but the BAR was better than nothing.

I was wounded on the 23rd of December in 1944 while we were fighting in the Colmar Pocket. It was the last German stronghold in France and they fought hard. We were fighting through a small town; there had been heavy fighting there and just about the whole town was rubble. We had been fighting there for about two hours, in some pretty close combat. A German Mark IV tank came forward and we took cover in a cellar. We had been out on the wall of the courtyard firing at the Germans, but when the tank appeared it looked bad for us. I called for artillery on our position and we moved down into the cellar. The tank fired three rounds into the cellar and I was hit in the face. There were two wounded German soldiers in the cellar with us. I had them call out when the German infantry accompanying the tank appeared at the cellar entrance. They captured all eleven of us, with six of us wounded. A German private was leading us to the rear. The five healthy GIs were each helping one of the wounded guys. I was ambulatory and I was the last man in the column. A German corporal was bringing up the rear and he had an American carbine. I didn't think much of the carbine, but he must have liked it. I had my hands in the air about level with my ears when the corporal came up and shoved me on my left shoulder to move faster. Some artillery rounds came in and I wheeled around and hit him in the face with the palm of my right hand. I'm pretty sure I knocked him out. I ran off and hid in the rubble, no one fired at me. I was able to make my way back and find friendly troops.

I was sent to England for treatment of my wounds. I finally returned to the regiment in March 1945. When I returned, I was given a section of heavy, water-cooled machine guns in the weapons company. I really didn't know anything about them; I'm not sure why they did that, maybe they thought it would be safer for me. It was safer; we were mostly used in support. Fortunately, we often supported I Company, so I stayed pretty much with the company I knew. I received a battlefield commission just before the war ended.

After the war ended I became the company commander of L Company during the occupation. We guarded some large dams and made sweeps through the towns looking for weapons or Nazi insignia. There were a lot of people coming into the unit and others leaving when they got enough points. I was sent home in November of 1945 and discharged.

# Personal Experiences

*Gerald Gwaltney, photo taken just after the war ended.*

**Gerald Gwaltney** *joined the Marines in July of 1942 and went to boot camp at Parris Island, SC. After completing his initial training he was assigned to the 23rd Marines at Camp Lejeune, NC. Later as the 4th Marine Division was being formed, he was transferred to the 25th Marine Regiment. He participated in amphibious landings in the Marshall Islands, Saipan and Tinian and then Iwo Jima. Near the end of the campaign on Iwo Jima, he was wounded. He was evacuated from the island and passed through a series of hospitals until he ended up at the Naval Medical Center at Bethesda, MD. He was discharged from the Marines after his medical treatment was completed in March 1946.*

When I was in boot camp at Parris Island, we carried the Springfield 03. We were the first boot camp crew to go through the new firing range at Camp Lejeune. It was a known distance type of range, with targets at 200, 300 and 500 yards. We fired the Springfield 03 for record on that range. I liked the Springfield; it was a very accurate rifle, but it had a lot of kick to it.

When I got to the 23rd Marine Regiment at Camp Lejeune, I went into machine guns. I was assigned to H Company, 2nd Battalion, which was a weapons company. The company consisted of 81 mm mortars, .50 caliber machine guns and .30 caliber machine guns. We had the Browning water-cooled .30 caliber machine gun, the Model 1917. It was the same machine gun they had in World War One. We later had both the water-cooled and light air-cooled guns. We had a heavy tripod with the water-cooled gun, I believe it weighed 51 pounds. Sometimes we used the light tripod that was issued with the air-cooled gun. In the Marshall Islands, we carried the water-cooled gun with the light tripod. On Saipan, we used the air-cooled gun and on Iwo, we went back to the water-cooled.

When we first started training with the water-cooled gun, they trained us like they had trained for World War One trench warfare. We took training on firing the guns in battery. We would sandbag each machine gun in line and have a forward observer to direct our fire. He would give us directions and we'd set the traverse and elevation and do plunging fire across a hill into the target area. We never fired the guns in battery in combat.

In the beginning of the war we were short of a lot of things. When we first fired the heavy water-cooled gun we shot it on a 1,000-inch range using .22 ammunition. It was good training for learning to fire three to four round bursts and learning to traverse the gun across the target. There was just one group of us that used the .22 adapter with the gun. When we fired for record, we used .30 caliber ammunition.

We had some really good training and I think that it saved some lives. We'd lay out our poncho and while blindfolded, we would detail strip the machine gun. You would practice putting the parts in the same spot on the poncho every time. The purpose of doing that was if you had a gun failure at night and had to tear the gun down, you'd do the same thing. The difference between field stripping and detail stripping was when you field stripped the gun, you broke it down into the three major groups. With detail stripping, you take the major groups apart.

When they were forming the 4th Division, they split the 23rd Regiment right down the middle and half of us went to form the 25th Regiment. I went from H Company, 2nd Battalion, 23rd Marines to H Company, 2nd Battalion, 25th Marines. Before we went to the Marshall Islands, each battalion had a weapons company. What they did was take a platoon of .30 calibers and attach one of them to each rifle company. After the Marshall Islands, they streamlined the division and changed the weapons companies. They took the .30 caliber machine gun platoons and assigned them to the rifle companies. The first platoon became part of E Company, the second platoon, which I was in, became part of F Company and the third platoon part of G Company. Before that, the rifle companies only had one section of light machine guns, so when we became part of the company we doubled their firepower.

I was first gunner when we landed in the Marshall Islands, but I didn't do a lot of shooting. Our battalion landed on a smaller island off Roi-Namur to capture a Japanese communications building and secure the island for our artillery. As soon as we got on the beach, they started bringing the artillery pieces in. From the island, the artillery could support the landing on Roi-Namur. We secured the island a little after lunchtime.

When I was the number one gunner, I also had a carbine. I first trained with the carbine at Camp Lejeune in 1942. We got carbines before we got M1s, although the M1s came in soon after. I got one of the first Winchester carbines that came out. Later on, Nickelodeon and everyone else started putting them out. I really liked my carbine; some of the others weren't as accurate. We only fired them at two and three hundred yards. At two hundred yards it did real well, at three hundred yards it did OK, but the rounds were a little scattered. I never ever had any misfires with mine.

I was a squad leader when we invaded Saipan. As a squad leader, I was issued an M1. I particularly liked that Winchester carbine, so whenever we went back into combat I would trade with the first gunner. He liked the M1, so he'd take my M1 and I'd take the carbine. We did the same thing on Iwo. When I got hit on Iwo, I was still carrying that same carbine; by then, all the bluing had been wore off. I usually carried three to four clips for it. The carbine didn't have the knocking down power that a .45 or a full-sized .30 caliber round had, but it was good enough.

I never carried an M1 into combat. I had fired an M1 during training and all the guys in the squad had them. The thing I wasn't particularly enthused about with the M1 was when you loaded the clip; you'd pinch your thumb if you weren't careful. It also made a terrible noise after the last round was fired and the clip flew out. Anything that made noise at night was bad. During those fights at night we fought with our bayonets fixed, although the carbine didn't have a bayonet.

On the first night on Tinian, we had a big *banzai* attack and they used tanks against us. I had a grenade launcher on my carbine. We had trained shooting rifle grenades from the M1 and the carbine. These were the anti-tank grenades; I usually carried two of them. During the attack, the Japanese were using knee mortars off to the left about 150 feet from our gun position in a cane field. I fired a rifle grenade at them and there was a pretty good explosion. I may have hit some of their ammo; it wiped out the mortar team. It was a lucky shot. We had our machine gun belts loaded so that every seventh round was a tracer. That night, we could see the tracer rounds go through their bodies as they were attacking. Their momentum would carry them several steps on before they went down. I had a buddy who had "found" a whole case of grenades and brought them to our position during the afternoon. I couldn't believe it when he brought them up. You know Marines have a certain ingenuity for finding stuff like that. During the attack he threw every one of them. If he hadn't got that case of grenades, I don't think I'd be talking to you today. Some of the Japs got right up to the parapet of our machine gun before we got them.

We used our machine guns a lot on Saipan and Tinian, more so than we did on Iwo. On Iwo, we didn't have a field of fire most of the time because of the terrain. Everything was all tore up from the shelling. I never had any failures with the gun, I always made sure it was clean and in good shape. Most of the time the squad leader and first gunner maintained the gun. We could field strip the air-cooled to clean it, but we couldn't do that with the water-cooled. You didn't want to field strip it and lose the water by breaking the seal on the water jacket. We just kept it clean the best we could. All of my training before I went into combat was with the water-cooled gun and I thought a lot of that gun. But after using the air-cooled gun on Saipan and Tinian, I really liked it. We did a lot of firing with it and I never had a barrel heat up too badly. It was a lot less bulky too.

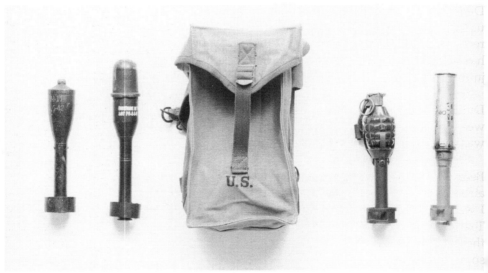

Rifle grenades, left to right: M11 practice, M11A1 practice, rifle grenade carrying bag, Mk II fragmentation hand grenade on M1 adapter, ground signal parachute flare. Photo courtesy of Bruce N. Canfield.

I was wounded on Iwo on what was supposed to be the last day. As it turned out, it wasn't the last day of fighting; it went on a few days after that. I was running with my carbine in my right hand ahead of me and a round hit me in the right forearm. I guess the Jap was leading me too much. I always had in mind that after the war, I was going to take my carbine back home with me somehow or another. When I got hit, it went flipping through the air and that was the last I saw of it.

Personal Experiences

> **Bob Nesbitt** *joined the Army in February 1950 and took his basic training at Fort Dix, NJ. While he was at Fort Dix, he volunteered for airborne school. After completing airborne school, he was assigned to G Company, 187th Regimental Combat Team (Airborne) which was at Fort Campbell, KY at the time. Several weeks after he arrived with the unit it was deployed to Japan and then air-landed in Korea. The regiment served as a theater reserve unit and was shuttled to hot spots back forth across the Korean Peninsula. Mr. Nesbitt made two combat jumps with the regiment and was severely wounded on Easter Sunday 1951, three days after his second combat jump.*

I was 17 when I enlisted. I had just graduated from high school and didn't have any money. I thought the Army would be a good career. My father had to sign to let me join at that age. I was at basic training at Fort Dix and the 11th Airborne Division had sent a recruiter to talk to the trainees. They talked to us and showed us some movies. I was dozing through them, not really paying attention. Then the recruiter mentioned that upon graduation from jump school, paratroopers received hazardous duty pay. I signed right up! Back then privates got $75 a month and jump pay was an extra $50!

During basic, my weapons training was strictly with the M1 rifle. It was the only weapon that was ever issued to me. I thought it was a very powerful rifle, the recoil was pretty tough. It was hard to qualify expert, but I did become an expert with it.

Because the Korean War had started and they had already decided to send an airborne regiment over, I never trained with any other weapons. After jump school, I was sent to Fort Campbell, Kentucky and joined the 187th Regimental Combat Team. I was only with the 187th for three weeks before we got on a troop train for the West Coast. We took a Merchant Marine ship to Japan. I remember we did some rifle training on the ship. We practiced our firing techniques from different positions firing live ammo into the sea. After we arrived in Japan, they flew us over to Kimpo airbase in Korea. It was just after the Inchon landings. They had just recaptured the airfield and we got in a firefight right after we got off the plane.

We skirmished with the North Koreans before we made our combat jumps. The regiment was used more or less as a backup force. If there was a breakthrough along the line or if a unit needed support, they'd send us over to help. We'd jump on trucks and they'd drive us over to the action. We crossed that peninsula many times. I made two combat jumps with the 187th. For the jumps, I didn't use any kind of case for my M1. I just strapped the rifle to my side, muzzle down. We'd put a covering on the muzzle so that nothing would get in the bore when we landed. We wanted it on the outside so we could get to it fast if we needed it.

Since I was just a rifleman, the sergeants pretty much told us what to carry as far as ammo goes. I had a heavy load, I think I had about 400 rounds of ammo for my rifle. The M1 was a good rifle. It was much better than the bolt action rifles most of the North Koreans were using. They couldn't match the firepower we had with our semi-automatic M1s. I was fortunate, my rifle never gave me a bit of trouble. Some guys would have a problem once in a while, a broken firing pin or whatever. On the average, it was just a superior weapon. You did have to keep it clean or it wouldn't work, especially with us living in the elements. I cleaned mine whenever I had the time. If I was in a foxhole with nothing to do, I'd clean my rifle. I kept my rifle in tiptop shape so I could rely on it when I needed it.

Most of the combat engagements were 300 yards or less. When we got in a firefight, it was usually pretty close. The North Koreans and the Chinese had the numbers, but we had the firepower. We could get off five times as many rounds as they could. I didn't think they were well trained troops. If their commanders told them to charge, they charged. They just kept coming and we just kept letting them have it and pretty soon they'd back off. It wasn't so much aimed fire during those attacks, you pretty much fired as fast as you could. I didn't have any problems reloading with the clips. Once you learned how to handle it and load it without getting your thumb caught in it, you could load them really fast. Like I said, the M1 was a very reliable weapon. I used it a lot and never had nickel's worth of problems with it.

Personal Experiences

> **Rudy Haynes** *was drafted in October 1942 and was assigned to the newly formed 83rd Division at Camp Atterbury, IN. He became a member of the Division Recon Troop and took his basic training with them. After extensive training in the States, the division was sent to England in April 1944. They landed in France on D+12 and went up on the line shortly thereafter. Mr. Haynes fought with the recon troop through France, Belgium, Luxembourg, and Germany. When the war ended they were deep in Germany, on the Elbe River, waiting to meet the Russian Army. He returned to the US and was discharged in November 1945.*

I turned 20 in February 1942 and in those days, once you turned 20, you were eligible for the draft. I got the letter from Uncle Sam in June and had my preliminary physical in August. I was classified 1A and ordered to report for my final physical 13 October where I was accepted and sworn into the Army that afternoon. I went to Camp Atterbury, Indiana for basic training. The camp had been built in early 1942 and the 83rd Infantry Division was being formed there. We were the first unit to be based there. I was assigned to the 83rd Cavalry Reconnaissance Troop along with about 175 other guys. We started our basic training in early November and finished in February. Our first rifles were M1917 Enfields, the ones used in World War One. We were taught the manual of arms and did close order drill with them. We even went out to the range once and fired them.

Once we finished our basic training, we advanced to what they called Corps training. It was more specialized training, mechanics went to maintenance school, radio operators went to radio school, etc. We ran through exercises with our vehicles, we were totally mechanized. We had M8 armored cars, half-tracks, jeeps and trucks. In June, we went down to army maneuvers in Tennessee with three other divisions. After the maneuvers, we moved to Camp Breckenridge in Kentucky, and continued training.

Insofar as weapons proficiency, once we got up to Camp Breckenridge we trained with the M1, the carbine, the Colt .45, the .30 caliber machine gun, the .50 caliber machine gun, the 60 mm and 81 mm mortars. We even had some of the old Thompson submachine guns that we fired. I qualified with the M1 and the carbine while we were at Camp Breckenridge. On rainy or cold days, we would break down the machine guns and put them back together again. In fact, sometimes we broke down our M1s, carbines and .45s and we'd put them back together blindfolded. The reason for doing that was if something happened to it at night, you could break it down to replace a part. Being trained on the use of all those weapons was useful later, when we were overseas.

# US Infantry Weapons In Combat

Our M8 armored cars had a 37 mm cannon, which was in the turret and rotated just like a tank turret. It was synchronized with a .30 caliber machine gun, so they would both hit the same target. Then around the top of the turret, we had a ring mount with the .50 caliber mounted. Although the armor wasn't very thick on those things they were well armed. In the troop, we had eight armored cars, 8 to 10 three-quarter-ton trucks, two 6x6s, and probably 15 to 20 jeeps. We were totally mobile. The infantry guys didn't like us very well. They would be marching down some of those dusty roads and we'd go flying by in our vehicles and throw dust up in their faces.

We went overseas in April 1944. When we left the States, we didn't have any weapons. We turned all our weapons and vehicles in before we left. All I had when I got on the ship was the clothes on my back and a barracks bag over my shoulder. When we got to England we were issued all new equipment. It used to be an old joke that we almost sank that island with all the men and equipment we had over there. They took us to an open field where they had armored cars lined up in a row, literally as far as you could see. Also, they had jeeps and tanks and trucks. It was fantastic! Everything was new! The M8s 37 mm gun, the .50 caliber and .30 caliber machine guns all still had cosmoline on them. The first thing we had to do was clean all that crap off the guns. We were also issued new M1 rifles and carbines.

I was issued a carbine. It wasn't the greatest weapon that was ever invented. Later after we got over into France, sleeping on the ground, and in foxholes, if you got a little dirt in the breech, the carbines jammed rather easily. It was also terribly inaccurate when compared with the M1. If you had zeroed your M1 and you were shooting at 300 yards, you could line it up and hit a bullseye every time. But with those carbines, forget it. They weren't worth the effort to ship them overseas. I never met anyone who liked the carbine. They were not good weapons, period. A lot of the guys got rid of their carbines as soon as they could get their hands on an M1. Some of the guys were issued .45 caliber grease guns. We called it the "Buck Rogers" because we thought it was typical of the old Buck Rogers science fiction movies. It was a strange looking weapon. The biggest problem with it was when you fired it you couldn't hold it down. It kept rising up from the force of the recoil.

We landed on Omaha Beach on the 18th of June. We went into the line to relieve the 101st Airborne during the nights of the 26th and 27th of June. That was our first combat experience. We fought in hedgerow country until late July and then we went down into Brittany.

I did get rid of my carbine and picked up an M1. I didn't use it very often though. Usually when I was involved in any action, I was firing the .30 caliber or the .50 caliber mounted on the ring mount of the armored car. I remember using the M1 a few times in Germany. I thought the M1 was probably the best individual weapon that we had over there. You couldn't tear that thing up. I didn't really carry much ammunition for my M1; usually I just had a bandoleer. I was always very near my vehicle and there was ammunition in the vehicle. I picked a .45 up along the way and carried it through the war, but I never used it in combat. I just had it in case I needed it.

On July 19, we were ordered to support one of the infantry battalions on La Varde Peninsula. For some reason, they took the recon troop over there and dismounted us. We took all the weapons we could get off the vehicles and sent the vehicles back to the rear. We were placed in a position along a hedgerow, on the left flank of the infantry battalion. We got into a big firefight when the Germans counterattacked. I had a machine gun at the hedgerow and I remember firing over at the next hedgerow where I knew the Germans were. I would move from time to time so they couldn't zero in on me. I was down behind the machine gun and I saw the leaves jumping beside me on the right. All of a sudden, I realized those were bullets making those leaves jump. I got down behind the hedgerow for a little while and thought about it. Then I thought, I can't do any good down here, so I started firing the machine gun again. Then the cover latch on the gun jumped up and I couldn't keep it down. If the cover latch won't stay down, the gun won't fire. I took it down off the hedgerow and was looking at it and I noticed that a bullet had hit the cover latch spring and broken it. A half-inch up or down and the bullet would have hit me right in the head. I never noticed the bullet hitting the gun. The machine gun was no good, so I tossed it aside in the roadway.

I remembered that earlier I had seen one of my comrades running along the hedgerow behind me with a machine gun and a mortar shell had exploded by him. I knew that he had a machine gun and I wondered if it was still over there. I went over to where I had seen him get hit and I found the machine gun on top of a hedgerow. I tried to get it down, but it wouldn't come down. The ammo belt was caught on something. I climbed up on the hedgerow to see what it was caught on and my comrade was dead on the other side on the hedgerow with his body lying on the belt. I had to get over and yank the belt from underneath him. Then I took the machine gun back over to my position and started firing again. Another guy in the outfit came up on my left and started firing his M1. I yelled at him to be careful, that I had just been fired on from the opposite hedgerow. The words were barely out of my mouth when a bullet hit him right in the forehead. He was dead before he hit the ground. I didn't know at the time, but on the right flank the Germans had hit the infantry pretty hard with some tanks. We had to retreat from our positions because we didn't have any tank support.

The air-cooled .30 caliber was a very good machine gun. It was a very reliable weapon; I never had any complaints with it. It was easy to take care of, although you had to be careful not to fire it too rapidly or it would overheat and lose some of its accuracy. I found the .50 was even more reliable. That was a powerful weapon.

We had four or five types of ammunition for it. We had armor piercing, tracer, incendiary, HE and rounds with a regular bullet all in the same ammunition belt.

Later in the war, we were fighting across Northern Germany and we pulled into this little town. I was standing in the armored car leaning up against the ring mount for the .50 caliber. I saw this airplane coming down the street towards me at tree top level. As it got closer, I could see that it was a German artillery spotter plane. I immediately grabbed the handles on the .50 caliber and started pumping lead into the plane. As it went by me, it wasn't any more than 40 to 50 feet above me. I could see the tracers tearing through the fuselage. It went down just off to my left. It crashed on top of some telephone wires running along some railroad tracks and hung up there and burned. That .50 caliber machine gun really ripped that plane apart.

On another occasion in the war, farther into Germany, we were reconnoitering in front of the 331$^{st}$ Infantry Regiment. They were riding on tanks, trucks and anything that was mobile following us up the road. We overtook some Germans on the road and I told our vehicle driver to stop. I stood up with this .50 caliber and they ran off the road into some woods on the right. I didn't want to shoot those guys with a .50 caliber at that stage of the war. I deliberately fired the .50 over their heads into the trees. I can imagine what it would be like with the sound of the lead from that .50 tearing through those trees over your head. I yelled for them to come out and they all stopped, turned around and came out. There must have been about 40 of them. I could have slaughtered them or at least part of them if I had fired into them with the .50. I told them to throw their guns on the engine of the armored car and I got a nice collection of P38s and Lugers.

I never had the kind of action that the rifle companies in the Infantry Regiments faced. They were the guys who took all the beating and pounding. In the final analysis, they were the guys who really won the war. They suffered most of the casualties.

Before the war ended, we had crossed the Elbe River and there we were told to halt. The word came down to wait for the Russians. After the war, we stayed in Germany for several months. You needed 85 points to go home and when they added mine up, I had 87. We drove our vehicles to France and turned them in to a depot. Then we waited 35 days for an available ship. We finally sailed from La Havre, France in early November, landing in Newport News, Virginia six days later. I was discharged at Camp Atterbury, 18 November 1945, and was home for Thanksgiving.

Personal Experiences

> **Howard Gaertner** *was drafted in March 1943 and took his basic training at Camp Butner, NC with the 78th Division. After a year of training he was sent to England as an infantry replacement just prior to the D-Day invasion. After D-Day, he was sent to France where he was assigned to the 9th Division. He was badly wounded in September 1944 and evacuated to England to recover. He was reclassified and returned to Europe to serve with a quartermaster unit until the end of the war.*

After I was drafted, I went to Camp Butner, North Carolina for basic training. It was a camp that was built expressly for an infantry division. I joined the 78th Division there. Our basic training lasted about four months and then we got into more specialized training. In the beginning, everyone took the same training. We all trained with the M1 rifle, the BAR and the carbine. Then if you were assigned into the weapons platoon, you trained with other weapons. Once you got into a specialty weapon, you stayed with that. I wound up training with the 60 mm mortar and the light machine gun. I became a mortar man while I was in the 78th Division.

I was with the 78th Division for about a year. In March of 1944 we went on Tennessee Maneuvers and we were down there training for a good two months. After the maneuvers, we were bussed up to Camp Pickett, Virginia and went right into more advanced training. Then all the privates and PFCs were given furloughs and when we came back, they had us pack up and get ready to go to England. They replaced us in the division with ASTP people and Air Corps recruits. We arrived in England in May, a few weeks before D-Day. We waited for the invasion in replacement camps, waiting to be sent over to a unit.

I was sent over to France a few weeks after the invasion and assigned to the 9th Infantry Division. I went to M Company, 47th Infantry, which was the 3rd Battalion's weapons company. They had heavy machine guns and 81 mm mortars. I became a machine gunner on a water-cooled .30 caliber machine gun. We were normally attached to one of the infantry companies, usually to the one that was first in line.

The water-cooled machine gun wasn't very good, it was too heavy. The German machine guns were better. We had a water can that we had to carry for the gun, but we would use our urine in it so we wouldn't have to carry water for it. That way we could carry another can of ammo instead. We would always carry as much ammo as we could. We were always short guys; it was rare when we had a full crew. The gun was reliable to a point, everybody in the squad helped to keep it clean. We didn't shoot it that often. For us it was moving, setting the gun up, guarding and then doing a little shooting here and there.

Normally we would have carried a pistol, but they wouldn't allow us to carry them. Everybody had a carbine. I thought the carbine was a fine gun. It was reliable and it was a lot lighter than the M1. I carried two magazines in a pouch that fit on the stock and one in the gun. It was enough ammo. With the carbines we could move around and act more like an infantryman. We used the carbines out to no more than 100 yards.

I was wounded on September 9th while crossing the Meuse River. I was hospitalized in England for two months before I returned to Europe. I was reclassified after recovering from my wound and assigned to non-combat duty in a quartermaster truck company. I served with the truck company for the rest of the war. I returned to the US and was discharged in November of 1945.

Personal Experiences

> **Oliver Green** enlisted in the Army in June of 1950, just before the outbreak of the Korean War. He took basic training at Fort Knox, KY and upon completion of his training, was sent to Japan. In Japan, he was assigned to the 3rd Infantry Division and landed in North Korea with his unit in November 1950. He served with the division during the harsh and brutal fighting in North Korea until they were withdrawn by the Navy and relocated to South Korea. He fought up the Korean peninsula until he was badly wounded in February 1951. He was evacuated to the US where he spent 20 months in various hospitals recovering from his wounds. He was discharged from the Army in 1953.

In June 1950 I didn't have anything else going for me, so I joined the Army. I had a military background: my father was a career soldier, who ended up spending 32 years in the Army. I had just finished high school, went to the prom and the next morning caught a train to Fort Knox, Kentucky for basic training. As far as small arms training, we trained with all of them. We trained with the Garand, the carbine, the BAR, and the light and heavy machine guns. The only thing we didn't train with that I used in Korea was the Thompson submachine gun. We didn't train with any submachine guns. Of all those weapons, I was most comfortable with the Garand. It fit me like a glove, I shot expert with it. While we were in training a lot of the rifles were second hand rifles, but I had a good one and took good care of it.

After I finished basic, I caught a train to Seattle and then a DC-4 to Japan. I was placed in D Company, 1st Battalion, 7th Infantry Regiment in the 3rd Division. D Company was a heavy weapons company. We had an 81 mm mortar platoon, we had a recoilless rifle platoon and we had a machine gun platoon. I was assigned to the machine gun platoon. We took our combat training at Camp Chickamagua in Japan, which was a joke. They pushed us through the training too fast. I'd had good basic training at Fort Knox and that's the only thing that saved my life. We were issued rifles in Japan and mine as I recall was virtually new.

We landed in North Korea in November. After we landed and were moving inland, we had some skirmishes with the North Koreans and had some artillery duels. I saw my first live Chinese when they hit us on the 24th of November.

We had a section sergeant who had been a tanker in World War Two. He would not let us place our weapons around a fire or into a building. If we went into a building we left our weapon outside with another man. The reason for that was if the weapon got warm it would "sweat" once it was back in the cold. The worst thing was that the firing pins would freeze. If the bolt froze shut you could usually break it free, but there was no cure for a frozen firing pin, except possibly some antifreeze.

Our machine gun platoon had four squads and we were normally assigned to rifle companies. We would rarely see the other squads. At first I was an ammo bearer, although I was classified as a gunner. I got my machine gun training on the job once I was in Korea. I did get to fire sometimes, but not like the squad corporal. We each carried two 250-round boxes of machine gun ammo and frequently we would go back to the trailer and get more. I normally carried two bandoleers of rifle ammunition; I never used my belt. Most of the ammo we got was primarily the black-tipped stuff. We preferred it because of the penetration. We noticed the difference. We learned from our section sergeant that the object wasn't necessarily to kill the enemy, just put a bullet through him.

We had both the water-cooled and air-cooled guns in the platoon; we had them available in our trailers. We used the water-cooled for the defense and the air-cooled for assaults. You couldn't take a water-cooled gun on the advance; it was too heavy. Also, we didn't use water in those heavy machine guns, we used antifreeze. You couldn't use water in that Siberian weather; the water freezes in the jacket. The jacket was never full; it's usually 40 to 70 percent full, but when the water freezes it splits the jacket. As long as we had anti-freeze in the jacket, we could fire them all night.

During the day, the platoon lieutenants would tell us what areas to sight on. If they called for a fire mission in a particular area, you had to be able to traverse your gun and give them some fire. We used a T&E (traverse and elevation) mechanism to line the gun up to fire into the area. The discipline was 20-round bursts from the water-cooled and eight-round bursts from the air-cooled. We actually tried to maintain that, but it wasn't always possible. When the gun got too hot those tracers would corkscrew out of the barrel, but you could let the barrel cool and it would be just fine.

We didn't do anything special to those weapons to keep them working except keep them away from the heat. The extreme cold won't keep a weapon from working as long as the weapon is dry. At the direction of our sergeant, we never took apart our machine gun or rifles. We would clean the bore and make sure there was no oil in the mechanism. That was it, I never took a weapon apart the whole time I was in Korea. We were fighting in relatively clean conditions in that winter weather. There wasn't much dust.

For a while I used a Thompson that I took off of a Chinese soldier that he'd put down. It was a bad mistake. One time we got hit while we were in column on a road. I was shooting from behind our trailer; each machine gun squad had a jeep and trailer. My Garand was in the trailer and I couldn't get to it. I knocked a Chinese soldier out of some bushes with the Thompson 75 to 100 yards up a hill, which was way out of range for that Thompson. I did it by dropping the rounds in on him. With a Garand, it would have been child's play. I didn't make that mistake again. There was no question, the Garand was a much better weapon than the Thompson. One time I took two sandbags and laid them back to back and I emptied a Thompson magazine into them. It made a real good mess of the surface of the first sandbag. Then I took my Garand and fired one black-tipped bullet into the sandbags and it went through both bags. That's all you need to know. Range and penetration was the key factor. After that, I used the Garand and kept the Thompson around my foxhole to cover my backside. I had that Thompson until mid-February when they had us turn in all unauthorized weapons.

We usually let the Chinese or North Koreans do their assaults and we just cut them down. We learned that if we got in their face and made a problem for them and they'd come at you. Having enough ammunition wasn't a problem. What would happen is the enemy would infiltrate and get behind you. Some units would panic when that happened. It really wasn't a bad situation if you kept your head and kept shooting. They just had more people than we did and some units couldn't take that. They just wanted a nice, neat battle. If we could go toe-to-toe with them, we had superior small arms.

The Chinese were well armed. A lot of them had those bolt action Russian rifles, but the vast majority had that drum fed submachine gun. It was an effective weapon. When they hit our guys, usually it was a wounding shot, even if you got hit two or three times. We had on this heavy winter clothing, which helped. But that's all you needed to stop a man in combat, then it took at least two men to take care of him. They also used American weapons: Thompsons, carbines and Garands. The two Thompsons I took were brand new, I mean brand new. They were probably lend-lease guns we had given the Nationalist Chinese.

As I mentioned, I don't recall ever carrying more than two bandoleers of rifle ammunition; it was enough ammunition for me. We didn't waste rifle fire; you had to see something to pull the trigger. We didn't use rifles for suppression; we used machine guns for that. The engagement range could run from 500 yards down to right outside my hole. I knocked people down right outside my foxhole and I shot at them at 500 yards.

In February, we were south of the Han River when I was hit. We were on an assault, but we had planned our defensive line, hoping they would charge us. I was talking to a lieutenant about where to put our machine gun when I was wounded by a shell burst. I was evacuated to Japan and after a month, I was sent back to the States. I was in different hospitals for 20 months and 27 days. I was discharged in 1953.

## US Infantry Weapons In Combat

*Article from Stars and Stripes dated December 8, 1950:*

HQ, X CORPS IN KOREA- An 18-year-old American GI killed six curious Chinese Communists-and left them all kneeling, X Corps PIO reported.

A 3rd Division Rifle Company was defending its command post from attacking Chinese when the Reds broke through and infiltrated.

PFC Oliver Green Jr. of Huntsville, AL saw one of the enemy soldiers kneel to peer into a house opposite his position. Green fired and the soldier slumped forward, still kneeling.

Green watched as another Red approached the house, quizzically eyed his dead buddy and kneeled to look over his shoulder. Green fired again and the second victim died kneeling, leaning against the first. It happened four more times.

When the infantryman stopped shooting, all six were neatly stacked up.

*Article from the Huntsville Times quoting a letter written home by Mr. Green during the war:*

PFC Green and a buddy were left behind at a command post when "everyone took off for the hills," during a night attack by the Chinese.
He wrote: "We climbed in a hole right outside the C.P. The bullets were popping inches over our heads. The five Chinese came running up to the C.P. about 15 yards away from us.

"I cut them all down at once with my M1...I wounded one, and I could hear him moaning and crawling over the frozen ground.

"I was afraid he was going to throw a grenade, so I raised up and put two more bullets in his back.

"Then the sixth one ran up, and I cut him down.

" It wasn't very pretty the next morning."

Personal Experiences

Bill True, 1945

**Bill True** *joined the Army in August 1942 and volunteered for the Airborne. He arrived at Camp Toccoa, GA as F Company, 506th Parachute Infantry Regiment was being formed. Following extensive training in the US and England, he jumped with the 101st Airborne Division into Normandy during the D-Day invasion. After fighting in France until mid-July, the unit was returned to England. The next big operation was Operation Market Garden, the airborne assault into Holland. The 506th saw heavy fighting during the battle and was redrawn to France for rest and refitting in November 1944. The division was hurriedly committed to Bastogne during the German Ardennes offensive. Mr. True fought with the division until the war ended.*

When I arrived at Camp Toccoa, the regiment was just forming F Company, so I ended up with the first platoon in F Company. That's the way they did it; as guys arrived, they formed the platoons and companies. As soon as they had enough men arrive to fill a company, they formed one. We trained about a month without any weapons; there just weren't enough to go around at first. We concentrated on doing physical training. It seemed if we didn't have anything to do, they'd take us on a run or have us go though the obstacle course. I remember when the rifles came in, they were brand new M1s all covered with cosmoline. I carried the rifle I was issued at Toccoa for the whole time I was with the unit. We also got some training with the pistol, the Thompson submachine gun, the machine gun, the mortar and some BAR training. Not extensive, but some. The BAR wasn't a standard weapon for us, but I can remember having one in my group while in Normandy. I don't know where they got it.

After training in the States, we went overseas to England. We continued training in England preparing for the jump into Normandy. We were really loaded down for the Normandy jump. The one thing that seemed funny was jumping with a land mine. We had never had anything to do with mines before and each one of us jumped with what they called a Hawkins land mine. I believe it was an anti-tank mine. The rifle was disassembled into three pieces and packed into a canvas bag that strapped across your chest. When you landed, you didn't immediately have a weapon handy other than your knife and hand grenades. Although once on the ground, it didn't take long to reassemble the rifle. That's the way we jumped at Normandy, we didn't thereafter. That was the only time we jumped with it disassembled. I had a full cartridge belt of clips, two bandoleers of ammo and a few grenades. We were really loaded down. I was also assigned to a mortar section, so I had either a piece of the mortar or some mortar rounds too.

We landed a few miles away from our objective. I remember that before noon that day, we met infantry coming up from the beach. The different units were considerably mixed up until late in the day. But before D-Day was over, I was back with my company. We weren't fully assembled, but we probably had half the company. My section's mortar was lost in the jump, so I ended up as second gunner on a machine gun for much of the time.

The M1 was a good weapon. I was on a patrol on the second or third day and had an occasion to fire at a German who wasn't too far away. I missed him with the first shot and as I started to squeeze off the second shot, I had a jam. It probably took me all of two seconds to clear the jam, but by that time the other guys had hit him and he went down. It was the only time in either training or in combat that I ever had a malfunction like that. When I think back on it, I should have tried harder to clean my rifle after the jump. That first night was a wet one and I just never had the chance to clean the rifle over the next few days. It was carelessness on my part; I'd never had the rifle misfire before and never even thought about it. We stayed in France until about the middle of July and then went back to England.

I also participated in the jump into Holland in September. On that jump, I kept my M1 fully assembled and ready to go and didn't use a case. I think I just slipped it between the parachute straps and didn't have any problems with it. I felt more comfortable having it out. It was a lot handier and ready to use once I landed. The jump into Holland was made during the day. It was a nice day and I had a good landing. I was slightly wounded by some German flak while I was on the plane on the way to the drop zone. The guy behind me took the brunt of it and was badly wounded. He wasn't able to jump. I only had a small piece of shrapnel from the round hit me in the hand. I landed next to a medic and he bandaged it up for me and I forgot all about it. Later when the war was over, I was waiting to get enough points to rotate home and I found out I had been awarded the Purple Heart. The medic had reported my wound and it gave me five extra points and I got to go home a little earlier. I'll always be grateful to that medic for recording that wound. We did see a lot of fighting in Holland; we didn't get relieved until the end of November. I was still in the mortar section, carrying an M1. Our basic load was still a full cartridge belt and two bandoleers of ammo. It was also normal for us to carry a few grenades and a can of machine gun ammo or several mortar rounds.

After we were withdrawn from Holland, we were sent to France for some rest. We weren't there more than a few weeks before we got involved in the Battle of the Bulge and ended up in Bastogne. I don't remember having any trouble with the weapons in the winter weather during the Bulge. We cleaned our rifles fairly frequently; it was important to keep them in first rate condition. I don't recall doing anything different because of the weather conditions. My rifle fired any time I needed it to fire.

I was with the unit for the whole campaign, although I was off the line for a few weeks after I wrecked my knee during an artillery barrage. After the war I had enough points to go home with the first group to return to the States.

## US Infantry Weapons In Combat

*Len Lazerick*

**Len Lazerick** *was called to active duty in the Army in April of 1943 and initially attended basic training for medics. Upon completion of that training he was accepted to participate in the Army Specialized Training Program (ASTP). When that program was closed down, he was assigned to K Company, 382nd Infantry Regiment, of the 96th Division as an infantryman. He fought in the Pacific Theater with the division, making amphibious landings on Leyte in the Philippines and on Okinawa. He was wounded once on Leyte and twice on Okinawa. He returned to the US in December of 1945 and was discharged.*

When I first came into the Army, I went to Camp Grant, Illinois and took medic's basic training. I didn't do any weapons training at all during that course. Then

# Personal Experiences

went into the ASTP and went to college to study engineering. When that program was closed down, we all wound up in the infantry. When I got to the 96th Division, they took all of us with previous military training but no infantry training and put us through a crash course in the basics of infantry. It was a six-week course. During that course, I trained with the M1 and the carbine. I qualified with both weapons. They had different known distance ranges for each. I think with the M1 we fired at 100, 200 and 500 yards and with the carbine it was only 100 and 200 yards. I thought the carbine was a peashooter, but the M1 was outstanding. I only qualified as marksman with the M1, but I was very confident with my ability to shoot with it. Going to the Pacific, we wouldn't be shooting at any great distance. My first M1 was so old and worn that it hardly had any rifling in the barrel. It was so bad it could have passed for a mortar. Before I went overseas, I got a brand new M1.

The division went overseas to Hawaii in July 1944. While we were there, we did some additional training. We did some practice landings, some jungle training and spent some more time on the rifle ranges. I also received training on demolitions, the flame thrower and the bangalore torpedo. I was never called upon to use the flame thrower in a combat situation and I was happy about that. We had a fellow in our company who just loved using the flame thrower. Most people weren't thrilled about having to carry that heavy, clumsy thing.

M2-2 flame thrower. Hayes Otoupalik collection. Photo courtesy of Bruce N. Canfield.

I was in the first wave on the beach during the invasion on Leyte in the Philippines. I carried my M1, a full cartridge belt of ammo along with two bandoleers, two fragmentation grenades and two concussion grenades. Some guys carried smoke grenades and some carried front line marking panels. I only lasted about 15 minutes on the beach before I was wounded. We were attacking three pillboxes and had thrown a couple of grenades in them. I was firing into the front of one of the pillboxes while in a prone position behind a coconut tree stump. When I went to reload, rather than pull the rifle back, I leaned forward from behind the stump to load the clip. That's when a Jap inside the pillbox shot me. If I had pulled the rifle back, I don't think he would have had a shot at me. It was carelessness on my part. After I was wounded, I was evacuated from the beach by ship. When they evacuated me, they made me leave all my ammunition and my rifle on the beach. I have no idea what happened to my rifle after that, for all I know some sailor picked it up as a souvenir. They sent me to the Admiral Islands, where I was hospitalized for about two weeks. I returned to my company in December 1944, while they were still in combat on Leyte.

The Okinawa landing was much different for me. My regiment was in reserve and the landing was hardly opposed. It wasn't until we moved to the south when the Japanese put their plan into effect. I think they wanted to make the island as costly as possible for the Army and the Marines. I was equipped the same as I was when I landed on Leyte. On Okinawa it was rare to actually see a Jap, we didn't see them often. If you came upon a hole or a cave, you just assumed it was occupied. You fired into it and then you'd throw a grenade or satchel charge into it and blow it up.

I had one situation where I had to use a BAR during a *banzai* attack, on April 21, 1945 in a village called Nishibaru. Our company was in reserve at the time, but we were called forward to fill a gap that L Company had made. We went down into the village and a couple of our platoons got trapped there. At that point, on one of the rare occasions on Okinawa, the Japs launched a *banzai* attack. The machine gunner on our light machine gun was killed and my buddy, who was carrying a BAR, took over the machine gun and slid the BAR over to me. We pumped out lead as fast as we could. Things happened so fast, I don't think I fired any more than four magazines. I learned later as the adrenaline subsided that I had burned my hands on the hot barrel of the BAR. A sergeant in M Company fired a water-cooled machine gun from the hip with the ammunition belt strapped around his shoulder. One of the Japs crawled up right next to him and was ready to lay a grenade in his hip pocket when someone saw him and mowed him down. The Japs came within 20 feet of us, I remember we could clearly see their faces. I don't know if they were hopped up or something, they came on pretty good. I guess we had too much firepower for them, all of a sudden they backed off. They dropped down to the ground into the tall grass. We kept firing into the grass until the attack was over. It was the only time I ever used a BAR and it probably saved my skin that day. The BARs we had were the old World War One kind. They could shoot one round at a time or fully automatic. I was wounded for the second time during that attack by grenade fragments.

The M1, as good as it was, had to be kept clean. If you didn't keep it clean, eventually the humidity would get to it. We had constant moisture on that island. There were a couple episodes of rifles misfiring. The carbines were much worse; they required a lot of care, as did the BARs. In the butt stock of the M1, we kept a brush, some bore patches and a little bit of oil. With that stuff, you could keep your rifle in half decent shape. I also had a shaving brush that I used to keep my rifle free of grit. Your rifle was your best buddy; you had to take care of it. Once you got used to loading the M1 and learned to get your thumb out of the way, we got pretty good at it and could reload very fast. What we did to make sure we wouldn't have to fumble or fish around for another clip, we carried a clip in a rubber band on our helmet. All I had to do was to reach up on the right side of my helmet and pull a second clip down. I heard stories that guys would put a round in the chamber of their rifle and then load a clip of eight rounds, which would give them nine shots. I never experimented with that, I just did it by the numbers. We used to get both the black-tipped armor piercing ammo and the regular ball ammunition. We pretty much took what we got; I didn't have any preference.

Our squad of 12 men had two BARs and the rest carried M1s. The only guy who carried a carbine was the lieutenant. I didn't see too many submachine guns. One of the platoon leaders had one, but he didn't last too long. I had the equipment to launch rifle grenades; I had the launcher and the blanks. I never used rifle grenades and I never talked to anyone who did. In the rifle company, we had the 60 mm mortars right behind us and those guys knew their business.

I was wounded for the third time on Okinawa on the 12$^{th}$ of May. I think a guy from L Company shot me, although I'm not sure. We were attacking and as I was running forward, I could hear the bullets cracking over my head. A bullet doesn't whine when it's close, it cracks. Finally, one caught me in the left shoulder and knocked me down. That's why I think it was a guy from L Company, we were attacking at right angles to each other, we were going to go so far and then swing right to be parallel to them. I think one of them saw us out there a few hundred yards and thought I was a Jap. At that range, you couldn't be sure and I guess he figured shoot first, ask questions later. Whoever it was made a good shot. That wound got me all the way to Guam. I was in the hospital for two months.

When the war ended, the division was in the Philippines. I was on an LST on the way back to the division when the ship's captain announced that the war had ended. They gave each man two cans of beer. With three Purple Hearts, I had enough points where I was among the first from the division to go home.

## US Infantry Weapons In Combat

> **Jim Kendall** *entered the Army in January 1943. After an initial assignment in an anti-aircraft unit in California, he was accepted into the Army Specialized Training Program (ASTP). After the ASTP was canceled in early 1944, he was assigned to the 384th Artillery Battalion in the 103rd Infantry Division. After training in the States, the division landed in France in November 1944 and fought across Europe. After the war ended, he was transferred to the 5th Division and returned to the US to train for the invasion of Japan. However, the war ended before the division was sent to the Pacific and he was discharged in December 1945.*

I entered the Army in January 1943 at Fort Devens, Massachusetts. A group of us were put on a train across the country to Camp Hahn, California. We were assigned to a 90 mm anti-aircraft battalion. I didn't have a regular basic training; I just started training with the unit. We didn't do a lot of weapons training; the concentration was on the operation of the guns. We were out training in the California desert when I experienced my first weapons training. We were issued M1917 Enfield rifles and conducted some squad live fire maneuver drills. I got a little excited during one of the drills and got too far out in front of the others. I guess it scared the lieutenant in charge because he stopped the drill thinking I was about to get shot. We only had the rifles for about a week before they took them away.

I spent four or five months with that unit before I went off to school as part of the Army Specialized Training Program. I went to study engineering at Northeast Junior College in Monroe, Louisiana, which was part of LSU. When the program ended in the spring of 1944, we were sent to a camp near Gainesville, Texas. I can't remember the name of the camp. About half our group was sent to the 103rd Division and the other half went to the 106th Division. I was dumped into the 103rd Division and assigned to the 384th Field Artillery Battalion. I'm not sure why I was put in an artillery unit. In the Army, I've seen cooks driving trucks and truck drivers acting as cooks. I assume because I had been in anti-aircraft, the nearest thing they could get to that was the artillery, so that's where I ended up.

The 384th was a 155 outfit and I was assigned to the detail section in a firing battery of four guns. The section ran the wires to the field phones in the battery and occasionally we furnished people for forward parties. I didn't work with the guns.

During our training, we were issued brand new carbines. We had to clean all the cosmoline off them and I remember we did it using gasoline, which was strictly a no-no. We'd have a bucket of gas in the middle of the room and we'd all throw the parts in it. The parts would get swapped around, but the guns worked just fine.

Personal Experiences

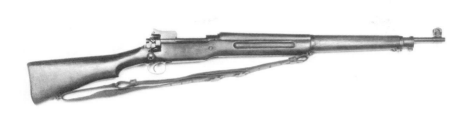

*M1917 rifle. Photo courtesy of Scott A. Duff*

They took us to the range and let us shoot them, but there was minimal training. It wasn't as it should have been at all; it was a real hurry up operation. I was familiar with weapons anyway, there was no problem with how the thing operated, it was a simple little gun. We did go through one of those infiltration courses when they fired live rounds over our heads. They didn't concentrate on any infantry tactics at all because we were in the artillery. I thought the basic training should have been more thorough. I never received any formal marksmanship training during any of my training. I think part of the problem was I joined the outfit as a replacement and I missed out on some of the training.

We landed in Marseille, France in November 1944 and went into the line. We usually set up behind a terrain feature, that's the way a howitzer works best. That way, the flat firing Kraut artillery can't get at you. Sometimes there was no terrain feature in front of us and we would setup a mile or two behind the infantry, sometimes not even that far. Other than pulling guard duty at night around the gun, things were very casual. There probably should have been a lot more security, but we were lucky, nobody gave us a problem. I tried to stay away from the guns as much as I could. Once we got the lines laid, they left our section alone, so we had a lot of freedom. We were able to roam around and explore.

We felt like we weren't armed enough for our defense. Most of us were only armed with carbines; I don't remember anybody even having an M1 rifle. I never fired an M1 rifle during my time in the Army. I remember there was some training on the bazooka. We had one of those in the truck and some of the other sections had them. I missed the training, but I talked to a couple of guys who had fired one, so I knew how to fire it. We had six or eight .50 caliber machine guns that were mounted on our trucks, but they weren't very mobile weapons. Since we'd be moving right in behind the infantry, there'd be dead Krauts and equipment scattered around. We picked weapons up along the way to augment our defenses. Anything that looked interesting, we picked up. At one time we had several German light machine guns that we used on our outposts. We found American weapons as well. There were several M3 grease guns in the unit and we had a Thompson submachine gun.

The grease gun was kind of hairy to operate. The only safety was the cover that was over the firing chamber. Once you opened that cover it was ready to fire and you had to be careful. The rate of fire was very slow, but they worked all right. I shot at a strafing fighter plane with the grease gun one time. I know I didn't have any chance of hitting it, but it made me feel good to shoot. We found the Thompson on a dead American sergeant who had five dead Krauts around him. I thought it was a pretty good ratio if you had to go. I even carried a Springfield sniper rifle that I picked up for a while. Then one day the officers came down and confiscated all our "unauthorized" weapons. Luckily, we never got in a situation where we needed to defend ourselves, although there were some tense times during the Battle of the Bulge.

When the war ended in Europe, we were in Austria. Shortly thereafter, a bunch of us were reassigned to the 5th Infantry Division and came back to the US as part of that unit. The ones with the least amount of points from the 103rd Division came home the soonest because we were supposedly going to the Pacific. They sent us to Camp Campbell, Kentucky, but before we got there they had dropped the A-bomb and the war ended. They kept us there for several months before they discharged us.

Personal Experiences

> **John Taylor** *joined the Army in March 1952 and took his basic training at Camp Breckenridge, KY. Upon completion of his training, he was sent overseas to Japan and then on to Korea. In Korea, he was assigned to the 40th Infantry Division. He spent a little over ten months in Korea before he was returned to the US. He completed his enlistment at Camp Atterberry, IN and was discharged in February 1954.*

I took my basic at Camp Breckenridge, Kentucky, which was a 101st Airborne Division camp. The 101st ran the camp and they trained us. We trained on all the infantry weapons, but very little. Not enough for us to say we were experts on any of them. It was more a familiarization on most of them. I did qualify with the M1 rifle and the machine gun, but we didn't do much live firing beyond the qualifications.

After 16 weeks of basic training, I took leave and then reported to Seattle, Washington where I got on a ship for Japan. I spent about a month in Japan and then I was sent over to Korea. When I got to Korea, I was sent to the 40th Infantry Division and assigned to M Company, 160th Infantry Regiment. When I reported to the company commander, I was in there with three other guys. He asked us which weapons we were proficient in and he got four "mortar" responses. Everyone wanted to be with the mortars. He didn't believe any of us, so he just assigned us where we were needed. He told me I was going to be a machine gunner on a heavy machine gun.

I never received any additional training on the machine gun before I went up on the line. I had learned the basics on the gun in basic training and knew how to break it down and put it back together. I was the gunner, there was an assistant gunner and we had two Koreans who hauled the ammo. My assistant gunner didn't know any more about the gun than I did. I guess we were lucky, we didn't get in any situations where we really had to know what we were doing.

The company occupied its own part of the line, at that time it was strictly a defensive position. When we first went up on line we relieved troops from the 3rd Division. The gun was already in place in a fortified bunker. The positions were permanent positions and the gun always stayed there. The only thing that moved in and out was the people. When we went off the line we left the gun there for the next unit. The company had equipment that was kept in the rear, so when we got back to the rear we always had a gun.

We had searchlights in the hills behind our lines. They would shine their light down the valley towards the Chinese lines almost every night. It would be like day in front of our position. Our patrols would have to move around the illuminated area when they went out. The Chinese never attacked us when the light was on, they only hit us when the lights weren't in operation.

I did do a little bit of shooting over there. We never had any problems with the gun. With it being in the bunker it didn't get very dirty; we would clean it after we fired it. We had the gun hooked up to two or three thousand rounds that we had strung together and stacked on the side. I shot the bunker down one time. It was braced on the corners with angle iron and while I was firing the gun, I fired through the angle iron in one of the corners and collapsed the roof. All it did was give me a smaller hole to shoot through.

Most of the fighting we did was at night. We had one occasion where some Chinese got up by the gun, but they didn't get past it. Our position was on the bank of a river, but up a little bit. A group of them were trying to come through our lines chasing after one of our patrols. They got up pretty close to us and we got six of them with our gun. I think they got careless and didn't know where they were to get that close to us.

We had a crazy, absolutely down right stupid lieutenant, who would get on top of my bunker and fire his rifle with tracer rounds to mark targets for a tank. The tank would fire at the Chinese positions he marked. The Chinese would return fire with mortars and every night the tank would have to go down the hill to be repaired. The mortars couldn't knock it out, but it would suffer damage.

M2 Carbine, selective fire, with 30-round magazine and M4 bayonet affixed. Photo courtesy of Bruce N. Canfield.

They also issued us M1s, carbines and .45s. We only used the .45s when we went to the showers or something like that. We often had to lend our carbines to the infantry because when they went on patrol, they didn't want to go with their M1s. On the patrols, everything was close up and M1s were not good for close up. They were too bulky and hard to handle. You wanted all the firepower you could get. They didn't have enough carbines of their own and needed ours. These were M2 carbines and I had three of those 30-round magazines taped together. I always thought it was unusual that they didn't have carbines of their own. They would come by almost every night and borrow the weapon and ammo. It was weird to loan your rifle to someone. They'd come back after the patrol, give me my carbine and take their M1 back. I was fortunate, since I was in the machine gun squad I didn't have to go on patrols.

After about ten months in Korea, I had enough points to return to the US. I was sent to Camp Atterberry, Indiana and I became a motor sergeant for a medical battalion until my time ran out. I got out just short of two years from the time I enlisted.

# Personal Experiences

> **Don Owens** *was drafted just after his eighteenth birthday in November of 1943. In January 1944, he was sent to Camp McCain, MS and joined the already formed 94th Infantry Division. He took basic and combat training with his unit. The division landed in France in September 1944 and fought through France, in the Battle of the Bulge and then into Germany. Once the war ended, he served in the occupation force in Czechoslovakia. He returned to the US in late 1945 and was discharged in February 1946.*

After a few days at the Induction Center, I left for Camp McCain, Mississippi and joined up with the 94th Division. They had just recently arrived at Camp McCain after completing the Tennessee Maneuvers. So it was with the 94th that I took my basic training. I was assigned to what was called a provisional battalion. There were about fifty of us, and due to the fact that the division had already received their basic training and were then getting their combat training, we were trained separately. That training lasted about ten weeks. We had all been assigned to companies and I was assigned to K Company, 302nd Infantry Regiment. I remained with that company for the duration of the war.

After our basic training with the provisional battalion, we joined assigned companies. Then we received our combat training, which lasted about five months until we went overseas in September of 1944. My MOS at the time was "Rifleman." Then it was changed to "Basic," a different MOS. The definition of a "Basic" was a rifleman who had been trained in the use of all infantry company weapons. So in the event of injuries or the death of a man, the "Basic" could temporarily fill that position until a replacement could be found. That training lasted about a month. I trained with the light .30 cal machine gun, the .50 cal machine gun, the rocket launcher, the flame thrower and rifle grenades.

When we fired the rifle grenades, we were taught to plant the butt of the M1 on the ground and fire it that way. That was unless you thought you were man enough to shoulder fire it. Of course, I had to try it that way. It knocked me back a couple of steps and I had a sore shoulder for a couple of days. It was much more accurate fired from the shoulder, but you had to be a muscle man to do it. Back then I only weighed about 115 pounds. My primary weapon was the M1 Garand, which I qualified expert with. After my MOS change, I also had to qualify with the M1 carbine, which I also made expert with.

The 94th arrived in France shortly after D-Day and remained in France until the December Offensive in the Ardennes. The division went immediately into the thick of it, in the Saar-Moselle triangle, with the responsibility of cracking the Siegfried

# US Infantry Weapons In Combat

Line in that area. I was still carrying the M1 at that time. As far as I'm concerned, the Garand was one of the finest military rifles ever made. Naturally any weapon I carried, I considered reliable, if it was properly cleaned and cared for. Hell, you knew your life depended on that weapon. I normally carried 150 to 200 rounds of ammunition and two or three hand grenades.

Quite often I was carrying a SCR-300 radio. It was kind of cumbersome carrying it and an M1, so I was given a carbine instead. I would carry maybe 100 rounds of ammunition for it. At the same time, I picked up a .45 and carried that as well. Although the .45 was a formidable weapon, I couldn't hit the broad side of a barn door with it at any distance, so I never relied on it as a weapon of choice during combat. I wasn't too impressed with the carbine, though. One day I watched as one of our guys in the company fired about four rounds into an attacking German infantryman and he just kept on coming. Another one of the guys let loose with one round from an M1 and the German dropped like a sack of cement.

A good buddy of mine was a tank commander and when he was wounded, he gave me his Thompson to carry until he returned to the front. The Thompson was also a fine weapon, but not one to rely on for accuracy at any distances. At least, not for me. I did use it for a couple of days on some "harassment patrols"; I don't remember what the Army called it. You infiltrated into enemy territory and stirred up a little trouble. I think it was just to let them know that you were around. Nobody usually questioned which weapon you carried. I had my .45 with me and decided to bring the Thompson. My buddy only had four clips of ammo on his pistol belt when he let me use it, so that was all I carried. We got into a little firefight with the enemy which didn't last but a few minutes, so that was the extent of my using it in combat. However, I enjoyed playing with it and I think I reduced the rat population in Germany by a good margin. Quite often we were up against the 11th Panzer Division; many of their troops carried the 9 mm Schmeisser, which was also a very good weapon.

One time, one of the squad leaders asked me to grab a rocket launcher and said we were going to ambush a Kraut tank that had been reported near our area. He knew I had fired the bazooka many times in the States, but he had never fired one. I showed him how to load it and stay out of the back blast. We waited behind some bushes and sure enough, after about a half hour we heard it rumbling down the road. As the tank came toward us, he loaded the round and we waited for a shot. I fired and to our amazement, the rocket just glanced off of the turret, and didn't explode. Just as we were about to load and fire another round, the tank stopped. I guess they had heard the round hit the turret. We took one more shot and the same thing happened. This time the turret swung around in our direction, so we quickly beat feet. Some of the earlier bazooka rounds were round at the front, and there were many complaints from the troops that the rounds were just

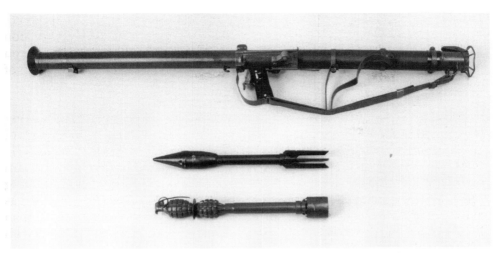

*M9A1 2.36-inch bazooka with sling, practice rocket and and twin piggyback fragmentation grenade rocket. Courtesy of the Robert G. Segel collection.*

glancing off of targets unless they were fired straight on and not at an angle. Later rounds were pointed on the front and proved to be more effective. As you probably know, many lessons in combat had to be learned the hard way.

During the war, I ended up as a communications sergeant. When the war ended, we went to Czechoslovakia in the Army of Occupation. I left the division to come home just after Thanksgiving 1945. I was subsequently discharged from Indiantown Gap, Pennsylvania in February 1946.

> **Tom Bartelson** *enlisted in the Marine Corps in August 1940. He took boot camp at Parris Island, SC and was sent to a Marine brigade on Guantanamo Bay for his first assignment. He returned to the US and joined the 1st Marine Division as it was forming at Quantico. The division was deployed overseas in April 1941. He landed with the 7th Marines on Guadalcanal in September 1942 and spent six months on the island. After resting and refitting in Australia, the division saw action in New Britain and Peleliu. Mr. Bartelson was wounded on Peleliu, which ended the war for him. He left the Marines in 1948 and later joined a reserve unit. During the Korean War, he was recalled to active duty. In 1953, he was sent to Korea and served a year with the 1st Marine Division. Mr. Bartelson spent a little over twenty-six years in the Marine Corps before he retired as a major in 1966.*

I enlisted in the Marine Corps on 27 August 1940, when I was 16 years old. I lied about my age; they took my word for it and let me in. Back then, the Marines had a recruiting poster that said "Travel, Adventure and Education." The Marines took on a high school drop out and when I left the Marine Corps, I had two college degrees and a good combat record.

I thought our training at Parris Island was excellent. We primarily trained with the M1903 Springfield rifle and the bayonet. They demonstrated the .45 caliber pistol, the BAR and the water-cooled M1917 machine gun for us. I thought the 03 was a monster! The recoil was so strong. If you didn't hold that rifle tight like we were taught, it would bite you. I thought that most of the young Marines were afraid of that weapon. There were many split lips and you'd get a big blue hickey on your arm if it wasn't held tight against your shoulder. Some guys shot well with it and some didn't. The best shots around to start off with were the country boys. They had rifles of their own for hunting and they knew how to shoot. I did awful when I first qualified with the 03; I only qualified as marksman. Over time, I eventually qualified as a sharpshooter and then as an expert. The 03 was an extremely accurate rifle; it was good we had it when we had it in World War One and early World War Two.

Back then, you were issued a rifle at Parris Island and it went with you wherever you went. Later they stopped doing that. When we got our rifles, they had been in cosmoline since World War One. When you went on liberty, you carried your full sea bag and a rifle. What did you need a rifle for in downtown San Diego? My rifle serial number was 858123. I kept that same 03 until I became a squad leader and was issued a .45 pistol.

Personal Experiences

My first assignment after boot camp was Guantanamo Bay where I was a rifleman in the 1st Marine Brigade. The brigade had about 1,500 men in it, but then we started expanding. Things were starting to happen over in Europe and we got more people and more weapons. While I was in Guantanamo, we did some training with the water-cooled .50 caliber machine gun. They qualified Marines with those weapons fleet wide because they had the same .50 caliber's on the ships back then.

I spent about eight months at Guantanamo and then I returned to the US. I was assigned to the 1st Antiaircraft Machine Gun Battery at Quantico. They used the water-cooled .50 caliber machine guns as anti-aircraft weapons. They were forming the 1st Marine Division while I was there and I transferred to the weapons company in the 3rd Battalion, 7th Marines. When I first got there, I was an ammo humper in a machine gun squad. I worked my way up to be the gunner and then squad leader. We still had the water-cooled .50 caliber machine gun. There were eight people in a machine gun squad; a squad leader, gunner, assistant gunner and the rest were ammo bearers. The squad leader and the gunner had pistols and the rest had rifles.

After Pearl Harbor, the 7th Marine Regiment was the first stateside Marine unit to be sent overseas. In late February or early March 1942, we got on a train and went to San Diego. From there, we got on a ship and we went to Samoa. I think at first they didn't know where they were going to send us, they just wanted to get some more Marines in the Pacific. They thought that the next move by the Japs would be in Samoa. But the Japs started to build that airstrip on Guadalcanal and that would have been a whole lot of trouble.

The division landed on Guadalcanal on August the 7th, 1942 minus my regiment, which was still in Samoa. The 7th Marines landed on the island on the 18th of September. By that time, Henderson Field had already been taken. Our weapons through the Guadalcanal Canal campaign were still the World War One era weapons. Our rifles were 03s, our pistols were M1911s, our .30 calibers were water-cooled and we were still using the water-cooled .50. When we landed, I was still the squad leader in the machine gun squad and being the squad leader, I carried a .45 pistol. My pistol's serial number was 22707. I never used my pistol in combat, but I did use an 03. I picked one up and used it during a Japanese attack one night, but I didn't keep it. All of our firefights with the Japs were at night; the Japs were night fighters. Because of that, the engagement ranges were short. Our platoon sergeant was killed in a Jap attack one night and I got his Thompson submachine gun. I carried that along with my pistol for a period of time. I had it if I needed it, but I never fired a shot out of that Tommy gun before I turned it in.

We'd dig our .50s in on top of hills, on the high ground. We dug holes for the guns where you could sweep the gun around 360 degrees. Jeeps would bring ammo up to our positions. I remember one day, it was about 1:00 in the afternoon, when everybody is looking around. This guy in his Betty bomber, some hot shot, went flying past us just above the jungle. We fired on him, but I don't think we hit him. Later on he came back and some of our guys on another hill got him. We fired at Jap airplanes any time they came near us. The .50 was a good reliable weapon; we never had any problems with them. In the Marine Corps, we always cleaned our weapons every day. In the machine gun squad, our gunner took care of the gun.

After six months on Guadalcanal, the division went to Australia to recuperate. While we were there we received new equipment. The M1 rifle, the carbine and the air-cooled .50 caliber replaced our older weapons. We were happy to get the M1; the 03 was an excellent weapon, but it didn't have the firepower. The M1 had an eight round clip and it was easier to load. It also didn't give you a split lip or bruise your shoulder.

While we were in Australia, the powers that be decided that the .50 was too big of a weapon for us to be hauling around. It was a big load, the weapon weighed about three or four hundred pounds. We had air superiority, so we didn't need anti-aircraft guns in an infantry battalion. When they took the .50s away from us, I didn't have anything to do. We were waiting to see what was going to happen to us. After working with the .50 all that time, I didn't really want to have to step down to the .30 caliber. One day, I happened to be looking at the battalion bulletin board and it said the intelligence section was looking for replacements. I went to the first sergeant and I got into the battalion intelligence section. When the division went to New Britain, I was a scout.

When the new weapons came in, the SOP was if a guy had a pistol, turn it in and get a carbine. It took me about five years to get good with that damned pistol. A lot of guys did it faster. I thought the carbine gave us a better weapon. It gave you more firepower. The pistol only held seven rounds, the carbine had a 15-round magazines. The pistol was only good out to 25 to 30 yards, but the carbine was effective well beyond that. I heard a story about a couple of gunnery sergeants who shot the carbine on the standard rifle range at Quantico. These were real dinger guys and they qualified expert with the carbine.

Something that people forget, the sole reason for the carbine was to replace the pistol. A lot of guys would say the carbine was no good. They said it was too small and it would jam on you if you didn't clean it every day. They would also say "A Jap was coming at me with his bayonet and I shot him three times in the belly with the carbine and he kept on coming." If you shoot someone in the belly with a .22 long rifle, he ain't going to be coming at you; he's going to be holding his belly. I thought the carbine was a good weapon, I never had any problems with mine. I killed Japs with the damned thing!

I served as a battalion scout through New Britain and then Peleliu. Peleliu was six miles long and two miles wide, but not a surveyor's six by two. The island was all hill. You went from the beach and went right up a hill. It was a bad place. When the 1st Marine Division left Peleliu, we had over 7,500 men wounded or killed. I was wounded by shrapnel on Peleliu and evacuated to a hospital on New Caledonia. That ended World War Two for me.

After the war I wanted to stay in the Marine Corps. As soon as the war ended, they started taking all of our people away from us and changing everything. The barracks were half-empty all the time. I wanted to be a platoon sergeant, but with the Corps getting so small I knew I'd never get promoted. So I reluctantly got out of the Marines and went to the University of Florida. A friend of mine was in a Marine Reserve aviation unit in Jacksonville and told me about it. I was able to get a billet in the unit as Intelligence NCO. Later I got a commission and then I was called back to active duty in February 1951.

I went over to Korea in 1953, the last year of the war. I went back to the $3^{rd}$ Battalion, $7^{th}$ Marines, the same outfit I was with in World War Two. When I reported in, I started looking around and there were a lot of people I knew from World War Two. I became the executive officer of the weapons company. Then I made captain and I became the commander of the company. In Korea, in our weapons company we had three machine gun platoons, an anti-tank platoon and an 81 mm mortar platoon.

We did a hell of a lot of fighting while I was there. It was trench warfare, which was stupid. We'd go out at night and kill their people and they'd come in the next night and kill your people. We moved around a little bit, but stayed on the same line up near the $38^{th}$ parallel. They signed the armistice while I was there, but it didn't change the length of my tour. I spent a year in Korea before I returned to the States.

# US Infantry Weapons In Combat

> **Bud Warnecke** *was drafted in October 1942 and joined the paratroops. He joined the 508th Parachute Infantry Regiment at Camp Blanding, FL and took his basic training there. After basic, the regiment went to Fort Benning, GA for parachute training and trained at Camp Mackall, NC until going overseas in December 1943. After additional training in the UK, the regiment was attached to the 82nd Airborne Division for the Normandy invasion. Mr. Warnecke made combat jumps into Normandy and Holland, receiving a battlefield commission after the Normandy campaign. He also fought with the regiment in the Battle of the Bulge. After World War Two he remained in the Army and served 10 months in Korea in 1952 with the 5th Combat Regiment Team. He retired from active duty in 1964 after 22 years of service.*

I was drafted in October 1942 and joined the parachute troops right from civilian life. I went to Camp Blanding, Florida where they organized the 508th Parachute Regiment. It was primarily made up of people coming directly from civilian life except the cadre. The cadre were all professional soldiers who were airborne qualified. We took our basic training there and then went to parachute school as a regiment.

At Camp Blanding, we trained basically with the M1 rifle and everyone qualified with it. We trained with the 03 some, but it all depended on what your job assignment was. The 03 was used as a sniper rifle. We didn't have very many of them, maybe one in every platoon. After we finished jump school, we went into advanced weapons training out at Camp MacKall, North Carolina. We learned to fire all the weapons in the battalion. We trained with the Thompson submachine gun, in fact that's what I carried into Normandy. We also trained with the 2.36-inch bazooka and the machine gun. The weapons company had the water-cooled machine gun and the rifle companies had the air-cooled guns. I was a 60 mm mortar squad leader in B Company. The 60 mm mortar was a good close in mortar for an infantry platoon; we trained quite a bit with the mortar before we went overseas. The Thompson was the standard issue weapon for the mortar squad leader.

We departed for overseas on the 28th of December 1943. We went to Ireland first and did a lot of night training and then we went on to England where we continued to train for the invasion. We were attached to the 82nd Airborne Division for the invasion and then for the duration of the war.

For the Normandy jump, I had a heavy load of equipment. I didn't put my Thompson in a case. I slung it over my shoulder with the barrel pointed down and then had the strap from my reserve chute around it. It was tight along my side. I also carried a .45 pistol, an anti-tank mine, hand grenades, gammon grenades and all kinds of ammunition for the Thompson. I think I had at least ten magazines for it.

On the drop into Normandy, we were scattered so much and so many people got lost that I wound up being designated a platoon leader and took a platoon all through Normandy. All we had were rifle squads; we didn't have any mortars or machine guns. We fought for 33 days without relief or replacements. We didn't run out of ammunition, there was plenty of it around. We picked it up off our casualties and found some equipment bundles. With attachments, our company jumped with 148 men and when we came out of there we only had 33 men. It was after that I received a battlefield commission to second lieutenant.

When we jumped into Holland in September 1944, I was a platoon leader in E Company. I had been issued a folding stock carbine that I thought was the worst weapon they ever came out with. I was on a combat patrol one night and I had a Kraut skylighted. It was the first time I had a good chance to use the carbine, but when I pulled the trigger all I got was a "click." The German heard the "click" and threw a potato masher at me. Luckily, it was a concussion grenade or I probably wouldn't be here talking to you. We got into a pretty good fight with the Germans after that. That was the last time I carried a carbine. I found another Thompson and carried it for the rest of the time.

We saw quite a bit of combat in Holland. After we jumped in, the Germans counterattacked and we had a good battle. We also did a lot of combat patrols. Holland was very flat and it was tough terrain to fight in. We weren't supposed to stay in Holland for very long, but we wound up staying until November.

I thought the Thompson was a really great weapon, especially close in. It didn't have the rapid fire that the German Schmeisser had, but when that .45 hit someone, they knew they were hit. For accuracy, it wasn't much good beyond 100 yards. It was a reliable weapon, although it wasn't as durable as the M1. You had to keep it clean.

Most of the Germans we fought were pretty good soldiers; their discipline was real good. Most of their weapons were superior to ours, especially their machine guns. The rate of fire from their guns was twice the rate of fire of ours. The only thing we had better was the M1 rifle; it was much better than their rifle. We had BARs in our unit, one per squad. It was an outstanding weapon.

After Holland we went to France and we received replacements and new equipment. Then we were called up for the Battle of the Bulge and went up into Belgium. We saw heavy fighting during that battle. After the Bulge, they detached us from the 82nd and we became a separate regiment again. We went back to France and prepared to jump on some POW camps in Germany. But the situation became so fluid in Germany we didn't make any of the drops.

When the war ended, we went to Frankfurt and became Eisenhower's honor guard. I came home in December 1945. I was hoping to make it home for Christmas, but that didn't work out. I met the 82nd Airborne Division in New York because they lead the Victory Parade down 5th Avenue. I didn't march in the parade, but I observed it. I was supposed to separate from the service, but I changed my mind. I got a letter of acceptance to get into one of the regiments and served with the 82nd for quite a while.

I went to Korea in January 1952; I served with the 5th Regimental Combat Team. It was a real good organization. The regiment was used like a "Fire Brigade"; we were attached to different divisions. The division commanders liked to use us in hot spots in their areas. I had a rifle company for a while, then I became a battalion executive officer. Things were pretty static in the war by then. I had enough points to return to the US in December.

Personal Experiences

*Earl Green while serving in Vietnam.*

**Earl E. Green** *entered the Army in 1949 and spent time at Fort Riley, KS in a training company. He was transferred to Japan and shipped to Korea as an infantry replacement. He was assigned as a rifleman to the Co. G, 35th Infantry Regiment, 25th Infantry Division while they were fighting delaying actions against the North Koreans. They eventually stood their ground in the Pusan Perimeter and made the breakout in September 1950. He spent 14 months in Korea fighting up and down the Peninsula. He arrived in Korea a private first class and departed a master sergeant. Master Sergeant Green spent 20 years in the Army.*

## US Infantry Weapons In Combat

I think I arrived at Camp Drake, Japan in August 1950. I was issued an M1 and was able to zero it while I was there. When I was assigned to G Company, they were somewhere in the boondocks in South Korea. About a week after I arrived, we assumed defensive positions on line in the Pusan Perimeter. In one of my first combat experiences, we were mortared and then attacked several times by the North Koreans during the night. As dawn was breaking, I saw two or three North Korean soldiers and a small horse with an enormous wheeled machine gun on it's back, moving along a ridge about 50 yards from my hole. Firing several clips rapidly with my M1, I shot the horse and several of the North Koreans. I felt bad about shooting the horse.

We received some heavy attacks while we were defending our positions on the Pusan Perimeter. One night during an attack, the enemy killed the guys in the foxhole to my left and got behind us. There was a small ridge between our holes. Somehow my instincts told me to look back and there was an enemy soldier with a burp gun standing on that ridge, skylighted against the starlit sky. We both started firing at about the same time. I took a round in the small of my rifle stock, which broke it. The enemy soldier took a round through the chest and rolled down within a few feet of my foxhole. I shot my rifle for the rest of the night with the broken stock. I swear, the M1 was the most dependable weapon that I was ever exposed to. In the morning, I was able to pick up another rifle.

I also carried a 3.5-inch rocket launcher for a short time. When we first received them to replace the 2.36-inch rocket launchers we had, the platoon had a competition to see who was going to carry it. We were shooting at 55-gallon drum targets. On my first attempt to fire, the guy loading for me didn't fasten one of the wires, so it didn't go off. He then rewired it and when I pulled the trigger again, the rocket fired. I was surprised when it went off and I really wasn't aiming at the time. The rocket struck the 55-gallon drum right at its base, which caused it to shoot up into the air. It was an accident, a lucky hit. With that, I became the platoon rocket man. I never got to shoot it at any enemy armor. When we were fighting the Chinese, one of our tanks threw a tread and it had to be abandoned. We were pulling back, so my commander told me to put a rocket in it so it wouldn't be captured. As I mentioned, I didn't carry the rocket launcher for long. While we were making our withdrawals from fighting the Chinese, I went back to carrying a rifle.

I really liked the M1, it was a tremendous weapon and it never failed me. I'm surprised they ever got rid of it. I normally would carry about 200 rounds of ammo. You had to be careful with loading the clips. Sometimes there would be a long round in the clip that could cause problems with loading. Since we mostly fought in the dark, you couldn't always see if the clip was loaded OK. I learned to always tap the clip against the stock to make sure the rounds were aligned.

We never had any problems with the M1s working in the cold weather, although some of the carbines had problems. Most of the fighting we did was at night, I only remember firing my rifle at the enemy a few times during the day. At night, most of the engagements were at about 30 to 40 yards. You really couldn't see beyond that range. The Chinese had quite a few burp guns and had a firepower advantage on us. I once saw a big .50 caliber rifle. It must have taken two guys to carry it. They also carried some really ancient bolt action rifles.

## US Infantry Weapons In Combat

> **Ralph Carmichael** *was drafted into the Army in 1943 when he was 19 years old. He took 17 weeks of basic training at Camp Blanding, FL. Upon completion of his training, he shipped overseas to England as an individual replacement. He was eventually assigned to the famous 1st Infantry Division, "The Big Red One." He ended up in H Company, 16th Infantry Regiment, which was the 2nd Battalions Heavy Weapons Company. He became an ammunition bearer in a machine gun squad. He landed on Omaha Beach during the D-Day assault on the afternoon of June 6th. He fought with the division through the hedgerow country of France, the breakout near St. Lo, across northern France and into Belgium. He was badly wounded by a shell burst while occupying a captured pillbox on the Siegfied Line just outside of Aachen, Germany. He was reclassified after recovering from his wounds and remained in England until the war ended. He returned to the US in 1946 and was discharged.*

I took the normal 17 weeks of training at Camp Blanding in Florida. They trained us on all the standard infantry weapons. We first qualified with M1903 rifles. They were used as training weapons for marksmanship training. We later qualified with the M1 too. I liked the M1 better than the 03 because it would shoot faster. I also remember shooting the carbine, the .45, the light and heavy machine guns, the 60 mm and 81 mm mortars. I think they trained us on everything because they didn't know where you were going or what kind of unit you would end up in.

After I finished training, I was shipped over to England in March 1943 and was put into a replacement company. Then I joined the 16th Infantry Regiment of the 1st Infantry Division. I was proud to join them; it was an old outfit that had fought in Africa and Sicily. I got in with some veterans and it was quite unique listening to their stories. I have no idea why, but I was sent to H Company, which was a heavy weapons company. I was assigned to a machine gun squad and became an ammo bearer. Since it was so close to the invasion, I didn't get to train much with the unit.

On D-Day, my section didn't go in until later in the afternoon. It was fortunate that we didn't land earlier. The first waves had a real tough time on the beach. As it was, I damned near drowned on the landing because I was weighed down with equipment. I was carrying two cans of ammo for the machine gun, an M1, rifle ammo, a gas mask and some grenades. I barely made it to shore and when I did, I had no rifle and no helmet. I picked another rifle up on the beach and moved inland with the unit.

There were seven men in the machine gun squad. There was the squad leader who was also the number one gunner, the second in command carried the tripod and the third guy carried the water can and a can of ammunition. The rest of the guys carried ammo. I can remember we'd pull the tracers out of the ammo belts. We didn't have flash hiders on our guns like the German machine guns did. If we were firing at night, you could easily pick us out. We thought there were too many tracers in the belts. We'd leave some tracers in the belt because you needed some so you could see where you were shooting. I think we would take two of the tracers out and then skip one and take the next two out and so forth. We'd replace them with regular rounds.

The water-cooled .30 caliber machine gun really was a heavy and cumbersome weapon. I think the whole thing weighed 52 pounds. It was too heavy and bulky and you had to carry water for it. The German machine guns were much lighter and fired faster. They could easily change the barrel quickly when it got hot. It was also very maneuverable too. It took a little time to move our gun around and get it set up. It was a reliable weapon though and was very effective for supporting the people in front of us. Although in my opinion, it wasn't used that much.

In hedgerow country, as a rule we generally had a .50 caliber machine gun in the field next to us to protect us against the Messerschmitts. In the early part of Normandy, they came over regularly.

One time in the town of Mons, Belgium, we set the machine gun up in the second story of a courthouse. We had Germans in the buildings all around the town square and they wouldn't surrender. We were firing into those buildings trying to get them out. We captured numerous prisoners during that battle.

I carried an M1 for most of the time. When we set up the machine gun, I'd drop the ammo off, dig in and then pull security for the gun. The M1 was a good gun, but it got too cumbersome. I traded it in for a carbine. It was lighter, but it didn't have the distance. If you had to go out beyond 200 yards, it wasn't any good. We didn't do too much long range shooting in combat. Most of the engagements were no more than 150 to 200 yards. For the type of fighting we were doing, the carbine did OK. My squad leader didn't care what kind of weapon we carried. One of the guys in the squad carried a Tommy gun.

I also had a .45 that I picked up after the Normandy landing. I had to use my .45 twice in combat. One time in Normandy, we were working from one hedgerow to the next. I can't remember why, but I had the pistol out. The sergeant told me to check around the corner of a hedgerow. When I walked around the corner, there was a wounded German soldier with his gun between his legs. He surprised me and I surprised him. He was sitting there with his gun and it was pointing right at me. I didn't know if he was waiting to ambush one of us, but I didn't wait to see. I shot him with my pistol and that was all she wrote. The .45 was a very effective round.

*M1911A1 .45 caliber pistol. Photo courtesy of Scott A. Duff.*

I got hit when we were fighting outside of Aachen. We had taken over an abandoned German pillbox and had set the gun up to fire out the rear embrasure, which was facing the German lines. We would take turns being on duty manning the gun. If something happened while you were on the gun, then you were the shooter. That night, I happened to be on the gun when I was knocked out with a German 88 shell or a mortar round. I woke up in a field hospital 20 miles behind the front lines not knowing how or who got me there. I didn't find out what had happened until later when I was in England. One of the sergeants wrote me a letter and told me. After that the Army reclassified me and I became an escort guard for the German prisoners and set up POW camps in England.

Personal Experiences

> **J.J. Witmeyer** *joined the Army the week following the attack on Pearl Harbor. In fact, he was so anxious to enter an armed service that he signed up with the Navy, the Marines and the Army. At the time the Army was less concerned with an astigmatism he had in his right eye than the other services, so he was inducted into the Army. While he was in basic training he received word that he had been accepted into the Navy as well. Too late, the Army had him. After his basic training he joined G Company, 314th Infantry Regiment, 79th Division at Camp Pickett, VA. He remained with that unit until the end of the war. The division landed on Utah Beach on the 14th of June and fought across Europe. Tech Sergeant Witmeyer received a battlefield commission during the summer of 1944. He was wounded twice while serving as a platoon leader.*

When I was in basic training, the first rifle I received was an Enfield rifle. It was a long rifle; it came all the way to my armpit. I remember we used them mostly for drill. We did fire them, but we didn't qualify with them. Then we got M1903 Springfield rifles, which we qualified with. The Springfield was the first real rifle I had been given and I really liked it.

I was very used to the Springfield when we were issued M1s in late 1942 while we were at Camp Blanding, Florida. I hated to give up my Springfield, the M1s seemed so different. I noticed that the first M1s were finely machined, nicely made rifles. I thought the later rifles were more crudely made. Once I got used to the M1, I really liked it. The first rifle I had didn't have a hinge on the buttplate like the later ones. At one time during our training, we had to turn the early rifles in for a reissue of newer rifles. I didn't want to exchange my rifle, so I changed the solid butt plate on mine to one of the hinged ones and kept my rifle, even though there wasn't a hole in the stock for the cleaning kit. The new butt plate didn't fit well, but since I was an NCO, I didn't have to stand inspections with it. If I had been a private, I never would have got away with it because there was a gap between the stock and the butt plate.

I fired thousands of rounds though that rifle before we went overseas. I had qualified expert and was a shooting coach for some of the guys who had problems qualifying. I got to do some extra shooting doing that. Most of the time my rifle stayed in the barracks rack. Because I was an NCO, I supervised the other guys during a lot of the training and I didn't carry my rifle. Because of that, my rifle was always in great shape because it was never out in the dirt and sand. One day I got a call to report to the company commander. He asked me where my rifle was and I told him it was in the rifle rack. Somebody had either used my rifle or deliberately took it and let it lay in the sand somewhere. The commander checked my rifle and it was very dirty.

Someone had either played a joke or was getting even with me for something. It took a little work to get it back in shape. Our rifles were kept in excellent condition while we were in training. I kept that rifle all the way through our landing at Normandy and into the fighting in the hedgerow country in France.

After we landed in France and were fighting though the hedgerow country, one of our sergeants had an interesting experience. He had slipped through a break in the hedgerow and had stopped to rest on one of the sunken roads between the hedgerows. He was lighting a cigarette with his rifle resting on his knee when a German officer with a machine pistol popped his head over the hedgerow on the opposite side of the road. The German was no more than 12 feet from the sergeant, but he didn't see him. It startled the heck out of the sergeant and he fired one quick shot from his M1 and scrambled back through the break in the hedgerow to get back with the rest of the platoon. We went back to check the area and found the German officer dead, clutching a machine pistol. The sergeant's one shot had shot him right through the head. I don't know what the German was doing all alone in that place, I guess he was doing a reconnaissance looking for us. He couldn't see us, you couldn't see though those hedgerows. Sometimes the Germans were so close, we could smell them. I'm sure they could smell us too.

One day, that same sergeant was shot through the chest. We made a stretcher by sliding two M1s through the sleeves of an overcoat. After they carried him to the rear, I couldn't find my rifle and realized that they had used it in making the stretcher. That's how I lost that rifle I'd been issued during training in the States.

I really liked the M1; it was a little heavy, but very reliable. The only thing I didn't like about it was the way it "clanged" when the clip flew out of it. It was too noisy. We got into a firefight with the Germans one night and I could hear the clanging of the clips hitting the ground. It was a funny story. We had two replacements in a hole together. One guy was supposed to sleep while the other guy was awake. There was a group of Germans and they must have been lost. As they were trying to find their way through the dark, one of Germans fell into the hole with these two new guys. Both of them must have been sleeping. When the German fell on top of him, one of the guys reached up and felt where the helmet curved in the front and knew it was a German helmet. He screamed! Then everybody starts shooting! I could hear the empty clips clanging. You almost had to go over and slap a guy across the face to get him to stop shooting. They were shooting, which was good, but they weren't shooting at anything. One of the problems we had was the American army didn't shoot enough.

I received a battlefield commission in August 1944. I still had the .45 I had been issued when I was at Camp Blanding in 1942. It was a Colt and it was a heck of a lot better than the Remington and other company's wartime production pistols. My Colt was nicely machined; it was probably a peacetime pistol. I still have it. Anyway, somewhere along the line, I don't remember the details, I commandeered a Thompson submachine gun from a German. He probably got it from a paratrooper or something. I carried that Thompson until I was wounded.

One night, a few of us were in an abandoned German dugout that was on the side of a hill. It was a very stormy and rainy night and the dugout started filling with water. We had to get our weapons and equipment off the floor because of all the water and I propped my Thompson on a shelf the Germans had dug in the wall of the dugout. It rained so hard that the rainwater caused the dugout to collapse. It almost caved in on us; we could barely keep our heads above water as we got out. It turned out that my Thompson had kept the whole wall from falling on us. It supported part of the wood frame when it caved in. It was so dark and there was so much water, I couldn't find it.

I spent that night with only my .45 for a weapon and we were attacked by a large group of Germans with tanks. It was a pretty bad situation. The next day, we counterattacked and I was able to go back to the dugout. There was still some water in it, but most of it had drained out. But I couldn't find my Thompson. A few days later someone told me that a sergeant from E Company had found a Thompson. So I went and paid him a visit and he told me he found the Thompson in the dugout. I told him it belonged to me and he didn't argue about it. So I got it back; it hadn't been damaged.

I really liked the Thompson; they weren't supposed to be good. I tested mine out regularly by throwing something out about 40 feet and making sure I could make it move. I kept my weapon clean, we all did. The Thompson was deadly at close range. One time, I had a German officer come out of a camouflaged foxhole at me. You know, when you're in combat, your weapon becomes part of you. It's like pointing your finger at something. You have no thoughts whatsoever, you just react. I turned and fired six to eight rounds into him and he went right back down into his hole. He was real close. There were at least eight Germans that got within 10 to 12 feet of me that my Thompson disposed of.

After I was wounded, a lieutenant from the Mountain Division asked if he could have my Thompson, so I gave it to him. After I recovered from my wound and was returning to the company, I was issued a carbine at the replacement depot. I never had any confidence in the carbine. After my experiences with the M1 and the Thompson, it seemed like a cap pistol in comparison. When I got back to the unit, I asked for another Thompson and they gave me a brand new one, still in cosmoline. I kept it for the rest of the war and I wanted to carry it home. I carried it all the way to the port when we were getting ready to go home. I was doing the inspecting of goods and souvenirs that people were taking home. I started thinking I was going to get myself in trouble, so I left it standing in the corner of the barracks when I moved out to get on the ship.

*A letter from **Jim Foster** who served with the 96th Division on Okinawa and then with the 86th Division.*

Dear Mark,

I read your request for comments on the Garand M1 rifle in the "Blackhawk Bugle" (86th Div.) I was with the 96th Division on Okinawa, having arrived as a replacement on April 28,1945. I was assigned to the 382nd Regiment, 3rd Battalion, Company L. Usually what stands out are the bad experiences. I called the M1 a "fair weather" piece.

I remember one morning on a hill in Okinawa. This was volcanic territory and this morning was misty. There were 8 or 10 of us on the front in that territory and none of our rifles would fire. We proceeded to tear our rifles down and started cleaning them. A Sergeant walked up and started chewing us out for all having our weapons torn down at one time. He wanted to know what we would do if Japs came of the hill now. I remember telling him, "Hell, we'll throw the pieces at them, for they won't work". He remembered that when he later picked me out for an assignment.

Later we were having a rough time and it started raining. Fellows in a hole next to mine kept cleaning rifles and passing them over to us. We were fortunate to get one shot off before they jammed. Fortunately, the Japs seemed to move further from us. I was hospitalized after that night for about two weeks.

When a group of us were released from the hospital, we were taken to a field ordnance depot. There were piles of different parts for M1s lying around. We were told to put together our own rifles. I remember looking for parts that would give my rifle a "sloppy" fit instead of a tight fit. I can never remember that rifle jamming, but I was never in such adverse conditions with it.

I hope this helps you.

Sincerely,

Jim Foster (former S.Sgt)

PS: When the war was over I did not have enough points to come home. I was transferred to the 86th Division to complete the rest of my service.

Personal Experiences

> **Lawrence D. Schubert** *volunteered for the draft after he turned 18 in June of 1943 and he was called to service in September 1943. He took basic training at Fort McClellan, AL and upon completion, was sent overseas as an infantry replacement. He was assigned to K Company, 16th Regiment, 1st Infantry Division as a replacement shortly after D-Day. He fought with that unit through France, Belgium and Germany until the conclusion of the war. He returned to the US in December 1945 and was mustered out of the Army.*

I trained with the Springfield 03 rifle in basic training. It was the first rifle I'd ever fired, I remember that it had a little bit of a kick. I qualified as a sharpshooter with it. We also learned to disassemble and assemble the air-cooled .30 caliber machine gun and fired it for familiarization. I never saw an M1 during training at Fort McClellan and I don't recall training with the BAR or the carbine, either.

I was sent overseas as an infantry replacement. I arrived in Ireland in April 1944 and was assigned to a replacement depot camp. After about a month, they moved us to another camp in England. We were trained on the M1 rifle while I was in the depot. We were taught how to take it apart, clean it and put it back together again. I don't remember firing it during training. I was issued my own M1 during that time as I remember that I had one when I boarded the ship to cross the channel over to France. I found out later that we were slated from the time we got on the troop ship to go to the 16th Regiment.

I joined K Company on D + 7 and was assigned as first scout. I guess the previous first scout was an invasion casualty. The first scout led the squad whenever we were on the attack. Later on during the campaign I became the bazooka man for our squad. I had never trained on the bazooka nor did I have an opportunity to fire the bazooka in combat. I just never saw any tanks. The bazooka was the single piece version and the sidearm was a .45 caliber grease gun. I heard it said that if you knocked out a tank with a bazooka, you received a Silver Star. The German tanks were almost impervious to our tank fire or bazooka fire. Your only chance was to hit a tread or some other lightly armored part of their tanks to effect damage, hence the award offer. On the other hand, the German 88 mm gun would punch a hole in our tanks. Or, their panzerfaust would open a large hole in the front armor of our tanks. I saw a tank hit by an 88 with an entry hole in the front and an exit hole in the back!

The grease gun, along with the bazooka, three rounds of bazooka ammo and ammo for the grease gun was a terrible load. I carried four magazines for the grease gun, one in the weapon and three more in a pouch. The gun and ammunition was heavy.

My sidearm should have been a carbine to save weight. I was a young guy back then and it never occurred to me to get rid of the grease gun and pick up a carbine. The guys in the 60 mm mortar squad had been issued carbines as a sidearm. They all decided that they would carry .45s instead. Then one time the Germans broke through our lines and they had to fight off an attack with those pistols. You couldn't hit a barn from the inside with one of those things. The next day, those guys all were carrying carbines again. As far as the grease gun was concerned, that thing was slow firing, not accurate at any distance and too heavy. I did fire it on a couple of occasions. We were doing marching fire during an attack across a large open field toward the Germans in a wooded area. We were marching along trying not to shoot the guy next to us. I found that if you didn't have tracers for it you couldn't tell where the rounds were going.

On one occasion, in Belgium, during the Battle of the Bulge, we attacked a German position in a wooded area on top of a hill overlooking our defense position. After securing the hill, we took turns using the bunkers the Germans had constructed to warm up. Remember that it was freezing cold during that campaign. Well, we made the mistake of bringing our weapons in with us. It was warm and humid in there and when we went outside, the condensation on our weapons froze. After a while, the Germans counterattacked. We tried to fire at them, but our weapons were frozen and would not function. I took my grease gun apart, in the dark, throwing all of the parts into my helmet, wiping off all the parts including the ammo in the magazines, but it still would not fire. My foxhole mate, who had a BAR, had the same problem. He urinated on the receiver and was able to thaw it out enough to get it working when the Germans were just a few feet away. We stalled their attack just long enough to call for mortar fire and were ordered to retreat to our previous position. The Germans chased us all the way down the hill with rifle and machine gun fire. I could see the tracers whizzing all around us. I'm sure we could have held that position if our guns had worked.

Later, I was assigned as wireman for the platoon and reverted to the M1 again. The M1 was a great rifle, although when the stock became water soaked it sometimes expanded. Then the trigger mechanism would become a "hair trigger." The only solution was to change stocks. I remained a wireman until the end of the war.

I spent about six months in Germany after the war ended. Then I was transferred to the 79th Division and we sailed out of Marseilles, France for the States in November 1945. Once we got to the US they mustered us out of the Army pretty quickly.

## Personal Experiences

> **Tom Twomey** enlisted in the Army in 1947. He took basic training at Fort Dix, NJ and following that, he went overseas. He served in Korea and Japan before he returned to the US with the intent of leaving the Army once his enlistment was up. When the Korean War broke out, he was involuntarily extended for one year. He went back overseas with the 15th Regiment of the 3rd Infantry Division. The division made the amphibious landing at Wonsan, North Korea with the X Corps in the fall of 1950. After heavy fighting with Chinese divisions in harsh winter conditions, the Corps was evacuated by sea to South Korea. They were landed at Pusan and began driving the Chinese north back to the 38th Parallel. After a year of combat duty, Mr. Twomey left Korea as a staff sergeant. He elected to stay in the Army and served in many different assignments over the years. After joining Special Forces, he served in Vietnam for a year. After 31 years of service he retired from the Army as a sergeant major.

I joined the Army on August 28th 1947 and went to Fort Dix for basic training. We did very little weapons training there. We didn't even have weapons until two weeks before range firing. Before that we just had sticks. When they gave us our M1 rifles, they took them out of a box and gave them to us to clean. These weren't new rifles, they were used rifles that were wrapped in protective paper and covered with cosmoline. There weren't enough soldiers to clean each rifle, so we each had to clean two rifles.

The marksmanship training we got wasn't very good. Most of it was on proper sight alignment, which was the most important thing. We also did a lot of dry firing behind the range. The bad thing was they didn't teach us proper zeroing techniques. The problem was they didn't have experienced cadre, most of the trainers were corporals.

Back then the standard qualification table was firing ten rounds standing at 100 yards, then you moved back to the 200-yard line and fired another ten rounds from the kneeling or sitting position. Then you went from the standing position to the sitting position, rapid fire. You fired two rounds, reloaded and fired eight more. From there you went to the 300-yard line and fired again from standing to the prone position, the same method, two rounds and then eight rounds. Finally, you moved back to the 500-yard line and did the same thing. I think I bolo'd the first time I fired qualification and had to go back and requalify. Qualifying with the M1 was the only weapons training I did at Fort Dix.

After basic, I was sent to Korea and assigned to the 6th Division. It was 1948 when Syngman Rhee became the President of South Korea. There were no firing ranges in Korea, so we didn't do any weapons training. We did a lot of forced marches and riot control training. I was there for a year, then the Koreans threw us out and we went to Japan. In Japan, I was assigned to the 24th Division. There was very little training there; we didn't have much equipment. It's like they were downsizing from World War Two and all the equipment was in depots. I was in Japan for about a year and a half; it was beautiful duty. We never trained. The 24th was the first division to go to Korea when the war started. You know what happened to those untrained troops.

When I left Japan, I went to the 3rd Infantry Division at Fort Benning. While I was there we mostly did KP duty, range details and things to support the ROTC and Army Reserve training. That's about all we did. It was during that time while I was on range detail that I got to do a lot of firing. I would just go off to the side of the range, put down a sandbag and do my own shooting. I practiced and I got better. This was in 1950 and I was getting ready to get out of the Army. I was actually out-processing. When I was trying to get my final pay at the finance office, I found out that I'd been extended one year because of the war in Korea. We called that the "Truman Year." I was in the 30th Infantry Regiment and they transferred me to the 15th Regiment. They were deactivating the 30th and they wanted to fill up the 15th. We got on a troop train to California and from there we went to Japan. We were issued some weapons in California and everybody fired different weapons off the tail of the ship on the way to Japan. They'd throw trash over the side and we shot at it. We fired the BAR, the M1 and M2 carbine and the M1 rifle. We also familiarized with the 2.36 rocket launcher. We zeroed our rifles while we were on the ship or we attempted to zero them. It was real flaky, but when you're 19 years old it was a lot of fun. It really wasn't very effective though.

When we got to Japan, the division was at one-third strength; we picked up our up KATUSAs (Korean Augmentation United States Army) while we were there. For every rifle squad, there were ten KATUSAs per squad and an American squad leader and assistant squad leader. We didn't speak Korean and they didn't speak English, you can imagine how that went. We were reissued weapons and trained there for a few months.

From Japan, we landed in Wonsan, North Korea. At that point, we were still fighting the North Koreans. When we made the landing I was a rifleman, but when the guy with the 2.36 got killed, they gave it to me. I traded my rifle for a .45 caliber pistol. The 2.36-inch rocket launcher didn't work well, the rounds just bounced off their tanks. As soon as they figured out the 2.36 wasn't worth a damn, they issued us the 3.5-inch rocket launcher. I was the gunner and I had an assistant gunner/ammo bearer. I didn't carry any ammo for it; the ammo bearer had a vest that slipped over his head that carried six rounds. With the 3.5, you needed someone to load for you. We used those on people, even though the rockets had a shaped charge. The Chinese would come down at us in hordes and my job was to try to hit right into the mass of them. The problem we had with the 3.5 was they failed to tell us we had to bore-sight those things. I didn't know what bore-sighting was. So when I fired it, it wasn't effective because it wasn't bore sighted. We had to learn these things on the battlefield, which made it quite difficult.

Then I became a machine gunner with the M1919A4/A6 machine gun. The A4/A6 was the same basic machine gun; you just modified it as needed. It was the A4 when it was on the tripod, then you put on an extended stock and a bipod on it and it became the A6. In a defensive position, we put it on the tripod and in the offensive mode, you used the bipod and the extended stock. I was in the heavy weapons squad of a rifle platoon. In the platoon there were three rifle squads and a 12-man heavy weapons squad. There were two machine guns in the squad. I was the gunner; there was an assistant gunner and an ammo bearer. We carried quite a bit of ammunition. Each man carried four boxes of ammo, 250 rounds per box as I recall. They'd strap two of them around their shoulder on a belt and then they carried two. It was quite a load and we made some long marches carrying it all. I loved that weapon, although you had to keep it clean. I'd say for the conditions we were fighting in, it was pretty reliable. We had stoppages sometimes, but most of the stoppages were because of the ammunition they gave us. Some of the rounds just wouldn't fire and we'd have to recock and reload the gun. About half the time, we had to take rounds from M1 clips and reload the cloth belts. Sometimes we even got loose ammo in boxes.

A lot of the ammo, equipment and food we received was World War Two surplus that had been stockpiled somewhere. We got grenades that went off prematurely, artillery rounds that fell short or wouldn't fire at all. We got rations that were dated 1943! We used to get cases of World War Two ammo that came on Springfield five-round stripper clips. We'd have to take those rounds and load them into M1 clips while we were on the line fighting the Chinese. Sometimes we had problems with bent or dirty clips, causing malfunctions in our rifles. After about six or seven months, we finally started getting the stuff we needed over there. Most of the ammunition we used was standard ball ammunition, although sometimes we got the black tipped armor piercing rounds.

Later, when we were fighting in South Korea, I became the company sniper. At the time I was still the machine gunner, but I told them I could shoot and they gave me a rifle and the sniper job. The rifle was an M1 with a scope, a cheek pad and a cone shaped flash hider. The scope mounted on the side of the rifle with a few bolts. As I recall, it was very hard to zero with that scope. I was more comfortable shooting with open sights, so I didn't use the scope. It didn't make any difference to me because I was pretty good with the rifle. I'd go out at night and set up in a position overlooking the Han River. Then during the day, I would shoot at the Chinese on the other side of the river. The next night, I'd infiltrate back into our lines. If they didn't spot me, I'd stay out there for couple of days. Sometimes when I got up there, if there was no activity, I would fire a few rounds and zero in on certain points. Then I'd wait. If someone came into one of those points and started looking around with a pair of binoculars, like a lot of them did, I'd nail them. I made shots out to 600 to 700 yards. I felt like I was gifted to be able to shoot well that far. There was no doubt about it; I was good with the M1. It just fascinated me that the rifle could do those things at those ranges. I was only the sniper for about three weeks, as long as we were working in that AO that was my job. Then I went back to machine gun squad.

When I became an assistant platoon sergeant, I picked up an M1 again. While we were fighting in the mountains of North Korea, the conditions were awful. It got as cold as 22 degrees below zero. Because of the extreme cold we were wearing gloves, sometimes it was hard to load the M1. Most of the time, I had to remove my glove to reload. Other than that, I don't recall ever having any big problems with the rifles because of the cold. I remember we had problems with the machine guns, trying to keep them from freezing up on us. If the gun stopped, we'd just pee on the weapon and that took care of it. I treated my M1 like a baby; I slept with it, kept it in the sleeping bag with me. It was important to keep it dry and clean. My rifle never failed to fire. There were nights when the Chinese attacked that I fired hundreds of rounds and never had a problem. Now we did experience problems because of the ammunition, as I mentioned.

I thought that the M1 was more effective than any of the individual weapons carried by the Chinese. They had some old US grease guns, SKSs, Russian burp guns and a lot of different bolt-action rifles. They weren't very effective; sometimes it was hard to tell if they were shooting at you or someone else. That's how erratic their firing was. They would hit us in human wave attacks and a lot of times the first three ranks were the only ones who had weapons. The ones in the rear didn't have weapons. They would pick up weapons from their comrades who got shot and keep on going. They would overrun a lot of positions that way. Those attacks were scary; they blew bugles and whistles and always seemed to attack at two in the morning. If they failed to overrun the positions, they would back off and disappear by first light. You hardly ever saw them during the day.

I eventually became a platoon sergeant while I was in Korea. A lot of the other platoon sergeants carried the carbine; they were lighter and easy to carry. I didn't care too much for the carbine; I elected to stay with my M1 because I was comfortable with it. With the 30.06 round, once you hit an enemy soldier, he was down for the count.

After the war, I was assigned to the Berlin Brigade. When I was in Berlin, they had a place called Kerns Range. It was almost like an indoor KD range, although it only went out to 300 yards. For 100 to 300 yards, it was great. We did a lot of firing over there because there wasn't anything else for us to do. If we trained, we had to train in a park. So we did a lot of marching, a lot of drill, a lot of ceremonies and a lot of firing. I got married and back then a married soldier couldn't be stationed in Berlin, so I was transferred to an armored infantry battalion in the 2nd Armored Division.

While I was in there, I tried out for the Le Clerc Match Team. This is where you run and shoot while you are timed. It was a long time ago, but I think you started from the 100-yard line. You'd fire ten rounds from the standing position and run your ass off back to the 200-yard line. Then you'd get in the kneeling position and fire again. From there, you'd run like hell to the 300-yard and fired from the prone. Then you ran back to the 500 or 600-yard line and fired again. I think the total possible score was 131 or something and when I tried out, I scored a 129. I only missed two shots. So they put me on their Le Clerc Team. That's how I started firing on Army rifle teams. The first team I was on was the 2nd Armored Division's rifle team. We fired against the British, French and other European army teams. We used the standard M1s on the team. Although these were rifles that didn't get beat up or taken to the field. They were nice rifles that were only used for shooting.

After I left Germany, I went to Fort Meyer, Virginia and they immediately put me on the MDW (Military District of Washington) Rifle Team. The team had an assigned school trained armorer who was skilled in modifying the rifles. He modified the important parts of the rifle like the op rod, trigger and gas port. He also took the rear sight elevation and windage knobs and modified them so that one click was a quarter inch instead of an inch. That's when I first saw glass bedding on the rifles. If we were on the firing line and having problems with a rifle, a lot of times he could make adjustments right there. We had a large arms room and building for the team. One of our responsibilities was to teach marksmanship to the whole regiment. So we were instructors as well as being on the team. We would fire matches against everybody, other Army teams, the Marines and the Navy.

Before you could go to the Camp Perry match, you had to shoot in the All-Army Matches down at Fort Benning. This is where the all-army marksmanship detachment would pick up shooters for their teams. They selected the best shooters from all the division shooting teams and had them reassigned to the detachment. Getting assigned to the detachment was very prestigious and a great thing if you were single. Since I was married and had a family, I didn't want to be assigned to the detachment.

I fired in the National Matches at Camp Perry in 1958. I did quite well; I think I picked up 15 medals for different things. That was the first time we fired at 1,000 yards. We got some instruction on shooting at targets that far. When we got out there, I think I missed maybe one shot out of the bull. I thought it was fantastic! I couldn't believe we could shoot that far. We used a spotting scope to look at the

300-yard line and watched the mirage. That's how we determined which way we were going to set our sights. If you missed with the first two spotter rounds, you might as well pick up and go home. But if you hit anywhere on that frame, then you could make sight adjustments and get into the center of that bull. I hit ten bulls with ten shots at 1000 yards using an M1 rifle with open sights.

I used the M14 too, but I didn't like it as well as the M1. I used the M14 at Camp Perry one year because that's the rifle the army teams were using. I always liked the M1 better; to me the M14 didn't work as well. It wasn't as smooth. I also didn't like the magazine. I guess as a combat weapon the 20-round magazine was a good thing, but it made it harder to hold for competition shooting. If you wanted to have real good accuracy, it didn't compete with the M1.

I went to airborne school and was assigned to the 101st Airborne Division at Fort Campbell, Kentucky. When they found out about my shooting background, they put me on the division rifle team. The 101st competed with all the other units; it was a big thing. By then, every unit had their own specialized marksmanship unit with trained armorers to work on the weapons. It was also the first time I used a National Match M1. I was shooting pretty well back then. I think I was averaging about 248 points on the standard 250-point KD range tables.

We had a big division exercise and they made everyone go to it. So I missed getting my third leg at Camp Perry, which would have given me my third distinguished badge. Then I got orders to go to Germany and from that time on, I didn't fire in any more matches.

# Glossary

| | |
|---|---|
| AO | Area of Operations |
| AP | Armor Piercing |
| ASTP | Army Specialized Training Program |
| AWOL | Absent Without Leave |
| BAR | Browning Automatic Rifle |
| CP | Command Post |
| CO | Commanding Officer |
| DMZ | Demilitarized Zone |
| ETO | European Theater of Operations |
| FO | Forward Observer |
| HE | High Explosive |
| HEAT | High Explosive Anti-Tank |
| HQ | Headquarters |
| KD | Known Distance |
| KP | Kitchen Police |
| LP | Listening Post |
| LST | Landing Ship, Troops |
| LVT | Landing Vehicle, Tracked |
| MASH | Mobile Army Surgical Hospital |
| MG34/42 | German light machine gun |
| MLR | Main Line of Resistance |
| MOS | Military Occupational Specialty |
| MP | Military Police |
| NCO | Non Commissioned Officer |
| OCS | Officer Candidate School |
| OP | Observation Post |
| P38 | German pistol |
| PTO | Pacific Theater of Operations |
| POW | Prisoner Of War |
| ROTC | Reserve Officer Training Corps |
| S-3 | Unit Operations Officer |
| SKS | Russian Carbine |
| TO&E | Table of Organization and Equipment |
| UK | United Kingdom |
| VE Day | Victory Europe Day |
| VJ Day | Victory Japan Day |
| WP | White Phosphorus |
| XO | Executive Officer |

# About the Author

Mark G. Goodwin retired from the US Army after 20 years of active duty. He entered the Army in 1979, enlisting as an airborne infantryman. After completing basic training and airborne school at Fort Benning, GA, he was assigned to the 2nd Battalion, 505th Infantry, in the 82nd Airborne Division at Fort Bragg, NC. While serving with the 82nd Airborne, he applied for and was accepted to attend the Warrant Officer Rotary Wing course at Fort Rucker, AL. He graduated from flight school and was appointed as a Warrant Officer in 1982. His first aviation assignment was as an aeroscout pilot in the 2nd Squadron, 10th Cavalry, 7th Infantry Division at Ford Ord, CA. During the next 17 years, he served in various aviation units, which included three tours of duty with the 2nd Infantry Division in the Republic of Korea. He also participated in Operation Desert Shield and Desert Storm while serving with the 2nd Squadron, 17th Cavalry in the 101st Airborne Division. He completed his service as a Chief Warrant Officer (CW4) at Fort Bragg in 1999. CW4 Goodwin was awarded Master Aviator Wings, the Parachutist Badge, Air Assault Badge and the Expert Infantryman's Badge. He currently lives in Fayetteville, NC.

# Related M1 Garand Books from Scott A. Duff Publications

### THE M1 GARAND OWNER'S GUIDE

(Volume 1 of Owner's Guide Series)

by Scott A. Duff
ISBN 1-888722-03-7
6"x 9" softbound, 125 pages, 49 photos, 84 line drawings
$19.95 + shipping

Written specifically for the M1 Garand owner. Answers frequently asked questions such as: "Who made my rifle and when?" "How do I take it apart and put it back together?" "How do I clean, lubricate, and maintain it?" The civilian owner of an M1 rifle must understand its operation and function, be proficient at disassembly, assembly, inspection, and replacement of individual components. The purpose of the book is to provide the reader the information necessary to develop the knowledge and ability to perform these tasks. Acquisition of these skills will inspire confidence at the work bench and rifle range!

### THE M1 GARAND: SERIAL NUMBERS & DATA SHEETS

by Scott A. Duff

ISBN 1-888722-05-3
4" x 8" softbound, 101 pages, 84 Data sheets
$9.95 + shipping

Two of the most critical factors in collecting the M1 Garand are determining the dates of manufacture and identification of components correct for specific rifles. This is done through use of data sheets on original rifles. This book provides the reader with serial number tables and a large sampling of data sheets to aid in identification and restoration.

The M1 Garand: Serial Numbers & Data Sheets is in response to collectors requests for a "pocket format" reference book convenient for gun shows, auctions, estate sales, and gun shops.

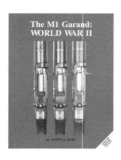

## THE M1 GARAND: WORLD WAR II

(Vol. 1, 1900-1945) Revised, updated edition

by Scott A. Duff
ISBN 1-888722-01-0
8 ½" x 11", softbound
320 pages, 230 photos
**$34.95** + shipping

Volume 1 of the definitive reference set for the Garand Collector. Examines development and production of the M1 rifle from conception through the closing days of WW II. Examines the first Garands - Gas Trap rifles. Chronicles evolution of Springfield Armory and Winchester produced M1s in data sheets and photos. Collectors are aided in ID of parts changes through detailed photos and explanations. Collectors can verify original rifles and/or restore M1s to correct configurations. Month-end serial number tables ID manufacturing dates. Bayonets, slings and cleaning kits examined in detail.

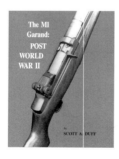

## THE M1 GARAND: POST WORLD WAR II

(Vol. 2, 1945-1957)

by Scott A. Duff
ISBN 1-888722-00-2
8 ½" x 11" softbound
139 pages, 99 photos
**$21.95** + shipping

Volume 2 of the definitive reference set for the Garand collector. Examines the post World War II rebuild program at Springfield Armory. Manufacture of M1s by Springfield, International Harvester, and Harrington & Richardson are chronicled in Data Sheets and photos. Component variation with period of use. Collectors are aided in ID of parts changes through detailed photos and explanations. Collectors can verify original rifles and/or restore M1s to correct configurations. Serial number tables ID manufacturing dates.

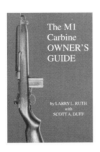

## THE M1 CARBINE OWNER'S GUIDE

by Larry L. Ruth with Scott A. Duff
ISBN 1-888722-09-6
6" x 9" softbound
136 pages, 106 photographs & drawings
$21.95 + shipping

For the Ml Carbine Enthusiast. Provides a detailed evaluation and selection process for both shooting and collecting. Serial numbers at the end of each Quarter for the various manufacturers are presented to date the Carbine. Details include parts identification, evolution of changes, operation, functioning, troubleshooting, disassembly, assembly, cleaning, lubricating, maintenance, and zeroing. The appendix provides the reader with names, addresses, and phone numbers of reputable gunsmiths and suppliers of books, parts, tools, and accessories.

## AMERICAN MILITARY BAYONETS OF THE 20TH CENTURY

by Gary M. Cunningham
ISBN 1-888722-08-8
8 1/2" x 11" softbound
115 pages
$21.95 + shipping

No military rifle is truly complete without its matching bayonet and scabbard. Combining bayonet and rifle not only enhances the appearance of the ensemble but also more closely represents its use by the infantryman. A single reference book that chronicles U.S. Military knife bayonets of the 20th Century. A guide for collectors, including notes on makers, markings, finishes, variations, scabbards, and production data. Covered are bayonets from the Model of 1892 used on the Krag rifle to the current issue M9 for the M16. Bayonets and scabbards are addressed in the order they were adopted. Computer-generated line drawings offer outstanding clarity. A detailed "Specifications Box" is included on each model to guide the reader through variations.

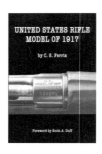

## UNITED STATES RIFLE MODEL OF 1917

by C.S. Ferris with Foreword
by Scott A. Duff
ISBN 1-888722 14-2
6" x 9" softbound
213 pages, 122 photographs
**$23.95** + shipping

This book informs the collector of details of an original M1917 rifle, including finish, dates of manufacture, serial number correlation, manufacturer and inspection markings, rebuild marks, and differences in parts between the three manufacturers: Winchester, Remington, and Eddystone. There is a detailed chapter on accoutrements. Dates of first shipments and dates of last manufacture are provided. Post World War One usage is addressed. If you are interested in the study of the M1917 rifle and have been disappointed by the lack of information available, then this book is for you!

## TM 9-270 U.S. RIFLE, CAL. .30, M1903A4 (SNIPERS)
### Characteristics and Operation; and Use of Telescopic Sight
**28 September 1943**
6" x 9" 30 pages
**$5.00** post-paid

A high quality reprint of the War Department Technical Manual on the most widely issued U.S. Sniper Rifle of World War II and the Korean War. This TM includes information on operation and care of the rifle and Weaver 330C (M73B1) telescopic sight.

# Scott A. Duff Publications Bookshelf

The M1 Garand: World War II ..................................$34.95
The M1 Garand: Post World War II ............................$21.95
The M1 Garand: Serial Numbers
  & Data Sheets ..............................................$9.95
The M1 Garand Owner's Guide ..................................$19.95
The M1 Garand Complete Assembly Guide ........................$22.95
The M1 Carbine Owner's Guide .................................$21.95
The M14 Owner's Guide and
  Match Conditioning Instructions ............................$19.95
The AR-15 Complete Owner's Guide
  Updated 2nd Edition ........................................$22.95
The AR-15 Complete Assembly Guide ............................$19.95
Rock Island Rifle Model 1903 .................................$22.95
United States Rifle Model of 1917 ............................$23.95
American Military Bayonets of
  the 20th Century ...........................................$21.95
US Infantry Weapons in Combat ................................$23.50
Arms For The Nation - Springfield Longarms ...................$9.95
U.S. Army Air Service Wing Badges -
  Uniforms and Insignia 1913-1919 ............................$29.95
Technical Manual 9-270 U.S. Rifle ............................$5.00

*...plus postage and PA sales tax for Pennsylvania residents*

## *Scott A. Duff Publications*
*website: www.scott-duff.com*
*P.O. Box 414 • Export, PA 15632*
*Phone: 724-327-8246    Fax: 724-327-4192*